"Writing is an act of hope. It is a means of carving order from chaos, of challenging one's own beliefs and assumptions, of facing the world with eyes and heart wide open. Through writing, we declare a personal identity amid faceless anonymity. We find purpose and beauty and meaning even when the rational mind argues that none of these exist."

— Jack Heffron,
from the Introduction

It all begins with the creation and development of ideas, the genesis of all great writing. To most, it is surrounded by an almost mystical aura. Regardless of how it may appear, there are no tricks, no best-selling nor Pulitzer Prize–winning concepts hidden up the writer's sleeve.

Inside, you'll find an abundance of playful, humorous—sometimes downright cranky—instruction that will enable you to generate new ideas and reinvigorate old ones. You'll learn how to determine which ideas engage you the most, ensuring that the ones you choose are the ones you're sure to develop into something extraordinary. You'll find a wealth of advice for getting started and writing with the right goals in mind.

(continued on back flap)

Praise for *The Writer's Idea Book*

Here is a writing book that has soul. You can tell it's been written by a true believer. It's such a wise and open-hearted book that even in the unlikely event that it fails to help you write better, it might enable you to live with a little more grace. Now how many books about writing can you say that about?

—WILL BLYTHE, CONTRIBUTING EDITOR FOR *HARPER'S* AND *MIRABELLA*

What an inspiring book! *The Writer's Idea Book* does exactly what it sets out to do—offer writers at all stages of their careers a seemingly endless variety of ideas to noodle around with, explore, and ultimately make their own. Jack Heffron's voice is so nurturing, funny, and wise that, as he guides you along the writer's path, you'll feel as though you've made a new best friend.

—JANICE EIDUS, AUTHOR OF *THE CELIBACY CLUB* AND *URBAN BLISS*

In a field crowded with disappointing tomes, what a joy to open *The Writer's Idea Book* and find vast regions of opinion and experience mined for creative fodder. As much fun to read as it is to use.

—JANET FITCH, AUTHOR OF *WHITE OLEANDER*

The Writer's Idea Book reads as fluently as a good novel, on every page offering the novice writer and seasoned pro alike all sorts of ingenious ways to unlock the stories in your head. It's a savvy, inspiring book full of practical wisdom, written by a writer who knows his craft inside out and also happens to be one of the best editors in the business. I'm recommending it to all my students at every level.

—PHILIP GERARD, AUTHOR OF *HATTERAS LIGHT* AND *BRILLIANT PASSAGE*

The Writer's Idea Book is an excellent workbook for people interested in any kind of writing. The advice is helpful and practical, without making grand promises or arousing inflated expectations in the writer. I recommend it highly.

—JOANNE GREENBERG, AUTHOR OF *I NEVER PROMISED YOU A ROSE GARDEN* AND *WHERE THE ROAD GOES*

The Writer's Idea Book is a fascinating, no-nonsense, sit-your-butt-down-and-work approach invaluable to all writers hoping to stretch their imaginations, deepen their understanding of experience, and explore their moral visions. Not since John Gardner's *The Art of Fiction* has there been such a useful and informative and comprehensive resource book. In fact, if writers have only one book about writing on their shelves, it should be this one.

—LAURA HENDRIE, AUTHOR OF *STYGO* AND *REMEMBER ME*

Every writer out there will benefit from *The Writer's Idea Book*. Whether you are just starting out, are immersed in a project, or simply feeling stuck, Jack Heffron has an idea to help you along. This is a book to keep close at hand as you will be referring to it often!

—ANN HOOD, AUTHOR OF *THE PROPERTIES OF WATER* AND *SOMEWHERE OFF THE COAST OF MAINE*

Jack Heffron's *The Writer's Idea Book* is the literary equivalent of attending the Actor's Studio. Wise, entertaining, and inventive, the book liberates beginning and advanced writers alike, helping them get to the heart of their story.

—DAVID MORRELL, AUTHOR OF *FIRST BLOOD* AND *BROTHERHOOD OF THE ROSE*

Jack Heffron manages a sly trick here by offering *The Writer's Idea Book* as a how-to for beginning or fearful writers. In pleasing, trustworthy prose, he lures writers into thinking they're just practicing, but at the end they'll have enough material for a lifetime and a new way of being in the world.

—MONICA WOOD, AUTHOR OF *MY ONLY STORY* AND *SECRET LANGUAGE*

The Writer's

Idea Book

Jack Heffron

![W] **WRITER'S DIGEST BOOKS**
CINCINNATI, OHIO
www.writersdigest.com

Visit our Web site at www.writersdigest.com for information on more resources for writers.

To receive a free weekly E-mail newsletter delivering tips and updates about writing and about Writer's Digest products, send an E-mail with "Subscribe Newsletter" in the body of the message to newsletter-request@writersdigest .com, or register directly at our Web site at www.writersdigest.com.

04   03   02   01   00   5   4   3   2   1

Library of Congress Cataloging-in-Publication Data

Heffron, Jack
    The writer's idea book / by Jack Heffron.
      p.   cm.
    Includes index.
    ISBN 0-89879-873-6
      1. Authorship. 2. Creative writing. I. Title.

PN147 .H36 2000
808'.02—dc21   00-035939
                                                          CIP

Editor: Michelle Howry
Designer: Sandy Conopeotis Kent
Cover design and illustration: Chris Gliebe/Tin Box Studio
Production coordinator: Mark Griffin

Acknowledgments

Thanks to the posse, the editorial team at Writer's Digest Books—Dave Borcherding, Michelle Howry, Meg Leder—without whom this book could not have been written. And thanks to David Lewis. Thanks, too, to Anne Bowling and Deb Garvey, for invaluable editorial assistance. Thanks to the sales and marketing folks at WDB, whose savvy and hard work will play a key role in the life of this book, and who too often remain unacknowledged. Thanks to my writer friends, too numerous to mention, who through the years have been great companions as well as trusted advisors about the art and craft of writing, especially Rick Stansberger and John Tibbetts. Thanks to my writing teachers: the late Andre Dubus, the late Don Hendrie, Chase Twichell, Dallas Wiebe, Alan Wier, Austin Wright. Special thanks to Sheila Bender, Jamie Braga, Mark Garvey, Wendy Knerr, Jen Lile, Karen Lound, Don Prues and Robyn Weaver. Thanks, finally, to Mary, Joe and Anne Marie Heffron, to Ghette and Mercedes, and to Kim and Dot.

About the Author

Jack Heffron is the senior acquisitions editor for Writer's Digest Books, Story Press, Walking Stick Press, and Betterway Books. He was the series editor for *Best Writing on Writing*, the associate editor of *Story* magazine, and he is a contributing editor for *Fiction Writer*. His short stories have appeared in numerous literary magazines, including *North American Review* and *TriQuarterly*, have been reprinted in anthologies, and twice been nominated for the Pushcart Prize. His nonfiction has appeared in *ESPN's Total Sports Magazine*, *Oxford American*, *Utne Reader* and other publications. He has taught writing at the University of Alabama and the University of Cincinnati. He lives in Cincinnati, Ohio.

Table of Contents

Introduction . . . 1

5 | Part I
Bending and Stretching

CHAPTER ONE
Making Your Way to Schenectady . . . 6

CHAPTER TWO
Enemies of Creativity . . . 12

CHAPTER THREE
Leading a Creative Life . . . 25

CHAPTER FOUR
Getting Ready to Write . . . 34

43 | Part II
Exploring

CHAPTER FIVE
I Yam What I Yam and Other Lies . . . 44

CHAPTER SIX
Schnitzel With Noodles . . . 52

CHAPTER SEVEN
Nellie Malone From Fifth and Stone . . . 60

CHAPTER EIGHT
With a Banjo on My Knee . . . 67

CHAPTER NINE
Thoughts of a Sundrenched Elsewhere . . . 74

CHAPTER TEN
What's Your Road, Man? . . . 80

CHAPTER ELEVEN
The Love You Make . . . 88

CHAPTER TWELVE
Don't Get Me Started . . . 98

CHAPTER THIRTEEN
Your Fifteen Minutes . . . 105

CHAPTER FOURTEEN
All Our Secrets Are the Same . . . 113

CHAPTER FIFTEEN
Minding Other People's Business . . . 122

CHAPTER SIXTEEN
A Day in the Life of a Writer . . . 129

CHAPTER SEVENTEEN
A Life of the Spirit . . . 133

139 | Part III
Finding Form

CHAPTER EIGHTEEN
Of Sonnets and Toasters . . . 140

CHAPTER NINETEEN
Folks Like You . . . 148

CHAPTER TWENTY
The Shape of Things to Come . . . 163

CHAPTER TWENTY-ONE
It All Depends on Your Point of View . . . 171

CHAPTER TWENTY-TWO
Other Rooms, Other Voices . . . 181

CHAPTER TWENTY-THREE
Vast Is the Power of Cities . . . 190

CHAPTER TWENTY-FOUR
It Was the Best of Times . . . 199

CHAPTER TWENTY-FIVE
A Sort of Miracle . . . 208

217 | Part IV
Assessing and Developing

CHAPTER TWENTY-SIX
What's at Stake? . . . 218

CHAPTER TWENTY-SEVEN
Sitting Still . . . 226

CHAPTER TWENTY-EIGHT
Tell It Slant . . . 236

CHAPTER TWENTY-NINE
Anything Is Beautiful if You Say It Is . . . 244

A Final Word . . . 255

Index . . . 257

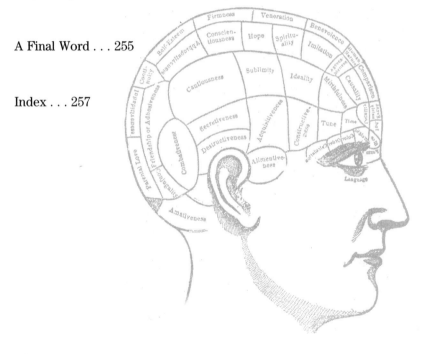

Introduction

Writing is an act of hope.

It is a means of carving order from chaos, of challenging one's own beliefs and assumptions, of facing the world with eyes and heart wide open. Through writing, we declare a personal identity amid faceless anonymity. We find purpose and beauty and meaning even when the rational mind argues that none of these exist.

Writing, therefore, is also an act of courage. How much easier is it to lead an unexamined life than to confront yourself on the page? How much easier is it to surrender to materialism or cynicism or to a hundred other ways of life that are, in fact, ways to hide from life and from our fears? When we write, we resist the facile seduction of these simpler roads. We insist on finding out and declaring the truths that we find, and we dare to put those truths on the page.

To get ideas and to write well, you have to risk opening yourself. In her book *When Things Fall Apart*, Buddhist teacher Pema Chödrön writes of this risk:

> When we regard thoughts and emotions with humor and openness, that's how we perceive the universe. . . . We begin to find that, to the degree that there is bravery in ourselves . . . and to the degree that there is kindness toward ourselves, there is confidence that we can actually forget ourselves and open to the world.

There must be that softness, that openness. Rather than making us weak, it makes us confident and fearless. The more confident we grow, the more open we can allow ourselves to be. If you can write even when your life seems dark and bleak, even if all you can write is "Life sucks," then you have the hope and courage necessary to keep moving, to persevere as an artist. In perseverence you will find your creative self.

Writing also is an act of joy and celebration. With it we say that life is worth preserving, worth exploring in all its facets, and to do it well we must have fun. It must be approached with a sense of play, of risk and experiment, openness and laughter. Throughout his book *Fiction*

Writer's Workshop, Josip Novakovich entreats the reader to "have fun." This is not a catchphrase. It's an important bit of writing advice.

Getting Ideas

Most writers have more ideas than they can explore in a lifetime—subjects and situations that someday will be short stories and novels, memoirs and poems and screenplays, bits of scene, a great zinger of a line, characters, moments of loss and triumph to capture on the page. This book will help you explore those ideas and help you generate new ones. It will help you push deeper into your ideas to plumb their possibilities.

The book is organized in four sections that follow the process of creation: warming up, deciding what you want to write about and beginning to generate ideas, finding a form for those ideas, developing those ideas. But you should feel free to open the book anywhere and find a prompt that interests you. If you respond to enough of the prompts, you will generate ideas for many new projects. You also can use the prompts to find new ways of seeing projects already underway. You might be stuck, for example, on a way to develop a minor character in your novel. Find a prompt that focuses on character and follow it. Then put the character into your novel.

A Few Points to Keep in Mind

In many of the prompts I use the word *story*. By *story*, I mean any sort of narrative—short story, short-short story, narrative essay, memoir, narrative poem, novel, script, even journal entry. Rather than repeat all of these forms again and again, I use *story* as a shorthand word. Work in whatever form interests you. I do suggest that you try your hand at a few forms rather than sticking to just one. A new form can suggest all sorts of new possibilities and can provide a fresh context for your ideas.

Sometimes I use the word *piece* to mean any type of writing—any "piece of writing." When possible, I try to avoid using *piece* in its current incarnation, denoting an arty form of nonfiction, or, more and more often, any type of nonfiction. Apparently the word *article* is now considered pedestrian. In his book *U and I*, Nicholson Baker takes umbrage with the word *piece* used in this way, calling it "a journalismoid word." And I agree with him. If, in a prompt, I want you to write an article, I'll say *article*.

Next, I've tried to vary gender-specific pronouns. Sometimes I use *she*; sometimes I use *he*. I've done this in an arbitrary way. If there are more of one than another, this is purely accidental. In my experience, I've found that writers can be either male or female, and I've tried to acknowledge that fact in as unobtrusive a way as possible.

As you can see from the introduction, the tone of the book will vary, from high-minded to playful to downright cranky. As for the content of the book, I hope you find it useful, that it sparks a great many ideas that lead to satisfying projects. Unfortunately, I can offer no hidden formulas, no *secrets* in this book. I don't know that any exist. The secrets to getting ideas aren't really secrets. Open your mind and heart. Open your eyes and ears. Take risks. Trust your talent and your instincts. Be willing to see your ideas—and your life, and the world around you—in new ways. Be patient. Be positive. Don't be distracted by the opinions of others, real or imagined. Don't worry about getting published—that's a whole new topic, and one worth investigating if that's your goal, but it's a needless and potentially harmful distraction when you're writing. Don't worry about "getting better" or fret about whether you're really any good. Read a lot. Write a lot.

Most of all, as I said earlier, have fun. Your sense of freedom and play will infuse your writing with energy, and that energy will make your words enjoyable to read. And you'll be having fun, which is an end in itself. You'll be learning about yourself and about others. You'll have a place to nurture yourself and explore your ideas. You'll have a place to investigate things in all their maddening ambiguity, to seek and find your own opinions and truths. You will expand your powers of empathy as well as your understanding of life. In empathy and understanding, we find compassion, for others and for ourselves. We grow. With those goals in mind, let's begin.

Part I
Bending and Stretching

Chapter One

Making Your Way to Schenectady

It is good to have an end to journey toward;
but it is the journey that matters, in the end.
—URSULA K. LEGUIN

I f you've been writing for any length of time, you've surely been asked this question by well-meaning friends and family: "Where do you get your ideas?" Perhaps you've even developed a stock, smart-ass reply, such as Robin Hemley's: "Joyce Carol Oates gives me her extras." Ray Bradbury has one, too: "I get them from the Schenectady Center for Ideas."

If you're feeling kinder, you might reply, "Dunno," with a shrug. "Everywhere, I guess. They just sort of come to me." And you'd probably be telling the truth. But even this straightforward pooh-poohing of any grand source of ideas won't demystify the creative process for your listener. Instead, she'll probably be awed, convinced that your self-effacing response is surely a sign of genius. "She's so creative," you will hear—and probably feel like the biggest fraud since Barnum and Bailey.

Fact is, there is no magic elixir we can brew to conjure ideas from the air, and though we've been told we're "so creative" since we were sucking on Tinker Toys, we often don't feel creative at all. Our ideas seem stale. Or we feel stuck, unable to get a pleasing voice on the page.

Or we feel blocked on a particular project. If only there were a real center for ideas in Schenectady. Oh, frabjous day—we'd write every morning and evening, pouring forth words of divine beauty.

But before we get to specific idea prompts, let's look at some general truths about writing more creatively, ways to keep your mind fresh and your imagination fertile. You possess the resources, you know you do, to come up with many good ideas. It's simply a matter of tapping into them and trusting them and understanding how your creative self works. To achieve these goals, you will need to help your creative self function at its best by shaping the way you perceive your writing and by structuring your life to write.

Show Up

Showing up is the main thing. Get to the desk regularly. You'll find you have no end of ideas if you can make writing a regular habit. Woody Allen once said that 80 percent of being successful in life is just showing up. We all know this is true. The writers we admire—or envy—might be geniuses whose talent dwarfs ours, but more often they're people who show up, with those seven-hundred-page novels they've been rising at five to write every morning for the past year. You think, *I'm as talented as Anne. I would have done that.* But alas, you have no seven-hundred-page novel. You have six novels, varying from twenty-five to sixty pages. They're in a drawer or file cabinet, or even still in computer files. Is the culprit writer's block? A dearth of ideas? Cruel and fickle fortune? Nope. If you want to write, you must begin by beginning, continue by continuing, finish by finishing. This is the great secret of it all. Tell no one.

PROMPT: Writer Thomas McGuane goes to his study at a certain time every day and stays there for a scheduled length of time. He sits at his desk. "I don't have to write," he explains, "but I can't do anything else." Try his approach for a week, scheduling a specific period of time, during which you must sit at your desk or wherever you write. You don't have to write, but you can't do anything else.

Acknowledge the Difficulty

People, like me, say, "Just show up," as if it were the easiest thing in the world to do. It's not. It's hard. Why? Writing creatively can be hard. It can empower you and free your spirit and can be a source of great joy, but it's not always easy. Sometimes we just don't feel creative. We're tired or bored. Also, as I said in the introduction, and many more brilliant folks than me have said before: Writing is an act of courage. Sometimes it's just too scary to face the page. Or too frustrating: We've worked hard, and still our skills seem small, our writing clumsy, our ideas foolish and hackneyed. Who needs it? Our friends get along just fine without opening the vein every day to pour their blood onto the page. They have more time to do things—have fun, enjoy themselves.

So if you fall away from your schedule, if you wake up at 5 A.M. but pop the snooze button six times rather than getting out of bed, don't beat yourself up. Telling yourself, "I'm lazy," "I have no willpower," "I'm not a writer," won't help you become a writer. That approach will convince you, instead, that you're a lazy loser with neither willpower nor talent. Such a person ain't flinging back the covers at 5 A.M. and striding to the coffeemaker. Such a person stays in bed. Give yourself positive messages.

PROMPT: List the positive messages you have received about writing or about any creative undertaking. What did people say? How did they say it? Then write about times when you felt good about your writing, such as when a great idea zipped into your mind or when you finished a project that turned out well. Keep these messages and memories handy. When you're feeling stale or want to berate yourself about your work, read about what you've done in the past and know you can do it again.

PROMPT: Acknowledge that writing is hard. Write it down. Then write about how you're going to make writing happen. How will you find the balance in yourself to combine willpower with relaxation, stubbornness with joy? Write about how you've struck this balance in the past, with writing, a sport, a musical instrument—anything you've done.

P R O M P T : If the McGuane approach mentioned previously doesn't work for you, create a writing schedule for the next three weeks. Start with five minutes per day. Add five minutes to every writing session. Note on your schedule how you're doing.

L ike many things, writing becomes a habit. If you do it, you just keep doing it. If you want to break a bad habit—smoking, watching television, eating chocolate—instead of trying to will yourself past the habit, cultivate the habit of not doing it. Get in the habit of not not writing. Sounds like psychobabble? All right, phrase it however you'd like. But it's one way to reframe the situation. I learned this from a friend who quit smoking. He told me he did it, gradually, by cultivating the habit of not smoking. True, this took willpower. But he started by not smoking in his car, then not smoking right before going to bed. The same can happen with writing! Start small. Start cultivating the habit of not not writing.

If this reframing approach doesn't work for you, don't worry about it. It probably sounds a little weird. But it does eliminate the structured, even puritanical implications of disciplining yourself. It takes from your hand the *I should be writing* stick with which we are tempted to beat ourselves. It keeps discipline in a more positive, nurturing context. A positive mind-set is important for sustaining joy in your writing. If you turn it into a teeth-grinding test of your willpower, you'll lose the fun. If you lose the joy and the fun, why bother?

P R O M P T : Collect some motivational statements about writing or about creativity or about perseverence. Choose ones that speak directly to your needs or beliefs, and post them where you write. You can find a number of these statements in this book. Use them to keep yourself writing.

Joy and Gratitude

There's no question that only through regular writing will you generate a lot of good ideas. But joy and fun are important, too. We must find a balance. As writers, we know what the "writer's high" feels like, the sense of elation we feel when we're cooking away on a project. The world and all of its problems melt away. Our lives have purpose, direction, meaning. We feel our passions rise within us. We tap into thoughts and emotions and feel restored. As Annie Dillard said, "It is life at its most free."

PROMPT: Write about a time when your creativity flowed, perhaps when you were immersed in a project or when you spent a few hours at a coffeehouse scribbling in your journal. Try to describe the feeling. Describe, too, the circumstances—the time of day, the location, your mood before beginning. In this exercise, try to get to know your creative self a bit better.

PROMPT: Celebrate your creative self, the writer inside you. Write about how writing is an important part of your life. Write about the pleasure it brings. Write about your gratitude in possessing such a gift. Shakespeare once wrote the following:

> This is a gift I have, simple, simple; a foolish extravagant spirit, full of forms, figures, shapes, objects, ideas, apprehensions, motions, revolutions. . . . But the gift is good in those in whom it is acute, and I am thankful for it.

Though it may sound stupid, cultivate gratitude even for the obstacles that stand in the way of your writing, the ones that sometimes impede your ideas and creativity. Recent psychological studies show that these obstacles actually aid creativity. The tension between your desire to be creative and the obstacles you have to overcome sparks ideas, like rubbing two rocks together to ignite a flame.

Difficult to believe? Consider: Have you ever suffered from too much time to write? Though we all wish we had much more time to spend writing, sometimes when we receive such a gift we find the well is dry. We don't feel creative. When we're snatching a desperate hour here and there, before work, during the kids' baseball practices, then the ideas seem to flow. We find a way to make it happen, and that fuels our imaginations. In a recent *New York Times* article, creativity consultant Roger von Oech sums up this idea well: "Skyscrapers weren't invented by people with a lot of land, but by those who had to figure out how to build more offices on tight and incredibly expensive real estate."

So instead of cursing your obstacles, be grateful for them. In chapter two, we'll discuss enemies of creativity, and you'll notice they share a common quality: They all exist inside us. Obstacles outside ourselves only make us more creative.

PROMPT: Reframe your view of the obstacles in your life that impede your writing. Make a list of these obstacles, then, next to each one, write about how you can overcome the obstacle and how it might be used as a tool for creativity.

PROMPT: Research a few inventions. Write about the circumstances of the inventions: How were they discovered or made? What obstacles did the inventors overcome? If you want, write an essay about an inventor or invention.

Now is the time to be more creative. Today. Trust that there is no better time, that no time in the future will offer you more of what you need. I often hear people talk about a time in the future when they will have time to write—when they retire, when the kids are grown and gone, or when they can quit that moonlighting job. My advice: Start now, if only in a limited way. A time in the future may exist that will hold fewer obstacles, but these can be dealt with today, and, as we've discussed, removing all the obstacles can hurt creativity. There's an old saying about life that applies to writing:

> Happiness is not a destination. It is a companion we can choose to accompany us on our journey.

You're not going to be a writer someday. You're a writer today. Discipline yourself to write and take time to enjoy writing. Do it a lot. Have fun with it. Begin now.

Chapter Two

Enemies of Creativity

What is needed is, in the end, simply this:
solitude, great inner solitude.
—RAINER MARIA RILKE

G etting ideas, as we've discussed, is largely a matter of showing up. As writer Ron Carlson says, it's the butt-in-the-chair approach. Waiting for inspiration is a loser's game, because without a work in progress, even if you're only doing some personal journaling and the work in progress is you, ideas that arise will have no context. They won't be recognizable as ideas. Or, they'll be great ideas for a novel or article that will never be written. And so at writers conferences and workshops, teachers will say the key is "Just do it."

And they're right. But "Just do it" is a slogan for shoes. And slogans work because they make things seem easier than they, in fact, are. If just doing it were simply a matter of deciding, anyone *could* do it. But sticking to a schedule goes beyond will. As we discussed in the previous chapter, it's a matter of consciously developing a writing habit.

But there are enemies to that habit, dark forces that keep us from writing creatively. Read this chapter to find out who they are—as if you didn't already know. Each has its strengths and weaknesses and all can be beaten. The key is awareness. Recognize the force at work against you. Recognition is a large part of the battle against these nefarious foes.

The Procrastinator

What a great word: *procrastinator*. All of those crashing consonants, the *c*, *s* and *t*s. The Procrastinator sounds like the name of a comic book super-villain. This guy should be kicking Spiderman's butt all over New York.

Instead, he's at my house. And your house. He's convincing us we will write, yes we will, and we'll get started next week. Absolutely. No exceptions this time, no way. Well. Next week may not be ideal because there's a big meeting at work on Tuesday, which means all of those reports have to be finished, and Wednesday is parent-teacher night, and then there's soccer practice and the appointment with the eye doctor and something has to be done before the first freeze with that tree branch hanging over the garage. But the week after, no problem. We're all over it.

This is the voice of The Procrastinator. He's merciless. Very tough to beat. He can hit you with excuses so good your priest, minister, mother and therapist would absolve you of your decision not to write. They'd even write a note for you. If you want, write your own, just like you used to do in grade school in your best Mom handwriting.

How does your excuse sound? Does it ring false in your ears? Will the muse believe this excuse? Like a clever truant, make a dozen of these notes, and when you miss a day or a week or whatever your schedule calls for, write a note to the muse explaining why. Look at your excuse on the cold white paper. Does it justify not writing? This strategy can keep The Procrastinator at bay.

But maybe your excuse really is valid. Stuff comes up. It really does. We all have worthwhile reasons not to write, and if we're not writing, we're not creating new ideas. If you made a list right now for why you can't write, or couldn't write the last time your schedule said you should, I'll bet you can come up with at least five reasons, three of them excellent.

PROMPT: The next time you skip a writing session, write five reasons, three of them excellent, for why you must skip. These reasons are The Procrastinator's power. Now, one by one, take back the power by writing a sentence or two explaining why each excuse is not good enough or how schedules could be shifted, arrangements made, to allow you to write some other time.

B y using these strategies, you can defeat The Procrastinator. Today. That's the key. Don't delay. Have you ever had a friend tell you that she's starting a diet "on Monday"? Usually she's crunching through a mouthful of Doritos at the time. Yep. Monday. That's when she's starting. Meanwhile, you couldn't be more sure that the diet will fail. You just know it. Why? Because the postponement shows the lack of commitment and desire necessary to make a diet work.

The Procrastinator feeds on delay. To vanquish him, start now. If only for five minutes. Then do five minutes tomorrow, until you're churning out ideas and writing pages. Go ahead, start now. Write a scene from your current story. Pull an unfinished poem from your files and tinker with it. Write anything. Make a list of your favorite foods or a list of your favorite friends, then explain why you like them. List ten things you hate about the holidays and explain why. Describe in detail the most romantic evening of your life. Open this book to nearly any page and follow the prompt. Do it now.

Really. Right now. What are you still doing here?

The Victim

All of us are, at times in our lives, victims. Life can be cruel. And we use the role of victim to stop being creative. We give up control of our creative selves because

- our families don't understand or appreciate us.
- our bosses are demanding and fill our lives with stress.
- our children are demanding and fill our lives with stress.
- our finances are a mess.
- our mates are insensitive to our needs for space to create.
- our cars refuse to run properly.
- our neighborhoods are noisy and overrun with children.

As with The Procrastinator and his excuses, The Victim makes some valid points. The key is taking back the power. In her book *Awakening the Warrior Within*, Dawn Callan speaks of "owning your victim self" as a way of finding one's inner warrior. How? Stop complaining about the forces victimizing you. Just stop. Stop making your lack of a creative life the fault of someone or something other than yourself. Any or all of the reasons on the list above might be true for you. But when you hear yourself complaining about them, hear the voice of The Victim. And, as with The Procrastinator, know that The Victim is inside you, under your control.

PROMPT: List the most common and frequent reasons you give for not spending enough time being creative. Next to each entry on the list, write who is in control of that situation. Now write a short plan for taking back control. It may require some tough admissions and a little creativity, but you're taking the first step toward opening your creative side.

PROMPT: Recognize victim talk when you hear it. Don't condemn yourself for it, just recognize what it is. Then stop. Take control. Give yourself a place to be creative again.

Taking back control is a wonderfully empowering experience. When you beat your victim self, you feel a sense of victory and you know that anything is possible. You *can* finish that novel. You *can* finish that screenplay. It really *is* within your power.

The Talker

Speaking of talk, this enemy just can't shut up. You've cooked up a great idea for a screenplay or an essay or you've made a revelation about your protagonist that will give your novel a much-needed new dimension . . . then The Talker takes over. She has to tell everyone in your writing group. She tells your mate. Or your mother. Or anyone at work who will listen. The Talker is an expert at squandering the creative nest egg. By the time you sit down to put this idea into action, it's dead, or at least not as zesty as it seemed to be a few days ago.

The Talker needs attention. The Talker needs validation. The Talker would rather talk about an idea than confront its complexities, its obstacles. The Talker wants the glory but none of the hard work that really lies at the heart of all creative efforts. The Talker is a bit of a coward, a narcissist, a layabout. If you want to develop your ideas to their full potential and to see a work through to completion, take control of The Talker. When writers tell me they can't help it, or that they *need* to talk it all out first, my advice is simple: Whenever you're talking about a work in progress, don't. Just shut up. Really. The story you're writing is a secret. Anne Tyler takes a somewhat gentler approach:

> It makes me so uncomfortable for them. If they're talking about a plot idea, I feel the idea is probably going to evaporate. I want to almost physically reach over and cover their mouths and say, "You'll lose it if you're not careful."

Writing is a private act. It is a way of communing with our imaginations, our subconscious minds, our secret lives. Bringing in a third party is almost always a bad idea. The sense of intimacy and revelation are lost, and you end up making small talk. By preserving the privacy of the creative process, you preserve the excitement of that intimacy. Getting back to that intimacy becomes a guilty pleasure, and it keeps the tension high. Ideas will spawn more ideas and you'll find yourself, and your project, rolling right along. Novelist Jay McInerney describes it this way:

> I find it helps to remove myself, as much as possible, from the world of daily life. Living in New York, it's tough to block out the din of the city. So I go away. I try to find a treehouse somewhere and pull the ladder up behind me. Once I have begun to believe in my alternate fictional universe, I can come and go from the treehouse. But it's a fragile state in the beginning.

Some writers simply think it's a jinx to talk about a work in progress. One writer I know was working on a novel for months and yet refused to even refer to the project as "a novel." She called it "this thing I'm working on" until, after more than a year, she finished it. She took care to avoid letting The Talker get so much as a toe in the door.

The best illustration of this process is also an admittedly silly one that I've used in classes and workshops for a number of years. It involves a TV commercial for grape juice. (Stick with me on this.) The commercial opened by demonstrating the way the competition made its grape juice—a rather primitive and cartoonish illustration of a big boiling vat of purple liquid. Above the boiling vat, smoke wafted into the air, and within the smoke sparkled little purple gems of flavor. Lost flavor. Flavor gone forever. Next, the illustration changed to show the sponsor's process. The vat of burbling purple stuff looked the same, but there was a cap on top of the vat, an inverted funnel with a pipe on the end that channeled the smoke (complete with sparkling purple gems of flavor) back into the vat, thus giving more flavor to the juice.

I can't believe this is how it's really done. But the ingenious ad person had created a good illustration of how The Talker can hinder the creative process. The Talker lets the steam out of your work, making it less rich and interesting. Your glistening purple gems of ideas are lost forever. Don't let that happen.

PROMPT: Remember some writing projects that were great at the start but stalled or remain unfinished. Write down why they weren't completed. Did you talk away any of them? Remind yourself when you're discussing a story in progress or an idea for a piece you've yet to begin that it's best to keep quiet. Tell yourself you'll talk about it after the next scene is written, then try to wait for the scene after that one.

The Critic

The biggest surprise I've found about The Critic is that he strikes every writer. As a young apprentice, I always thought that publishing a few stories would calm the critic, that I'd gain the confidence to know that I was good and wouldn't be plagued by doubt and frustration. Since then I've learned that's not the way it works. I've met esteemed writers, award winners, authors of best-selling books who still hear the voice of The Critic. As you get your chops and collect publications, your confidence grows but never to the point that The Critic is silenced. And maybe that's good, unless it's keeping you from writing, unless behind your chair The Critic is wailing an off-key version of Linda Ronstadt's classic "You're No Good."

In his book *Darkness Visible*, esteemed author William Styron discusses his nearly overwhelming feelings of self-doubt as he flies to Paris to accept an award. Despite tremendous reviews for her first novel, *A Bigamist's Daughter*, National Book Award–winner Alice McDermott still had such doubts about her ability that she considered quitting writing to attend law school.

The Critic is sometimes personified as a wicked English teacher from high school—Mrs. Crabass, she of the narrowed eyes and prodigious behind, she whose autocratic and hard-hearted insistence on rules of grammar and composition stripped us of our ability to let go, have fun and be creative. Alas, she ruined us, or nearly so, and we must fight her at every turn.

Maybe. For some reason I often hear a false note in this characterization. The majority of English teachers I've known and know would weep ecstatic tears if a student showed so much as a hint of an original thought. The Critic is, in fact, within us. We have, perhaps, absorbed the voice, from a teacher or a parent, or created the voice from our mythic personification of The Editor, who mocks with relish our feeble attempts at meaningful narrative. Once again, the voice of The Critic is our own voice. In fact, if we'd absorbed the lessons of composition from our English teachers, we may have fewer doubts about our ability.

The point here is not to "stop your whining." The Critic is a fearsome adversary, no question. And even after your flight to Stockholm to accept the Nobel prize in literature, after you win the favor and admiration of readers everywhere, that voice still will be there. Publication and praise help, no doubt. As you practice, you will gain confidence, allow yourself to experiment, even risk looking—gasp—stupid. But the real growth comes from inside, where The Critic resides. In an interview I conducted with David Guterson a couple of years ago, he spoke of this process:

The actual act of writing is no easier than it was. You can have all the awards and sales and reviews you want, it doesn't get any easier the next day. On the other hand, I feel a deeper confidence in myself. It doesn't come from *Snow Falling on Cedars*. It comes from the years going by. I feel more confident because I've practiced more.

When you hear the voice of The Critic telling you your idea is stupid, your writing dull and pedestrian, tell the voice to wait. He may, indeed, be right. And he will have his turn, you promise, but it's not his turn now. The early draft is not the place for The Critic. If he insists on interfering, try not to fight him directly. Instead, observe the voice, name it The Critic, and let it go. You will go on writing anyway, just as you've learned to write when your kids have the TV cranked and are fighting brutally over the remote control.

Listening and letting go is the process used in meditation to let go of your Thinking Mind. The meditator knows that thoughts will intrude. When they do, she simply tells herself, "Thinking," and lets the thoughts go, without labeling them good or bad, without labeling herself weak or scattered. Don't turn The Critic into that bifocaled, bun-haired termagant with a red pen; don't turn The Critic into that bald-headed editor with a blue pen. The Critic is a necessary voice, at times. As you grow as a writer, you cultivate an aesthetic, a criteria for recognizing strong writing and weak. With this growth you become a more useful reader, of your own work and the work of others. So resist labeling The Critic.

But in the early stages of a piece, send him to a movie or on a nature hike or into the other room where he might at least fold laundry. He'll probably pop his head in from time to time, asking, "Ready for me yet?" In as kind a voice as you can muster, simply say, "Not yet."

The Judge

This guy is your conscience. I see him as Judge Kennesaw Mountain Landis, the first commissioner of baseball. You've probably seen a picture of Landis in history books—a grim-faced, fierce-eyed gent, an old-time moralist, a hard-line arbiter of right and wrong. He appears when we feel guilty about spending time writing. Would our families be better served if we were with them instead of shut behind doors with "Do not disturb" signs warning intruders to stay away? Would our spouses be grateful if we didn't head off to bed early to get up and write in the morning? Shouldn't we, for heaven's sake, be

- raking the yard?
- playing with the kids?
- cleaning the furnace filters?
- making money?
- paying bills?

How selfish of us to demand this time to indulge pointless fantasies of publication. How silly to be working through yet another draft of the memoir, dredging through events that took place twenty years go. This is the voice of The Judge. His weapon: Writer's Guilt.

Women, especially, seem to have a wrangle on their hands with this guy. In our society, women, more so than men, have been raised to ignore their needs, to put themselves at the service of their families. And families, therefore, expect this behavior. Ask your family for an hour alone in the evenings, then watch their need to bond erupt. You'll field more questions and solve more dilemmas than if you'd plopped down in front of the television with them. Or, if you do get the quiet you ask for, the voice of The Judge might start speaking in your head.

In an interview with *Publishers Weekly*, fiction writer Gish Jen spoke of fighting The Judge, even after publishing three successful books:

Even today, I think my family would be more relieved than dismayed if I were to stop writing. I still struggle with the question, Is it selfish? It's hard on the people around me, it's hard on the children. Is it worth it? I was programmed to be selfless, and I go through periods where I wonder.

Men, too, suffer from Writer's Guilt. We feel we should be out there winning some bread, bringing home some bacon or, at the least, spending time with mate and kids. Our own fathers, by God, wouldn't be nursing along some narcissistic novel project when the grass could be cut or the garage painted. What a damp-souled, ineffectual man to have this need to create art at the expense of our dearest loved ones.

Of course, times have changed, and, I hope, things are not quite so regimented and old-fashioned in your world, but there's no denying that Writer's Guilt strikes often, and is an insidious enemy that is tough to beat. The Judge would seem to have bivouacked himself on the moral high ground with a phalanx of rocket launchers and barbed wire. To take back that ground, ask yourself why you're spending time writing rather than with family and friends and your ever-beckoning "To do" list. Is it because of your undying hope of fame and fortune? Are you seeking revenge on callous high school teachers who said you'd never be a writer? Are you intentionally hiding from responsibilities by using writing as a convenient shield?

Probably not.

If you're writing out of a need to communicate, to hear your own voice on the page, then you owe it to yourself—and to your family—to write. You have a moral imperative to do it. Try to ignore this imperative and you will unleash The Victim, the woeful sod who would write if only the world were a more understanding place. To be the best mother/father, husband/wife, son/daughter, brother/sister, friend or lover you can be, you need to have an outlet for your creativity. Even if those around you don't understand what you're doing, they should be able to understand that.

Of course, stealing creative time may require some sacrifices—getting up earlier, scheduling your time more tightly, delegating some responsibilities to family members. Can you do this and keep writing with a clear conscience? For most people, it's possible. But those blessed or cursed with an especially guilty conscience may have some trouble with The Judge. I may be one of that group. I've always admired people who put their writing first and live their lives accordingly. I remember reading John Gardner's *On Becoming a Novelist*, in which he says, in effect, use the people around you. Live off a spouse. Accept money from parents. Don't get a job. Write, write, write.

For some, this works. Books do get written that way. Take Gardner's advice at face value and make your own choices. My advice leans more to striking a balance between the needs of others and the needs of your creative life. As much as possible, meld them. Work to see them not as warring factions but as two key elements that make you a unique individual. If The Judge rears his tyrannical head, don't trust what he says. Insist upon your need for writing time. In fact, write about it.

PROMPT: Write about your need for a creative life or simply your need to write. Why do you do it? What needs are fulfilled through it? Call your essay "Why I Write." For examples, you can find an anthology of such essays—titled *Why I Write*, edited by Will Blythe—in which big-name authors explore their needs to write. In your essay, be honest, and be thorough. Try to achieve a better understanding of your impulse to write. Use this understanding to explain to The Judge, and to all the enemies, why you must write, despite blocks or guilt or a hundred really cool other things to do.

The following excerpt is taken from Lee Smith's essay, title "Everything Else Falls Away," which appeared in *Why I Write*. Throughout the essay, she gives a number of reasons for writing, but this reason stands at the core:

> For me, writing is a physical joy. It is almost sexual—not the moment of fulfillment, but the moment when you open the door to the room where your lover is waiting, and everything else falls away.
>
> It *does* fall away, too. For the time of the writing, I am nobody. Nobody at all. I am a conduit, nothing but a way for the story to come to the page. Oh, but I am terribly alive then, too, though I say I am no one at all; my every sense is keen and quivering.

The Author

Last year, in one of my idea workshops at a writers conference, I guided the conferees through a few prompts to help them generate ideas for essays and articles. When the session was nearly over, a woman in the back shot a vehement arm into the air and asked with barely contained frustration, "So now what do I do with it?" Of course, I hated her on the spot.

But that's beside the point. The true point is that she missed the purpose of the workshop. We were gathered to tap into our creative selves, to generate ideas for pieces that could be developed and completed later. Instead, she was under the spell of The Author, that part of ourselves that sees every moment of writing as important and valid only if it leads to publication. That goal can impede creativity. Instead of following our own desires to write, we write with the marketplace in mind. We write about what's hot. At nearly every writers conference I attend, I sit on an editor-agent panel, fielding questions about publication. Inevitably, many people want to know what's selling. It's good for any serious writer to understand the marketplace, but writing for the marketplace is usually a bad idea. If you don't feel passionately about a subject, you won't write well about it. If you're writing for a byline or simply to see your name in print, you're probably going to find yourself blocked on a regular basis. Again, the curse of The Author.

We all like to be published. It's fun to see our words in print; it's satisfying to reach an audience of readers; it's nice to make a little money for our literary efforts. We feel validated in some way. Publication makes us feel not simply like someone who writes but like A Real Writer. All of these desires are fine. They can help keep us motivated and focused. But in the early stages of a work, you'll be more creative and successful if you send The Author away. Allow her to return at the end of the session to embrace your great work and indulge you in daydreams of glory. When you've finished a project, put The Author to work zipping off your stories to magazines everywhere.

But when you're writing, write. Enjoy the work for its own sake. Relish the process itself. If you don't, The Author will become a voracious, nagging mate who is never satisfied. Publishing is a tough business, full of frustrations for even the most successful writers. If you write primarily to be published and to be An Author, you will never be a happy writer. I swear it. Nothing will be good enough. Publications will take far too long to respond; agents and editors will be hated enemies, fickle in their tastes, cryptic in their responses; less talented writers will get ahead because of their despicably sycophantic sucking up to every well-known writer who comes to town; your work won't receive the praise it deserves; your books will have terrible covers and the publishers will be out to cheat you on your royalty statements; and no one, no one, no one will ever have the human decency to call you back. In short, no matter how much success you achieve, everything will suck.

As Pema Chödrön says throughout her book *When Things Fall Apart*, give yourself a break. Be kind and compassionate to yourself. Give your creative side the love and respect it deserves. There will be time, if you want, to confront the business of publication. Publication can be a great motivator and is not a bad ambition. But when you're trying to get words on paper, to generate ideas that interest you and fill you with that feeling of elation that making art can inspire, push The Author away.

The Capricious Guest

The composer Peter Ilyich Tchaikovsky called inspiration The Capricious Guest. Wait for him to arrive and you may be waiting for a long time. Write regularly and you will find ideas flowing through you. In his book *The Craft of Fiction*, William Knott makes the point that The Capricious Guest usually arrives when you no longer need him, when you're doing just fine on your own. He makes the point, too, that when you compare pages you've written in moments of inspiration to those you've written when simply doing your daily work, you won't notice much difference.

The key to beating all of the enemies of creativity is to do your daily work. The experience of writing, as you already know, varies greatly, from times of exquisite, nearly sybaritic delight to spirit-pummeling slogs not unlike the Bataan Death March. Realize that both are part of the process. Some days the ideas will pour forth. Other days they won't. Enemies like those we've discussed in this chapter will appear. Know who they are, know where they come from and keep going.

Chapter Three

Leading a Creative Life

*The voyage of discovery lies not in finding new
landscapes, but in having new eyes.*
—MARCEL PROUST

Y ou are a creative person. You have the power to transform the raw
stuff of daily life into something beautiful. Trust yourself. When
you are trying to begin a new piece of writing, you needn't strive for
some gravity-defying idea. The strain will show. A new idea may appear
in something you've already written, a detail that was not explored, a
topic that was a small part of a larger one. When you feel blocked on a
project, read what you've written so far and focus on what is working
well. Push deeper into those ideas. "Creativity often consists of merely
turning up what is already there," wrote author Bernice Fitz-Gibbon,
adding that, "Right and left shoes were thought up only a little more
than a century ago."

We've discussed the need for balancing discipline and joy in your
writing, and we've looked at ways to silence the inner voices that hinder
creativity. Now let's explore ways to accomplish those goals by getting
to know your creative life more completely.

PROMPT: Write about the most creative person you've ever known.
Explain why you feel she is so creative, offering examples of her creative
accomplishments.

PROMPT: Write about a creative person you admire but don't know personally, such as a famous painter or musician or writer, living or dead. As in the previous prompt, explain why you feel this person is or was so creative. If necessary, do a little research to find out more about this person's creative gifts and habits. When you finish this piece, compare the people you wrote about in these two prompts. What qualities do they share? What qualities do you most admire in them?

PROMPT: Repeat the process one more time, though now put yourself at center stage. What qualities in your creative self do you most admire? List your own accomplishments, much as you did in the prompt in chapter one. Be direct and honest—no humility here, please. If necessary, describe your creative life through someone else's eyes. Perhaps this person can be more objective.

Where You Write

Let's begin evaluating your habits by giving you something else to worry about: where you write. This can be an important question or an irrelevant one. You decide how well it applies to you. I know writers who can plop down anywhere and start scribbling. Others need special spots, and more lucky talismans gathered around their computers than a bingo player. One person I knew was obsessed with her work space—a desk in her spare bedroom. This was her sanctified altar of creation, and woe be unto him who sat at the desk to sign a birthday card or write a check. Such a violation was catastrophic.

Think about where you write. There is no right or wrong place to do it. Legend has it that Thomas Wolfe wrote standing in his kitchen. And since Wolfe stood 6′6″, he usually wrote on top of his refrigerator. The only wrong place is a place you don't like. To write well and often, it must be a pleasure, and finding a place you love to be can be part of that pleasure.

***

PROMPT: Fantasy time. Describe your ideal writing space. Fill it in to the last detail. Perch yourself on a balcony overlooking the Pacific. Snuggle yourself next to a fire in a richly paneled study. When you finish the description, read it with an eye toward patterns and details. Do you prefer an open or a closed place? Light or dark colors? A sense of freedom or safety? Again, no right answers here.

***

PROMPT: As a way to help you notice your surroundings and work space (and, perhaps, improve them), write a detailed description of your work space. Pan your eyes all around you. Look out the window and describe the view. Again: details, details. To this writing, add a few paragraphs describing your feelings about the space. Is it a haven? Does it offer enough privacy? Do family and friends respect the boundaries of this space? If you often write in more than one place, do this exercise for each one.

Whatever space you use, fill it with things you love, things that make you feel happy, confident and creative. It's important to like the space. On the other hand, don't use the lack of a space as an excuse not to write. Many are the wanna-be writers who are waiting—probably still waiting—for an ideal space to write. When such a space is found or built, the making of literature will commence. Trust me. It won't happen. Waiting for a space is a reason to wait to write. And those who wait are not generating ideas, nor are they getting ideas on paper. The best writing room I ever had was in a house where I lived when I was married. A wonderful shelf ran along every wall, so that I was literally surrounded by books. I had room and an overstuffed reading chair, a reading lamp and two windows. I wrote there hardly at all. On the other hand, for a year I worked in a back room of an old house, a room that was added on, and had no heat and little light. I wrote five hours a day, every day. If you deeply want to write, you will write—no matter what type of space you have at your disposal. But, if possible, be good to yourself. Give yourself, as best you can, a space that is yours and that you like. It will make "showing up" that much easier.

PROMPT: Design the ideal writing space. Fill it with all the things you want and love. Take your time and really develop your descriptions. Ladle on the details. Now step back and look at your description. Does it tell you anything about your writing goals and dreams? Does it say anything about your vision of what a writer is? Does it tell you anything about how you see yourself as a writer? Consider these questions. They will help you design a good place for you to write and will help you understand better your own writing impulse.

So now you've imagined a great space for writing. Maybe you already have such a space, or one you like very much. If so, congratulations. If you don't, or even if you do, but feel stale sometimes, consider writing in other places—the library, the park, a bus. The strange surroundings can infuse your writing with new energy. New ideas pop up and a new zest enters the prose. I'm not, however, a big believer in coffeehouse writing. When you write where others can see you writing, a certain self-consciousness can enter the prose. You are a deep, dark, mysterious writer. For me, writing, in its generative stage, needs to be a private act, even a secret one. The secrecy adds power to the words. But that's my bias. Maybe you have found such a place that in the company of strangers you can create a keen sense of aloneness. If that works for you, by all means keep doing it. Each of us finds his own process, his own rituals that spark creativity.

PROMPT: In one week, write for at least a half hour in three different places. After the week is over, if not before, reread what you wrote. Look for variances in tone and voice. Are these differences the result of your moods at those times, or do they stem from the nature of what you were writing? Was one place more productive, more free than the others? If so, revisit that place, especially when you're feeling blocked or stale.

When You Write

Some of us are morning writers. We are sharpest then, perhaps still fresh from the night's sleep, or with our minds still partly in the world of dreams. We like morning light, the silence of the house before others awake. We enjoy the freedom from the noise of the day, the demands of family and work. We've yet to plug into our to-do self, who scurries about with a head full of errands. Our "monkey minds," as the Buddhists would call them, have not yet turned on.

Some of us prefer writing at night. The day's activities are behind us, our to-do list is completed (or, more likely, abandoned) for the day. This is our time. We can focus. The night brings with it mysteries and dreams of its own. Our imaginations are set free. Some of us find afternoons most productive. Certainly late afternoon, when the shadows grow long and sunlight takes on a golden hue, we feel drawn into ourselves. This feeling can coax ideas to the surface.

I know a few writers who find evenings great for first drafts, in which they make riskier moves, and they revise in the morning, when they feel better able to evaluate the quality of their ideas. One writer I know will not consider a short story finished until she has revised it at various times of day. She needs to see the story from all perspectives—"all her selves," as she says—to be sure she's found all the story's possibilities.

When do you prefer to write? When are you feeling most creative? Not many of us work well at all times. But by cultivating other sides of your creative self—the morning side if you're an evening writer, and vice versa—you can expand the range of your ideas and the tonalities of your world. If you're waking up feeling stale, try waiting until the evening. If you're stuck on a piece of writing, not sure where to go or just tired of it, try looking at it during a time of day when you normally don't write.

PROMPT: Begin a piece of writing in the evening. If you need an idea, flip to the prompts in the next section. Write at least a page. Put away the page. Then, in a few days, write on the same subject, as if starting it from scratch, during a morning session. Put away the page. After a few more days, pull out both pages and compare them. Which do you like better? Try this exercise a few times to help you gauge your best time for being creative.

P R O M P T : Write a scene that is set at night. It should possess an element of intrigue or mystery. Write this scene at night. Push yourself to take risks with the language or the images or simply with the events in the scene. Allow the scene to end without resolution so that at least one more scene will be needed to provide some sort of closure. Write that scene in the morning. Put the scenes away for a few days, then take them out and read them. Do they connect? Do the actions and the tone match?

How You Write

You'll be more creative if you approach writing in a healthy state of mind, one conducive to letting go of inhibitions. Some writers meditate to achieve this state; others drink a glass of wine. We'll explore specific ways to get started in the next chapter, but let's spend a few minutes examining the state of mind we're trying to achieve. I believe that we want to achieve an alert passivity, a state of mind that allows us to trust our instincts and frees us to take risks.

Yield

Ideas don't respond to the force of our wills—damn them. We can't make them appear. That's why when we're feeling blocked it does little good to try to pound our way through. It won't work. We'll grow even more frustrated and further away from where we need to be to find ideas (though I'll admit a good hard slam of fist onto table feels pretty good at those times).

Getting ideas requires allowing our minds to yield. The ideas are there, but we have to wait for them quietly. Poet William Stafford compared the creative process to fishing. We cast a line into the water, then wait silently, patiently, for a nibble. If we make a lot of noise, the fish won't bite. With experience, we learn how to read a nibble, how to wait for the right moment to pull the fish in.

The process also can be compared to yoga. We learn to resist the temptation to force a stretch or a twist. Our impulse is to push ourselves, to stretch or twist farther than we have before. But the teacher will tell us to yield to the stretch, to "breathe into it." Then we can go deeper because our bodies are not straining. They're relaxing into what they are able to do naturally.

Maintaining this mind-set is not easy. We live in a results-oriented society. We learn to be productive, to have something to show for our efforts. We want proof we are making progress, getting better. As writers, we want finished pieces and each piece should be better than the one before it. If we're going to the trouble of rising at the crack of dawn, we'd better get something out of it.

To be more creative, you need to resist these impulses. Some days will be effortless. Some days will be impossible, just as some days the fish bite and other days they don't. Your job is to show up, to write and enjoy, not to evaluate.

PROMPT: I used two metaphors for yielding—fishing and yoga. Think of a few of your own. What activities do you do that require this approach? Describe the process. Teach it to someone who has never done it.

Get in Your Belly

In her book *Awakening the Warrior Within*, Dawn Callan speaks of a warrior's ability to "get in the belly." By this she means the practice of trusting your instincts, depending upon them, to avoid the distractions of thought and emotion. If you've seen experienced martial artists spar, you've noticed that their bodies are loose and relaxed until the moment they strike. They breathe gently. They trust their training to defend them against an attack and disable the attacker. If they think too much, their bodies won't respond naturally. If they feel too much—anger, fear, aggression—they lose their balance, missing opportunities to strike and making themselves vulnerable to attack.

As writers, we can take a similar approach. Get in your belly. Trust your instincts. Don't listen to the voices we discussed in the last chapter. When an idea rises to the surface, be ready to seize it. If you practice your writing, read good work, build your vocabulary, study the craft, remain aware of the world around you, keep your imagination fresh and fertile, the ideas will come and you'll recognize them.

PROMPT: Open this book to any page and do one of the prompts. Don't consider if it interests you or is appropriate to your background. As you do it, try to move past distracting thoughts and feelings. Focus on the prompt and let yourself go.

Take Risks

Winston Churchill once said that the key to success for the beginning artist is audacity. I think that's the key to success of an artist at any level of experience. When you find an idea, push it to its limits. Explore all of its possibilities. Too often we decide what type of idea we want, knowing what will work for us. We reject other ideas before really digging around in them, especially if they demand that we go beyond where we normally go—in length, in depth, in emotional connection. An idea can seem "too crazy" or "impossible to pull off."

Compare this reaction to learning to do a somersault when you're a kid. Yeah, yeah, you were a plucky four-year-old and just flipped right over. But for the rest of us, that first trip over the top was a little scary. After we put our heads on the ground and kicked our legs up a bit, we let them fall back to the ground. Sometimes it takes someone to pull our legs over the first time. We felt sort of dizzy, but the movement was fun. Before we knew it, we were flipping backward off diving boards.

Many ideas never develop because we grow bored with them. We aren't blocked as much as we're just not interested anymore. This boredom could signal a weak idea not worth developing. But before abandoning it, try adding a new element. Take a risk. Up the stakes a bit. Surprise yourself. Risk embarrassment. When you hear yourself say, "I can't let anybody read this," or, "This is too weird," you've probably hit a vein worth mining a little deeper.

Sometimes you'll finish a piece and not like it. For some reason, it just doesn't shimmer. Perhaps the problem is that it's too safe, too pat. As an editor and contest judge, I've read hundreds of stories that were done well but weren't interesting. Of course, in some cases, it's a matter of taste. But sometimes the stories simply lacked the energy that comes from a writer's true and total engagement. My advice is to try to find the spark in the piece. Pull it out and pour some time into that place. If you widen your imaginative net, you'll catch more ideas. Follow Winnie's dictum: Risk audacity.

Chapter Four

Getting Ready to Write

*I have no warm-up exercises, other than to
take an occasional drink.*
—E.B. WHITE

B efore you exercise, lift weights, run or play a sport, you warm up. You move around a little bit to get the blood flowing into your muscles. Then you stretch those muscles, making sure your calves and hamstrings and Achilles tendons, your shoulders and arms are good and limber. Then you begin. That's our focus in this chapter: getting ready for individual writing sessions and getting ready to write on a regular basis.

What do you do to warm up before writing? Our imaginations need to be as limber as our bodies. If not, we can suffer the creative equivalent of muscle cramps. We struggle through a page, then grip our sides when an annoying stitch throbs. We try to run through it, but sometimes it's too much. We stop. I'll stop using the exercise metaphor before I really get on your nerves, and the point should be clear: Take time to warm up before beginning. Let's look at some ways to do that.

Warm-Ups

If you are writing a piece you hope to publish, you may have trouble getting started for fear of making a mistake or writing something that isn't good. Trying too hard can freeze your imagination. The words don't come to you. The writing is stiff and clumsy. The ideas don't make sense or hold together. You may grow so frustrated that you stop writing before you've had a chance to get started.

To move past these chilly moments, begin by writing on a less demanding piece. Try a prompt or two from this book, or write a brief journal entry. Then, when the words begin to flow, switch to the piece you want to write. Reading a page or two of a writer you admire can be another method for warming up. Reading switches your mind into "language mode." Your imagination warms up as it becomes engaged by what you're reading. After ten minutes or so, you should be ready to move to your own writing.

PROMPT: Warm up by writing at least three paragraphs in your journal. Write about the day's events or plans, ideas you've been thinking about, whatever. This will help you limber up without the pressure of writing well. It will also put you in touch with your natural writing voice. Sometimes we get mired in our "literary" voices, which prevents us from writing. In the journal, you can get your pen moving, then segue to the piece. If you find that this approach leads to long journal entries but no words on the piece of the day, set a limit: "I'll write one page in the journal, then move to the novel."

PROMPT: Warm up by reading one page from a book you enjoy. Reading can put you in touch with the language part of your brain, and put you in the mood for writing. This warm-up can be especially effective if you write at the end of the day. It helps you clear away the detail brain, the list-making, duty-performing, bill-paying, child-rearing brain. Reading poetry is especially effective, allowing you to focus on image and rhythm and cadence. Fiction writer Kate Braverman told me once she often begins writing by reading a poem or two by Octavio Paz.

B eware of a couple of dangers in reading before you begin. First, as with journaling, we easily can get caught up in what we're reading and use up our designated writing time. The remedy here is also to set limits: "I'll read these three poems, and then move to the memoir." The second, and more insidious, danger lies in the voice of the writer we're reading; it can invade our own writing. This danger is especially prevalent with less experienced writers who are still seeking their voices, but it can happen to all of us.

A couple of remedies: Read a form different from the one you're writing in. If you're writing a mystery novel, for example, read poetry or an essay. The voice of the writer you're reading still can invade, but the influence will be lessened. Or, read a writer whose style is significantly different from your own, a style you admire but don't feel drawn (or able) to imitate. If your own style is straightforward, perhaps a little Dylan Thomas and his lush lyricism will get you moving.

PROMPT: Not to wave my own flag here, but, again, diving into a prompt in this book can help you warm up. Any book with exercises will do. Like a musician zips through a few scales to get his fingers moving, try exercises. There's no pressure to "perform" in these exercises. You don't risk a wrong turn in your novel or memoir. You're not going to screw up your short story or script. So, right now, pick a prompt from anywhere in this book and follow it.

Creativity Techniques

You can use any number of techniques for storming the old brain bastille: freewriting, clustering, cut and paste, mix and match, cavewriting and a few others. You probably are familiar with these techniques, but let's review them.

Freewriting

Freewriting, often called automatic writing, though the two techniques vary slightly, is a process in which you focus on a specific topic and write everything you can think of, never lifting your pen. You don't worry about punctuation or grammar; you just keep writing. If you can't think of anything to write, don't stop your pen. Simply write "I can't think of anything to write" or whatever phrases come to mind. You may want to take a deep breath during this time, to relax into your blocked mind, freeing it, just as in yoga we're taught to breathe into the stretched muscle. The goal is to get the words on the page and to circumnavigate the critical part of your brain. By ignoring the rules of writing, you'll focus on the topic itself, capturing images and metaphors and memories that a more formal, structured approach can impede.

Throughout this book, in some of the prompts, I'll suggest freewriting as one way to generate material. Some freewriting, especially the kind done in school, is timed, which adds an urgency that can help you bypass the critic, distracting you from trying to perfect each sentence. If this approach works for you, time your writing. But for some people, the ticking clock adds an unnecessary frantic quality that may undermine their creative flow. Experiment with how freewriting can work best for you.

Brainstorming

Brainstorming is a technique similar to freewriting but is even less structured. You write as much as you can, ignoring all rules of grammar and punctuation, and you need not even focus on the topic. Instead, you write anything that comes into your mind. If you're brainstorming ideas for a particular project, you will be focused, but don't discard any ideas that seem unrelated. You're trying to bypass your critic and dig deeply into your unconscious mind, allowing that part of your brain to conjure images and connections that your conscious mind would discard.

Automatic Writing

The automatic writing approach was popularized by Jack Kerouac and the Beat writers of the 1950s. Though it is similar to freewriting, in automatic writing you do obey the basic rules of punctuation, grammar and sentence structure. In fact, your first draft can be your final draft. Also known as trance writing, this approach taps into the subconscious mind, disregarding the inner critic and allowing you to bend image, metaphor and language to your own whims. The writer falls into a somewhat hypnotic state and follows the lead of his subconscious, free-associating between ideas and images.

Perhaps due to my more formal education in writing, I believe in the power of editing and revising and doubt that automatic writing is somehow more pure and artistic. I would echo (if not completely) Truman Capote's famous line: "That's not writing, that's typing." But automatic writing can be a lot of fun, and it can be a great way to generate ideas and even entire pages in an early draft, especially for writers who tend to labor too long in getting everything perfect before moving on. Automatic writing can produce wonderfully lyrical passages and can inspire daring leaps of language and thought. If it works for you, use it. Just be willing to revise later.

Listing

As you'll notice as you work through this book, I'm a big fan of lists. I'll ask you to make a lot of them. It's simply a way of getting ideas on the page without even moving your pen or cursor from the left side of the page to the right. The lists I suggest in the prompts need not be hierarchical and need not even be in a straight line. They don't even have to be lists. They can appear any way you want them to appear. Straight lines work for me, allowing me to easily see patterns and connections. But if you tend to rely a lot on your left brain—the ordering, logical side—you may want to avoid lists. They will amplify your tendency toward linear thinking. You may want to try clustering instead.

Clustering

Also called webbing or web writing, clustering is an idea-generating device that taps into the right side of the brain by breaking down linear thinking. Instead of logical, cause-and-effect, top-to-bottom lines on the page, you draw circles. Place your keyword in the center of the page, circle it, then, as ideas flow into your mind, write them down in a word or phrase, circle them and radiate them around the keyword with connecting lines. See the example of the cluster on the following page.

As with freewriting and brainstorming, don't censor yourself. Write whatever comes into your mind. Clustering is especially good at generating images. These may seem unrelated when you write them down and circle them, but trust the process and your unconscious mind. If the image is vivid in your mind or nags at you as you're clustering, some

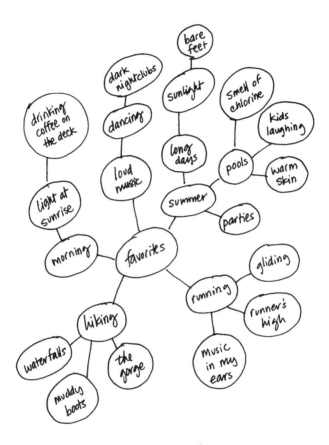

relationship exists with the keyword (sometimes called a nucleus word), and later you will have time to explore the connection.

Whenever I say, "Make a list" in a prompt, feel free to cluster. Find out what works best for you. In fact, vary your approach. The change could add freshness to your ideas.

Cavewriting

This approach was invented by Barry Lane and used in his book *Writing as a Road to Self-Discovery*. In cavewriting, you mix words and pictures. You draw pictures of things related to the subject and write words, well, anywhere you want on the page. Like clustering, it breaks down your left-brain need for order and control, allowing your right brain to play.

Just as you don't want to censor your words, don't censor your draw-ings. Draw whatever comes into your mind, much like a doodle, without giving it much thought. Write whatever words come to you, placing them around or even within the drawing. Lane based his approach on cave drawings, which are simple, primitive and often powerful. As a teacher, he noticed children had little problem mixing drawing and writing, and his approach attempts to recapture the creativity we all possessed as children. When I prompt you to make a list, feel free to do a cavewriting.

Cut and Paste

Another approach popularized by those knucklehead Beats. In this tech-nique, the brainchild of William Burroughs, the writer writes entire pages, maybe even entire stories and novels, then literally cuts the pages into pieces and rearranges them, sometimes simply throwing the pages into the air and organizing them according to where they fall on the floor. If you're blocked on a piece of writing, this can be a liberating exercise, giving you fresh insights into possible forms and shapes for the piece. You can discover interesting juxtapositions that otherwise would not have occurred to you. You could cut up a few freewritings from the prompts in this book, toss them into the air and find new ways of seeing the possibilities in your ideas.

Mix and Match

With mix and match, we do the one from column A, one from column B routine. Some writers would dismiss this approach as fatuous and arbitrary, useful only to hacks. But holster that gun for a second, pard-ner. This can be a fun way of seeing connections between seemingly unrelated things, which is one of the goals in creating art. I've read a few strikingly effective short stories begun using this method. In some of the prompts in this book, I'll suggest doing a mix and match, and you should feel free to try it whenever the mood strikes.

When You're Stuck

You can use any of the techniques discussed in the previous section to help you generate ideas in a focused way, that is, on a specific topic or project. But you can use them in a more general way, too, when you're having trouble getting started. You also can use them when you're stuck. You might be blocked on a scene or unable to decide what happens next in your story. Perhaps a character won't do what you ask of him.

If these techniques don't help you get unstuck, and you're using the approaches discussed in the previous chapter without success, try doing something else. Move away from your desk for awhile. Do something that doesn't require much thought, such as washing dishes or taking a walk. Have you ever noticed that some of your best ideas occur to you in the shower? Or when you're gardening? A writer I know breaks through blocks by kicking a soccer ball around his backyard. Something about repetitive motion allows you to drift past the block.

I have a basketball hoop on my garage, so when I'm blocked I shoot some baskets for a half hour. It nearly always helps. I don't force myself to think about the writing problem, but I don't force myself not to think about it, either. I let my mind drift where it will. Inevitably, it returns to the problem. Basketball has worked for me for years. My ten-year-old son has picked up the habit. Though he's not dealing with writer's block yet, and he doesn't even write down his stories, he makes them up while he shoots baskets. I can't even get him to play a little one-on-one anymore. "I can't, Dad," he tells me. "I'm thinking of my stories." So we shoot together and he tells me his stories, or sometimes we just shoot together, both of us far away in our minds, cooking up ideas. Do whatever works for you.

Begin

PROMPT: Write down every idea you've ever had but didn't use in a piece of writing. I'm serious. Get cracking. Note every one you can remember. Give yourself time to do this prompt. It might take days, even weeks. Make it an ongoing project. You'll never remember them all, but you'll be surprised by how many you do recall. Do a cluster or a freewrite or a brainstorm. As your list grows, choose ideas from it that still interest you. Write them on a new list of ideas for projects. If possible, dig up what you wrote before abandoning the ideas you like. Check the computer files or the pages in your notebook. In fact, pull out all of your old writing notebooks and read them. Again, you'll be surprised at what you find. You probably have enough good ideas to last you awhile. You'll see some of them through new eyes, perceiving possibilities that you missed before. Perhaps an old idea connects with a more recent one. Keep your list handy as you work your way through this book.

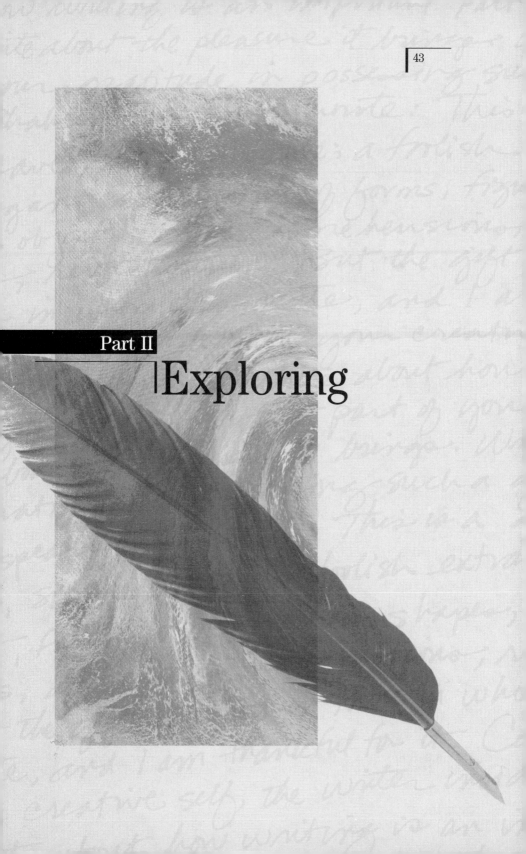

Part II

Exploring

Chapter Five

I Yam What I Yam and Other Lies

The writer can only explore the inner space of his characters by perceptively navigating his own.
—PETER DEVRIES

I love Popeye. I used to love him because someone I once loved collected Popeye memorabilia, and together we'd scour antique shops for Popeye stuff. We built a fine collection. Although the person is no longer in my life, the old sailor has sort of grown on me. Who, for heaven's sake, doesn't like Popeye? An even larger question is, Why do we like Popeye, this sketchy, quirky refugee from a seventy-year-old, long-forgotten comic strip? Most of his contemporaries have faded to obscurity or, in the case of superheroes, have been updated for today's audience. Not Popeye. He's still drawn in those primitive lines, still follows the single flimsy plotline of nabbing the fickle Olive Oyl from the hairy clutches of Bluto by glugging down a thatch of spinach.

His appeal, I think, is in his simplicity. He yis what he yis. That's comforting. We all would like to be that sure of who we are, but noncartoon characters like us are a lot more complicated. Getting at who we are is tough to do, and who we are changes depending on day, time, location and circumstance. We are parent, boss, motorist, son/daughter, employee, mate, shortstop, tourist, reader, writer, expert, novice and many other identities. As writers, we suffer from even more elusive identities. We are "the chameleon poet" and we "contain multitudes." There is a famous anecdote about the poet James Dickey nervously waiting backstage before a national television appearance. Someone told him, "Relax, just be yourself," and he answered, "Which one?"

So it's a bit troubling when books on writing and creativity urge us to write from our true self, as if there exists inside us a single real person, that the other selves are merely cranks and imposters who can be dismissed, leaving only the authentic person, from whom a tidal wave of words and ideas will rush forth. If the guy at the bookstore where you bought this book told you that would happen here, forget it. He was lying.

But getting to know who you are as a person is indeed helpful—and it's probably one of the reasons that you write. It's also helpful to get to know yourself better in order to find the sources of your creativity.

P R O M P T : List the top ten experiences of your life—*top* meaning significant. Wondrous. Glorious. Terrible. Illuminating. Demoralizing. Jubilant. Ten, of course, is an arbitrary number. But start there. Think about it for a moment, letting your mind roam free, keeping your pen on the page. There's no penalty for going beyond ten, but if you do, cut to ten when you review the list. Stop reading now and make your list.

How did you do? Did you stop at ten? Did you find yourself listing the *big* events—births of children, marriage, divorce, relocations, career moves? I did. Now take time to make another list of ten. We've cleared the monuments from the field and can now look at smaller ones.

P R O M P T : Brainstorm a new list of ten events.

P R O M P T : From your lists, pick one. Don't think about it for long. Choose the first one that pops into your head. Or, if you want, discard the first one and choose another. The second one is often better. Explore it in a piece of writing by recounting the event in a narrative—

first this happened, then this, then this, etc. Take your time and put yourself back in that place and time. Relax and allow the memories to trickle into your mind. You'll be surprised by what you remember. After you've finished telling the story, write a few paragraphs about why this was a significant moment, or, better, *how* it was significant. What did it mean to you? How did it change you? What does its significance say about you?

PROMPT: Spend a writing session making top ten lists of events in your life. Top ten happy times or enlightening times or whatever you want. Then look at these lists for patterns—recurring themes and images. Try to view them objectively, as if they happened to someone else. Who is this person? What do you like about her? What motivates this person? What mistakes does she continue to make? What demons dog her? What qualities does this person possess and how would you, as the objective writer, express these qualities?

PROMPT: Write about your first experience with death. Who died? When? What did you know about death before the event, and what did you come to learn about it after the event?

PROMPT: Write about your first experience with birth (not your own, of course). Who was born? What did you know about birth before the event, and what did you come to learn about it after the event?

PROMPT: Describe yourself from the perspective of someone you know, in a first-person monologue, as if the person were describing you to someone else. (To ensure your friend's candor, let's say you're not around when this description takes place.) Try this exercise a few times, choosing several people to describe you. Be faithful to the people you've chosen in all of these descriptions. Describe yourself in their voices, from their true perspectives.

PROMPT: Keep a grocery receipt—a long one. When you get home, put it away and then pull it out a few weeks from now. What does this person buy, and what can you tell about this person from what she buys?

PROMPT: Spend a few minutes looking in the mirror. Just stare back at your reflection. Then write a self-portrait, describing yourself in detail. Try to imagine that you're looking at a stranger. What assumptions would you make from this person's appearance?

PROMPT: Brainstorm a list, beginning each entry with the words "I am a..." Don't stop yourself during this brainstorm, even if you feel the word or phrase that comes to mind seems silly or just plain wrong. In a number of my workshops, this prompt has yielded some surprising results.

PROMPT: Make a list of the things in your home that are yours—furnishings, pictures on the walls, souvenirs. Go from room to room and write down what you find. Write about what these things say about the person. If you could pick one item from your list as emblematic of you, which one would you choose? Write about why you chose this item. Choose another item and try again.

PROMPT: Put together a resume and a cover letter to apply for your ideal job. Really sell yourself, detailing your professional skills and accomplishments. On a separate page, write your work history, listing jobs, places of employment, reasons why you left each job, how well you performed at each job.

PROMPT: Remember the old question that goes something like, "If you could be any kind of tree, what would you be?" Dumb, I know. But let's use it, changing it to, "If you *were* a tree, what kind would you be?"

How would you answer, and why do you think so? If you want, try it with car, animal, bird, food, color, era in history.

PROMPT: Mona Simpson begins her story "Lawns" with the sentence "I steal." Begin a story or essay or poem or journal entry with the line "I _____." Push forward from there. If you can think of one action that speaks to who you are, what would it be? Write at least a few paragraphs. Try this experiment a few times, using different actions.

PROMPT: Keep a dream journal for at least a week, preferably longer, waking up every morning and writing down what you can remember. Write about a character who appears in one of your dreams, someone who lingers in your mind or has appeared in past dreams. Who is this character? What can you learn about yourself from him?

PROMPT: Do you have a five-year plan? If not, take time and make one. Write down how you want your life to be in five years. When you finish, read what you've written and think about *why* you want to achieve these goals. What do the goals imply about your life as it is now? What do they suggest about you as a person?

PROMPT: Cast yourself five years into the future. You have achieved all the goals you wrote about in the previous prompt. In the persona of you-five-years-from-now, write a letter to the current you. Having achieved the goals, what advice would you impart to yourself? Explain how it feels to be living the life that you now hope to achieve?

The Many Faces of You

All of these prompts should help you begin exploring yourself in a variety of ways. The other chapters in this section will help, too, focusing on specific facets of your background, your experiences and your personality. In working through these chapters, allow yourself to have fun and to take risks. Enjoy the process. Be daring. Don't worry about sounding literary or angry or weak or whatever tag you're tempted to stick on yourself. In fact, avoid tags of any kind. The key is candor. You need only bring the courage to dig deep inside yourself.

And learn the lesson of Popeye: Don't worry about consistency. He is what he is, but you have many facets and dimensions. Need proof? Read your journal. Not only will you find yourself in many moods, your handwriting will change from day to day. Remember Emerson's line about consistency being "the hobgoblin of little minds."

PROMPT: You are afflicted with a rare (and getting rarer) disease in which you can only tell the truth, the whole truth. Now, introduce yourself to someone you don't know—on the page, of course. Explain to the stranger who you are. Go into detail. Tell your life story if you have to. The stranger is fictitious and will listen intently for hours.

PROMPT: Create two or three characters from facets of your personality. Put them in a car, driving to the coast (whichever coast is farthest from where you live). Who takes the wheel? Who navigates? Give them a topic of conversation, such as the best route to take or what they should do when they arrive.

PROMPT: Prepare questions for an interview with someone you admire. Try to get at what makes that person tick. Ask her probing, personal questions, no matter how inappropriate they might seem. When you've finished your script, ask these questions of yourself. And answer them.

PROMPT: Transport yourself back into the you at twelve years of age. Close your eyes and try to put yourself into your own twelve-year-old mind. Have that child prepare a list of questions for you—questions about life and what to expect, questions about love, questions seeking advice on the trials of a twelve-year-old. Now bring yourself back and respond to those questions. Explain why you've lived as you have, why you made the decisions you've made and how you feel about those decisions. Try the same experiment again, this time imagining yourself at seventy.

PROMPT: Write an alternate story of your life, like an alternate history book, in which the author changes one key fact of history, then explores the possible changes that would occur as a result. Change one key fact of your life, one decision that you made, and explore how your life would be different. If you hadn't committed to your mate, for example, or moved to a new city or passed up a certain opportunity, how would things change? You can do this in a serious way, striving for the most plausible possibilities, or you can go wild, concocting crazy scenarios. Better yet: Do it both ways.

PROMPT: You need a reference, someone to say what a wonderful person you are. Perhaps, you're at the gates of heaven and there's some question about letting you in. Pick the person you would ask for this reference and write what he'd say.

PROMPT: Wait a second. You're not past the pearly gates yet. A second reference has been found, someone you know who will not say good things about you. Write her rebuttal to the previous prompt.

PROMPT: Write a monologue in which a character describes herself, her nature rather than her appearance. As her description develops, begin to make clear that her self-portrait is not accurate. She might, for example, speak in a self-congratulatory tone about her humility, or she might mention events in her life to prove she is a terrible person, when in fact they show she was justified in her actions. Remember Huck Finn's self-accusatory description of himself as a bad person for hiding his friend Jim, the slave.

PROMPT: Begin a story with a character based closely on yourself. Put the character in a place you've never been and write about what happens.

PROMPT: For the last prompt in the chapter, let's return to where we started, with a comic strip character. Cast yourself in the starring role of a comic strip. It's called "Your Name." Describe this character, the supporting characters and the tone and focus of the comic strip. Would it offer trenchant political commentary? The foibles and frolics of family life? Whimsical wit about the single life? Daily life as viewed by a group of cats? A world of children coming of age? OK, I'm out of descriptions. You take it from here.

Chapter Six

Schnitzel With Noodles

If there's a book you really want to read but it hasn't been written yet, then you must write it.
—TONI MORRISON

Knowing what to write, as we've discussed, involves knowing yourself. You will write with passion if you write about topics and people close to your heart. I learned this truth again a year or two ago when a friend told me he wanted to be a writer but was struggling. He's been a cop for more than fifteen years but was tired of the job. In a few more years he could retire with a full pension, which he planned to use to support himself while he knocked out novels. Crime novels. He has the experience, we agreed. He should give it a try. But the pages of what I read were dull, larded with technical jargon and the accoutrements of police work. They were weak on plot and character. He clearly was not engaged by the stories. One night while we were talking about how to make his stories more interesting, we drifted to the subject of his collection of beer memorabilia. As he discussed the old beer bottles and vintage advertisements that filled his house, his eyes lit up. He was clearly engaged. We agreed that maybe he was writing about something he didn't really like—police work—and the novels reflected his disinterest.

He should try, instead, to write about beer stuff. He did, and he has since published several excellent articles in trade magazines.

The point is that the cliché about writing what you know is wrong. Instead, write about what you like. If you're afraid to write about what you know because you think readers will be bored, don't be so sure. If you're afraid to write about what you know because *you're* bored, trust your instincts. Avoid that subject. Too often we choose to write about what we think other people will like, or about what's hot in the marketplace. If writing about something feels like a guilty pleasure, you're on the right track.

PROMPT: I picked a corny title to this chapter, so let's use it. Write a list of a few of your favorite things. If possible, don't stop at a few. Write a list of a lot of your favorite things—foods, activities, possessions, seasons, settings, whatever comes to mind. Brainstorm your list and add to it later as more things occur to you. An artful example of this process occurs in Woody Allen's *Manhattan* when the protagonist is lying on a couch, speaking into a handheld recorder, rattling off the things he loves best, from Cezanne's still lifes to Willie Mays. With the list he slowly builds to whom he loves most of all, a woman he left earlier in the film for another woman. Pick an item from your list and explore it, giving your reasons for liking the item or developing a history, perhaps, of how long you've liked it, what associations it holds for you, particular memories of enjoying the item.

PROMPT: In *Manhattan*, another character builds a list of overrated people and things, popular favorites the character feels receive unwarranted praise. Compile your own list of overrated things. As with the previous prompt, look for patterns in the list, trends that say something about you as the compiler. Then choose an item and write about it as you did with the one above.

PROMPT: Pick an item from each list and write a piece comparing them in some way. Avoid simply making it "This is good; this is bad." What qualities do they share? How might someone dislike the thing you like and like the thing you don't? Try hard to make a fair, detailed assessment. Develop a convincing case, perhaps in a light, humorous way.

P R O M P T : Let's play the old "If you could take five things to a desert island, what would they be?" game. This will help narrow your list of favorites. Write about why you would choose these five things. Then imagine yourself on that island for six months or a year. Which items have grown dull in your eyes? Which ones continue to shine?

P R O M P T : Write about a favorite thing from your childhood. A doll you carried everywhere? A prized baseball card? If you want, explore what your attachment to this object suggests about you as a child. Why do you think it was such an important thing in your life?

P R O M P T : Write about a desired thing in your childhood that you didn't own, something you wanted—such as a toy or a trip to Disneyland—that you didn't get. Give us the details. How long did you covet this thing? What does your desire for it tell you about yourself as a child? If this focus interests you, do it again but explore your teens. What did you want during that time? If you want, push into your adulthood.

P R O M P T : Write about a favorite activity in your childhood, something you enjoyed and did as often as possible. As with the previous prompt, look for insights into yourself as a child through this examination of the activity. In his poem "The Hummer," William Matthews writes of a boy who plays countless baseball games in his mind while pitching a wet tennis ball against a toolshed door:

> Some days he pitched
> six games, the last in dusk,
> in tears, in rage, in the blue
> blackening joy of obsession.

PROMPT: Has anything ever been too much of a "favorite thing" in your life? An addiction? If so, write about the addiction and your experience with it. If you've never struggled with addiction, create a fictional character who is addicted to something and have him describe his feelings about his compulsion. In her memoir *Drinking: A Love Story*, Caroline Knapp chronicles her battle with alcoholism. In the following excerpt, she explores her love for alcohol:

> I loved the way drink made me feel, and I loved its special power of deflection, its ability to shift my focus away from my own awareness of self onto something else, something less painful than my own feelings. I loved the sounds of drink: the slide of a cork as it eased out of a wine bottle, the distinct glug-glug of booze pouring into a glass, the clatter of ice cubes in a tumbler. I loved the rituals, the camaraderie of drinking with others, the warming, melting feelings of ease and courage it gave me.

PROMPT: In the previous prompt, Caroline Knapp gives us specific details about the sound of her addiction. These sounds suggest her feelings about the subject. Use her example to write about a favorite activity by focusing on the sounds of it. No need to focus on an addiction. The activity can be something positive and beautiful in your life. The key is concentrating your imagination on the sounds.

PROMPT: Repeat the previous prompt, this time focusing on the smells involved in a favorite activity.

PROMPT: Repeat the previous prompt, this time focusing on the tastes involved in a favorite activity.

PROMPT: One more time, though now focus on the sense of touch.

You Are What You Like

Writing about favorites can be a way to characterize yourself as a writer to your audience and can be a way to see yourself from an oblique angle, or through the filter of an objective thing, so that you might better understand yourself. Anna Quindlen, for example, begins an essay with the sentence "I was a Paul girl," meaning that as a young girl her favorite Beatle was Paul McCartney. Girls who liked Paul were different from the ones who liked John, George or Ringo. Each musician, apparently, attracted a different type of girl. The essay establishes her childhood identity as a Paul type, a bit conventional and romantic, and explores the changes she's undergone since those days.

On the other hand, David Foster Wallace, in his essay "Shipping Out," writes a blistering and hilarious account of taking a Caribbean cruise, definitely not one of his favorite things. We learn much about him by what he notices and the attitude he expresses about these things. Through tone and selection of detail, rather than through direct statement, the narrative persona comes to life.

I now know every conceivable rationale for somebody spending more than $3,000 to go on a Caribbean cruise. To be specific; voluntarily and for pay, I underwent a 7-Night Caribbean (7NC) Cruise on board the m.v. *Zenith* (which no wag could resist immediately rechristening the m.v. *Nadir*), a 47,255-ton ship owned by Celebrity Cruises, Inc., one of the twenty-odd cruise lines that operate out of south Florida and specialize in "Megaships," the floating wedding cakes with occupancies in four figures and engines the size of branch banks.

The narrator clearly does not consider cruises one of his favorite things. His tone characterizes him, and we learn about him from what he doesn't like. (Author's note: "Shipping Out" is one of the funniest essays ever written.) Writing about things we don't like can be a delightful exercise, allowing us to indulge our dark sides without compunction. In fact . . .

PROMPT: Write about something you deeply dislike. Here's your chance to blast it. Go for the jugular on this one.

PROMPT: Write about yourself by writing in detail about one of your favorite things. Begin by only mentioning and describing the thing. Don't mention yourself at all. Then review these paragraphs. Make a general statement about the type of people who love this thing. Sophisticated and discerning? Simple and practical? We're dealing in stereotypes here, of course, but these could lead us to more sophisticated and discerning conclusions.

PROMPT: Follow Quindlen's lead. Describe yourself as a child or teen by filling in the blank of this sentence: "I was a _____ boy/girl." From there, write about your view of yourself as a child by refracting your view through the prism of this favorite person or object. If you want, keep going, exploring your childhood personality. If you want, continue the exploration by comparing your view of yourself today. What changes have occurred and why?

PROMPT: Continuing the theme of change in the previous prompt, pick something you used to like, in your adulthood, but now don't like nearly as much. A subject that has grown tiresome, perhaps. An activity that once consumed you and that now holds little interest. Explore the changes in you that may have caused this change in attitude toward the thing. You can take the opposite approach, too, if this topic engages you. Pick something that you used to not like and now enjoy quite a bit.

PROMPT: Follow the process of the previous prompt, but this time focus on a person. Is there someone you cared about or admired very much five or ten years ago who now does not appeal to you? How did this disillusionment occur? If possible, avoid choosing someone with whom you were involved in a romantic relationship. Choose a friend or, perhaps, someone you had a crush on but nothing came of it. What does this change in attitude suggest about changes you've undergone?

Literary Likes

In stories we can use favorite things to develop and show character. Laura Wingfield, in Tennessee Williams's play *The Glass Menagerie*, for example, loves her collection of glass animals. We cannot think of this character without thinking of her hobby. Williams uses the hobby to say much about Laura. She has no romantic interests, so her deep wells of love are spent on the glass figurines. The collection, therefore, reinforces our sense of her loneliness. The fragility and innocence of the figurines also mirrors Laura's fragility and innocence, giving the audience a sharper sense of these qualities without the playwright's stating them directly.

When using favorite things—hobbies, activities, possessions—in your work, consider what these things suggest and how they amplify your characters. If you're struggling with a character, give him a favorite song or a favorite food. Show him enjoying it. Without having to explain the character, you've shown your reader something significant about him. Avoid, of course, stereotypes: Construction guy loves guzzling six-packs while watching ESPN; soccer mom loves shopping at the mall and buying expensive clothes. Nor should you play too obviously against type: Construction guy loves making dried flower arrangements; soccer mom relishes weekend fly-fishing. Instead, get to know your character. Find out what works for that person.

PROMPT: Use the prompts above in a piece of fiction. Show the change in a character by showing how a once-loved hobby or object or activity now holds no interest. You may want to speculate in your mind upon the reasons for this change, but don't include these thoughts on the page. Show the character's change in attitude. The character might not even notice the change. For example, in Frank Norris's novel *McTeague*, the eponymous main character is a shy, oafish man, a not-very-good dentist with a taste for simple pleasures. Early in the novel, we learn that he delights in a Sunday afternoon ritual of eating a big lunch, buying a pitcher of steam beer at a saloon and returning to his office to nap and play "some half dozen very mournful airs" on his concertina:

> McTeague looked forward to these Sunday afternoons as a period of relaxation and enjoyment. These were his only pleasures—to eat, to smoke, to sleep, and to play upon his concertina.

Later in the novel, McTeague's fortunes change, which cause a change in him. He falls victim to his own avarice, a change shown through his growing dislike for steam beer and his other simple pleasures.

PROMPT: Let's follow the Wallace example again. Write about a character who clearly does not like a place or activity, but don't let the character speculate on what this dislike says about him. Allow the readers to draw their own conclusions. Indulge yourself. Take this thing to task. Excoriate it.

PROMPT: Review your list of things you like. How many of these items have you written about or used somewhere in your writing? With luck, quite a few. If not, keep this list handy so you can refer to it the next time you're feeling blocked or stale. Maybe you're feeling stale because the material does not engage you. Add some spice by bringing in something you enjoy or care more deeply about, something that, to you, is fun and interesting.

PROMPT: To help you write more about the things you like, write at least a paragraph about every item on your "favorites" list. If you want, add to the list, and write about those items, too. You might simply sketch a description of the thing or explain briefly why it's a favorite. You could cluster around the thing, generating details that could lead to further explorations. You could begin a poem or essay, attach the thing to a character and see where that leads you. You could put the thing in the middle of a room and begin a scene.

Chapter Seven

Nellie Malone From Fifth and Stone

They are passing, posthaste, the gliding years. . . .
The years are passing, my dear, and presently no one
will know what you and I know.
—VLADIMIR NABOKOV

M y grandmother grew up in the Irish ghetto of Cincinnati's West End at the turn of the century. She was poor, Catholic, and she dropped out of school in the seventh grade to go to work. Though her name was Helen, kids in the neighborhood called her Nellie and the name stuck. She was probably more a Nellie than a Helen. For a while the kids called her Nellie Malone from Fifth and Stone, chanted it sometimes, like a jump-rope singsong. My grandmother, from what I could discern, didn't really care much for the name, but bore it without complaint. She was Nellie or Nel to the people who knew her, right up until her death at the age of ninety-four. If I were to write about her, I might begin with those names, then characterize her as a woman who aspired to be a Helen but always was seen as a Nellie. Through those names, I could talk about her work ethic, her sense of humility and sacrifice, her eagerness and inability to dance, her desire to pull herself up from humble beginnings to be, as she constantly coaxed us to be, "refined."

A few years before Grandma was born, her mother had come to the United States from Ireland, traveling with a brother named Tom. Great-Grandma settled in Boston, working as a maid, then later moved to Cincinnati. Tom didn't settle at all. He left when the pair reached America, said he was heading for Australia and would write soon. No one in the family knows what happened to him. He was never heard from again.

There are a number of other family stories I could tell you. No doubt, you could tell me many stories of your own family and heritage. These stories offer great sources of ideas. In this chapter we'll look at those stories, exploring and developing them. Your goal is to use heritage—ethnic and familial—as material for your writing. It's probably the richest source you possess.

Family

You might think your family is deadly dull: Mr. and Mrs. Americana, two point five kiddies, a station wagon with wood-grain side panels, a house in the trim-lawn suburbs, a shaggy dog named Rex. OK, maybe not that dull. Probably not dull at all. Look closer. Dig deeper.

Or, you might have come to the opposite conclusion. You might think your family so strange, the relationships so convoluted and dysfunctional, the myriad battles so exhaustingly bitter and complicated, the interactions so fraught with shattered dreams, unfulfilled needs, grudges, rituals, secrets, lies, internecine feuds and chronic disappointments that you couldn't possibly cover it all in your lifetime. Hooray! Now you're thinking like a writer.

PROMPT: Tell a family story, one that gets passed around at holiday dinners more often than the gravy boat. Tell as many as you can recall. If you want, brainstorm for a while, tagging the stories with just a word or a phrase to help you remember them. Then pick a few and develop the narrative and the details.

PROMPT: Pick one family event that is emblematic of your family, something that happened once that sums up your family's general behavior and outlook. A trip? An emergency? Or perhaps something smaller, less significant to an outsider but freighted with meaning to those involved. If the event doesn't do your family justice, if it shows one side but ignores other sides, pick a second event, even a third one, and follow the same process. Can you combine these stories into a single story, a portrait of your family in its myriad guises?

PROMPT: Talk to family members in search of a mysterious relative from the past: someone who struck out on his own and was never heard from again; someone who lived modestly and died with a surprising amount of money; someone who abruptly left a marriage; someone who lived alone and rarely visited anyone in the family. Imagine a life for this person, the details, based on what you know but pushing beyond into the realm of fiction.

PROMPT: Write about a family ritual, something your family members do only with each other. How did it start? Why has it continued? Do your family members have nicknames for each other? Write about them. How did they start? Why did they stick? What do the nicknames suggest about the roles people play in your family?

PROMPT: Write short biographies of family members, living or dead, close or distant. Who is the black sheep? Who is the success story?

PROMPT: Write about a family secret. I'd give you an example from my own family, but they're secrets. If your family has no shared secrets, write about a family shame, something that simply isn't discussed, such as Aunt Alice's two-week affair in Atlantic City with the dashing Fuller Brush Man.

PROMPT: Find some family photos and use them as sources for writing ideas. Describe the people in the photos—what they're wearing and what they're doing. If you know the circumstances, write about where it was taken and why and what it suggests about your family. Impromptu photos probably will work better than studio portraits, but use whatever you can find. If the photos are very old, find out about the people. Photos are a great way to get older family members talking about the past, and surely you will hear fascinating stories that you'd never been told before. Write them down.

PROMPT: Describe your family to a future family member, an unborn or recently born child. Tell her about the legacy she inherits. What qualities do members of your family usually possess—industry, creativity, good teeth? What qualities bear close awareness—fiery tempers, moodiness, large appetites? If you want, read your piece onto a cassette or videotape. Share it with other family members, and use their thoughts to help you revise.

PROMPT: Write a eulogy for a family member who has passed away. Be honest, bringing up flaws as well as good qualities. Tell a story that is emblematic of the person's nature.

PROMPT: Create a family crest, if you don't have one. What animal—or charge, as it's known in heraldry—best represents your family? What color?

PROMPT: Write about your family, making them the First Family, plopping them into the White House. How well do they represent the country? Which member becomes the media darling? Which member causes no end of embarrassment?

PROMPT: Write about your family, making them the very first family, living in a cave, killing the occasional mastodon. How long could your family survive? Have fun with this one. Stretch your imagination.

PROMPT: Begin a story with a statement about the nature of family. The most famous one (so famous I'm loath to use it for fear of appearing ponderous and ill-read) opens Tolstoy's great novel *Anna Karenina*: "All happy families are alike, but each unhappy family is unhappy in its own way." Your statement could be more upbeat, but it should be broad and sweeping in this way. You could follow the statement with an essayistic investigation of families, or you could glide into fiction, introducing characters in a family, perhaps in a scene.

PROMPT: Make a general statement about motherhood or fatherhood, and follow the same process you used above. You could write an essay or poem, taking a more direct approach, or you could follow the statement with a fictional story using a mother or father as the central character.

Ethnicity

If your family has lived in America for more than a few generations, you probably feel about as ethnic as hot dogs and apple pie. But if you look closely, you may notice that a few ethnic traits and traditions still linger. Explore them. If you want, do a little genealogical research.

PROMPT: Find out about an ancestor's arrival in America. Dig up as many details as possible, then write a piece—true or fictionalized— based on the ancestor's experience. To develop this piece, research a bit of social history. Find out what people wore and ate during the time when your ancestor arrived.

PROMPT: Read a book by someone from a culture far different from your own, a book that explores that culture. Write about the differences between the cultures. Or, if you prefer, begin a piece similar to the book, but focus on your own culture.

PROMPT: In a single sentence, declare who you are—your ethnic and regional background, your social class, your religion or whatever is appropriate to you. For example: "I am a third-generation American of Irish-German heritage, raised Catholic in the middle-class suburbs of the Midwest." Follow this sentence with an autobiographical paragraph or two, perhaps shifting back to the time you were born, or perhaps showing how your background influences your beliefs and actions today. If this interests you, keep going. You may have begun your life story.

PROMPT: Substitute a character for yourself and do the prompt above, this time embellishing it, allowing the character to declare who he is beyond ethnicity. If you want a model, read the opening of *The Adventures of Augie March*, by Saul Bellow. (In fact, read the whole book. It's a masterpiece.) The novel opens using the declarative approach:

> I am an American, Chicago born—Chicago, that somber city—and go at things as I have taught myself, freestyle, and will make the record in my own way: first to knock, first admitted; sometimes an innocent knock, sometimes not so innocent.

PROMPT: Give a tour of your childhood home, focusing on details that portray your ethnic background or family history. You can do this as a narrative or simply in lists or in a freewrite. If you want, draw a blueprint of the house, noting in the floor plan where objects were placed or where old photographs were hung.

PROMPT: Give the tour again, this time focusing on your family's more recent history: events, social class and background, tastes. And be honest. Admit to that avocado fridge with the goofy magnets from all the states you visited on vacations. Draw a blueprint or floor plan of your house, noting where things occurred and how rooms were furnished and decorated. Take your time with this one. Allow it to spark memories and stories. Write them down.

PROMPT: Write a bigoted diatribe against your ethnic heritage. Use all the common myths and stereotypes. Then write a defense. If you want, create a dialogue between two characters, each one giving voice to one of the viewpoints.

PROMPT: Explain your heritage and upbringing to someone from a decidedly different one. You might write to someone from a different country or different part of the United States, someone from a different planet, someone interviewing you on TV. If you want, use a script format or a question-and-answer approach. Turn it into a scene.

PROMPT: Write a scene in which an American family is visited by a relative from a different country. If you want, base the family on your own. Quickly establish a conflict: The relative plans to live with the family; the relative is of a higher or lower social class; the family is in a state of crisis and has no time or energy for visitors.

Chapter Eight

With a Banjo on My Knee

Whatever our theme in writing, it is old and tired. Whatever our place, it has been visited by the stranger, it will never be new again. It is only the vision that can be new; but that is enough.

—EUDORA WELTY

M ining the places you have lived can be a great way to unearth ideas. Too often we feel that the places we were born and raised lack the sort of exoticism that will attract readers. We think this because the places are not exotic to us. We take them for granted. Believe me, I share this feeling. I was born and raised in Ohio, which is synonymous with, even symbolic of, bland America.

Of course, what is ordinary to us can be exotic to someone else. The key is being able to truly see the world around you, finding the details that evoke it. A world that is keenly evoked will be exotic to those who don't know it well and will allow those who do know it well to see it with fresh eyes. So don't dismiss the place where you live or where you grew up as bereft of idea possibilities. In fact, it's probably full of them. If you aren't seeing them, look harder. If you hear yourself say, "Nothing happened where I grew up," or, "It was just a normal, typical place," then you're missing something. In my creative writing classes, I always stopped students who wrote of—or even spoke of—something as "normal" or "typical." These words are a writer's enemies. They tell us you're not seeing beneath the surface, and readers come to writers for help in seeing beneath the surface.

When evoking a sense of place, writers today, unfortunately, must look harder than writers of fifty to one hundred years ago. They must peer deeply through the filter of what writer Max Apple called "the oranging of America." By this he meant the disappearance of regional and ethnic nuance. The melting pot of the world was melting into one giant franchise. His story with that title chronicles the quest of Howard Johnson, restaurant owner and hotelier, to erect his orange-roofed establishments from coast to coast as beacons of reassuring sameness to comfort weary, hungry travelers. This trend is truer now than when Apple wrote of it in the 1970s. In your own travels you've surely noticed that towns from Maine to California all have the same Blockbuster Video, Burger King, Kmart, Hallmark, Service Merchandise, not to mention the ubiquitous Golden Arches.

The proliferation of this franchise mentality, strip-mall America, makes it more difficult than ever for writers to see and to evoke a particular sense of place in their work. And yet our jobs as writers—whether poets or playwrights, novelists or essayists—is to make the world new again for our readers, to allow for fresh insights and discoveries. Avoid the shorthand, brand-name approach, which too easily characterizes a place. Instead, look for ways to follow Ezra Pound's artistic commandment to "make it new."

PROMPT: (This one is borrowed from Bill Roorbach's *Writing Life Stories*.) Draw a map of the neighborhood where you grew up. If you grew up in several neighborhoods, draw maps for each or choose one from among them. On the map, write who lived where, note places where events, large or small, took place. The process of detailing your map will spark memories of time and place that can lead to ideas for writing.

PROMPT: Continuing the map theme, find your city and state in a road atlas. Look at the place through the eyes of a traveler, someone who has never been there before. Note the names of highways and counties, rivers and places of interest. Write these down as though they are unfamiliar to you. Which ones would you like to see? Continue your investigation of this place by thumbing through a travel guide. Note places of interest, and note details that you didn't know about or had forgotten. If you want, send for state or local tourism brochures. These brochures can lead to article ideas that you might have overlooked or story settings and details that, again, were right in front of your nose.

PROMPT: Research the history of the places you lived. Find out how they were settled, which tribes of American Indians lived there. What events in the past helped to shape the identity of this place? What cultural forces helped shape it? Of course, take notes. Use your writer's instincts for story. You may find an interesting historical character upon whom to base a fictional one. Or you can enrich a character's background by linking her to a particular ethnic movement that occurred in real life. By linking the particulars of your characters to the context of place, you anchor the reader more firmly in the world of your story. You create a sharper sense of texture and immediacy.

PROMPT: What is the public perception of your city, state or region? In other words, what do people who don't live there think about—or think they know about—where you live? For example, those of us not from the South believe it to be a backward, slow-paced world of politically conservative views. We think of southern California as a place of glamour and hedonism. How is your area perceived? Start big, with a region or state, and move to the small. For example, I live on the west side of Cincinnati, which is seen as less sophisticated and interesting by snobby east-siders.

The Eyes of a Native

Of course, most of these prompts will offer a broad historical, geographical or sociological perspective. This can give a strong context to your character, but you'll now need to push deeper, looking for the particular details and rhythms of life that make a place truly unique. Otherwise your writing can sound like travelogue—researched rather than lived. Elsewhere in this book I mention Richard Russo's essay "Location, Location, Location: Depicting Character Through Place," in which he praises John Cheever's ability to evoke the world of Shady Hill, his fictional commuter town. In the same essay, however, Russo takes Cheever to task for his less compelling evocations of Italy, where the Cheevers spent time later in the author's life:

> The later Cheever stories, many of which take place in Italy, are much more descriptive, but there's a touristy feel to them, as if the author feels compelled to give us what filmmakers call "establishing shots." The film takes place in New Orleans? Then you open with a shot of the bridge over Lake Pontchartrain, Cajun music in the background, then obligatory shots of the French Quarter.

We do need, at times, an "establishing shot" or two in our stories, a detail to quickly place the reader. But Russo makes an important point. Too often we reach for the easy description, the "touristy" detail that simply tells the reader what she knows already rather than evoking a vivid world where the reader can settle in and view the people and events of the story you're telling.

PROMPT: Cruise around your city or neighborhood, keeping a sharp eye for interesting details. If you can, have someone drive you. Even better, ride a bus, especially if you rarely ride buses. The novelty of the experience will freshen your view. Note details—storefronts, faces, places where things have happened, in your life or in the news. And really try to see. Note patterns of architecture and dress; note the types of cars people drive. Imagine yourself, if you can, a stranger to the place, just arriving to take residence here. If you're focusing on your neighborhood, walk it, especially if you don't normally do that. If you do walk your neighborhood, you know that it's amazing how you're able to notice things that, while driving, escape your attention.

P R O M P T : Write a letter describing your place to someone who has never been there. "What is Idaho like?" they've asked. They think of mountains and potatoes. Fill in the blanks. Give them an insider's view of the place, while keeping in mind they know nothing about it. Take time to linger, elaborate. You will avoid the clichés of the place because you know the particulars. In fact, take time to explode the clichés. If you're from Georgia, explain how the myths of the South, or Georgia, or your city, just don't apply anymore. Is Nebraska really the breadbasket of Bible-beating boredom, or does some pretty interesting stuff occur there?

P R O M P T : Write a letter describing your neighborhood, town, city, state or region from the point of view of someone who has just arrived. Though this persona will lack your insider's knowledge, he will be wide-eyed at the world he's discovering. And he will notice different things from what you notice, if you can push yourself deeply enough into the persona. To him, this place *is* exotic.

P R O M P T : Write about how you are an ideal representative of the place where you were raised—your ethnicity, ideas, values, likes and dislikes. Then write about how you are an anomaly to your place of origin, utterly unlike the other people who live there. Put these pieces away for a few days, then return to them and look for ways to fuse them into a piece about how you are both like and unlike the stereotype of people in your place.

P R O M P T : If you need more distance, move your town to a different state in a different part of the country but be true to the smaller details. Use it as a setting for fictional events. How easily does it move? What changes—such as accents or weather—need to be made to fit the new part of the country? Or move a troubled story to a new place, one based on a place where you've lived, one you know well.

PROMPT: Sometimes it's easier to write about a place where you no longer live. If you grew up in one place and now live in another, write from memory about the place where you grew up. Don't look at old pictures or use an atlas. Rely solely on what you remember. Feel free to exaggerate.

PROMPT: Characterize a place by focusing on its predominant industry or business. Try to use the industry to suggest the nature of the place. For example, I live in Cincinnati, where one of the major businesses is Procter and Gamble, maker of soap, detergent and toothpaste, an interesting fit in a city that prides itself on cleanliness—physical and moral. For an example of how to do this in fiction, in his novel *The Nephew*, James Purdy places a ketchup factory in his small town. The industry helps characterize the town as a bland place—the factory isn't, after all, churning out spicy mustard. The blandness and conformity of the town oppress its citizens, making them emotionally ill, just as the pervasive odor of brewing tomatoes from the ketchup factor makes them physically ill.

PROMPT: Write a scene in which a character returns home after an extended absence. Tour the character through the streets. What has changed and what has stayed the same? If you want, heighten the tension by creating a disparity between the descriptive details as seen by the character and the character's reaction to them. The character, for example, could view sad, shabby storefronts as quaint and cozy or look-alike suburban streets as unique and distinctive.

PROMPT: Create a fictional hometown. Draw a map of it, creating the streets and noting the stores and the homes where people live. If you want, base this fictional place on your own hometown—or part of town if you live in a city. Write a description of the town. Give it a history. Give it landmarks, noting where certain fictional events took place.

PROMPT: If you had fun with the previous prompt, put some people in that fictional hometown. Write some character sketches of these people. If you catch a spark, begin a story. You may want to collect the stories into a single work. A famous example of this type of book is Sherwood Anderson's *Winesburg, Ohio*. A more recent example is Laura Hendrie's *Stygo*.

PROMPT: Write about a place you haven't seen for many years, preferably not since you were a child. Then, if possible, visit that place. How close does your description from memory match the reality? You may be surprised how your memory has changed it. Writer Wright Morris wrote of a favorite child place he remembered well, a cool, dark spot under the porch of his boyhood home in Nebraska. He remembered hiding in this spot, and even in his middle age still could see the flat sweep of land fanning out in front of the house. When he returned to the house for a visit, his family long since moved away, he was shocked to find the space beneath the porch far too small to accommodate even a child. He had made it up. Over time, his imagination had created a place that didn't exist.

Chapter Nine

Thoughts of a Sundrenched Elsewhere

Go slowly, breathe and smile.
—THICH NHAT HANH

I n the previous chapter, we examined places you know well, places you've lived for an extended period of time. In this chapter, we'll continue investigating ideas of place by focusing on where you *want* to go and on places you've been and would like to see again. As we saw in Wright Morris's anecdote, places exist in our minds as much as they exist in the corporeal world. We can tell much about ourselves by how we relate to place. Can't stand that one-horse town where you grew up? Perhaps this suggests feelings of inadequacy about your background. Dreaming of a move to Montana? Does this dream embody your hope of embracing a more adventuresome life?

I won't dispense any nickel psychology about your relation to place. You must discover the relationships for yourself. For myself, I find great insight in Isabelle Eberhardt's line from *The Passionate Nomad*: "I shall always be haunted by thoughts of a sundrenched elsewhere." Does this speak to my desire to go to the Caribbean, lie on the beach and stick my toes in the warm sand? Yes. Does this desire also speak to my romantic nature, ever wistful for a place that is not where I am, one that holds the promise of unfulfillable fulfillment? Yep.

Let's start there.

PROMPT: Write about the best place you've ever been. "Best" can have a few meanings: most exciting, most fulfilling, most interesting. It could mean the place where you felt most in sync with the world, where you had the keenest sense of belonging, coming home to a place you've never been. Or it could mean the most exciting place, or the one where you had a great time. You choose. Take time to describe it in detail, beginning with those details that first come to mind. Avoid, at first, explaining why you liked the place. Just describe it. After you have a few pages of description, you can begin to explain and speculate upon why this place had such a profound impact on you.

PROMPT: Write about the place you most want to go—for a visit or to live. It must be a place you've never been before. As with the previous prompt, open with details, unbarnacled with explanation. Describe what you know of the place, what you've seen in photographs or on television. Then, move to exploring why this place appeals to you so much. Which elements of your personality are hooked into this place?

PROMPT: Sometimes places hold more appeal when they remain in our minds. The reality doesn't match our romantic notions of the places. Has this disillusioning experience ever happened to you? Write about it. Begin with what you believed the place would be, then move to the reality you found. How were they different? Were the people less charming? Was the weather too hot? The streets too dirty? Or maybe your expectations were simply too high.

Highs and Lows

High expectations can lead to disappointment. They also can tell us about ourselves by shedding light on what we seek, what we feel is missing in our lives and in ourselves. I knew a woman who for many years wanted to see the Taj Mahal in India. When she finally visited this great Wonder of the World, she found it not so wonderful. I remember her telling me, "It was great, but not really great like you'd think it would be." I thought this was a great line, a telling statement that exemplified the woman's romantic nature, which, by the time I met her, was beginning to sour into cynicism and disillusionment. I used the line verbatim in a short story, placing it in the mouth of a character who possessed a similar mix of romantic notions and cynicism.

Maybe all places we visit are a bit disillusioning if we have wanted to see them for a long time. Like the Tom Waits song says of wanderlust, "The obsession's in the chasing, and not the apprehending, the pursuit, you see, and never the arrest." Of course, he is comparing wanderlust to romantic love, and maybe at some level they are not so different. Is there often not a fantasy person tucked away in your fantasy destination? Or, perhaps, the fantasy person is you, the worldly you who has been to myriad exotic spots and thus can move with the grace of royalty through any place or situation.

Pico Iyer investigates the nature of our love for travel and its associations with romance in his essay "Why We Travel: A Love Affair With the World":

> We travel, initially, to lose ourselves; and we travel, next, to find ourselves. We travel to open our hearts and eyes and learn more about the world than our newspapers will accommodate. . . . And we travel, in essence, to become young fools again—to slow time down and get taken in, and fall in love once more.

PROMPT: Write about your desire for travel, be it great or small. Perhaps you have traveled extensively in your life and are a little jaded. If so, write about that. If not, pour forth on where you want to go and why.

PROMPT: Write a scene in which a character arrives in a new place, one where she has longed to be but now finds disappointing. Suggest the reasons for her disappointment through descriptive detail—what she sees, the people she meets. Or, if her problem is that she's dragging more emotional baggage than physical luggage, intimate this situation. What is she running from?

PROMPT: Put a character in a place where he doesn't speak the native language. Explore the problems this barrier creates.

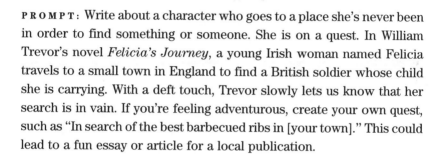

PROMPT: Write about a character who goes to a place she's never been in order to find something or someone. She is on a quest. In William Trevor's novel *Felicia's Journey*, a young Irish woman named Felicia travels to a small town in England to find a British soldier whose child she is carrying. With a deft touch, Trevor slowly lets us know that her search is in vain. If you're feeling adventurous, create your own quest, such as "In search of the best barbecued ribs in [your town]." This could lead to a fun essay or article for a local publication.

The way characters relate to place can be an avenue of development. A character who is yearning constantly for "a sundrenched elsewhere" is different from one who has never been out of the state where she was born and doesn't feel much need to go. A person who carries a clear sense of self wherever she goes is different from one too anxious to fit into new cultures by taking on all the trappings of that culture—suffering from "when in Rome" syndrome.

Young Fools

Experiencing a new place can be a wonderful experience for a writer, because everything is so fresh and new. Your soul is wide open to notice all that's around you. If you're feeling stale in your writing, take time for a trip, even if just a day-trip, to a place you've never been. It doesn't matter where you go. Take a notebook to write down your impressions, and use these in your current project or to start new ones. They need not lead to a nonfiction piece about the trip itself. As with all excursions of this kind, use it to load your arsenal of impressions and details, people and dialogue and scenes. When you need them, they will be there. They may end up in something completely different from where you found them.

P R O M P T : Write about a public gathering you attended in a place you visited. A baseball game or street fair, an outdoor concert or historical reenactment. Put yourself there by freewriting or clustering, allowing your mind to wander back. Write about the people you saw, the smells in the air. You'll be amazed by how much you remember once you begin writing about it. To help you develop this description into something richer, look for similar descriptions in books you've read. The one that comes first to mind is the Pamplona street celebration in Ernest Hemingway's *The Sun Also Rises*, at which Jake Barnes and his crew of lost generationers dance and drink in exquisitely rendered moments of color and exoticism. Of course, many such moments are captured in books. Which ones are your favorites?

P R O M P T : Use the description above as a backdrop for fiction, writing at least one scene in which characters deal with some sort of conflict while attending the event.

P R O M P T : Write about a private moment you've experienced in a distant place. Perhaps a solitary walk along a beach or a glass of wine in a restaurant far from home. Your goal, first, is to transport yourself back to this moment, then to put your reader there. If you want, use this moment in time and place for a fictional story, creating a character who experiences the same moment for reasons different from yours.

P R O M P T : Write about someone you met while traveling. Pick someone strange and eccentric, if you've met such a person, or pick someone with whom there was an undercurrent or confusion. Perhaps a language barrier made communication difficult. Perhaps you were looked on with suspicion as a visitor. Or pick someone who made a strong impression on you, someone who, perhaps, taught you something or who filters back into your memory now and then. Write down as much of the meeting as you can remember, taking time to set the scene in all its details.

PROMPT: Practice describing places by doing a sketch of each of the following: a place next to an ocean or some large body of water; a place in or very near mountains; a large city; a small town. Try to avoid the clichés of these places. Use specific, particular details.

PROMPT: Choose one of the places you described in a previous prompt as a background for a scene. In the scene, one character lives in the place; the other character has just arrived, for reasons I'll leave to your imagination.

PROMPT: Write about a character who visits a place for a practical reason, such as a business meeting or conference, but allows the trip to become something more (in a positive or negative way). At least for the length of his stay, the character's life changes significantly. He is transformed. In the essay mentioned above, Pico Iyer writes that our desire for transformation lies at the heart of our desire to travel:

> For me the first great joy of traveling is simply the luxury of leaving all my beliefs and certainties at home, and seeing everything I thought I knew in a different light, and from a crooked angle. . . . And if travel is like love, it is in the end, mostly because it's a heightened state of awareness, in which we are mindful, receptive, undimmed by familiarity and ready to be transformed.

Chapter Ten

What's Your Road, Man?

In many ways writing is the act of saying I, of imposing oneself upon other people, of saying listen to me, see it my way, change your mind.

—JOAN DIDION

The characters in Jack Kerouac's novel *On the Road* ask each other the chapter title's question while on their coast-to-coast road trips. They want to know, of course, each other's philosophy of life, primary set of beliefs, path to enlightenment. If you want to get to know someone, find out what he believes in. If you want to get to know yourself better, explore your own beliefs. That's our focus in this chapter. Through a clearer understanding of your own beliefs—be they ever so vague and contradictory or so deeply held—you can generate writing ideas.

Let's run through a series of prompts. They offer a variety of ways to ask yourself, "What's your road, man?" In fact, we'll begin with that question, but ask it in whatever language is most natural for you. You don't have to use the word "road" or call yourself "man," but it feels kind of cool if you do.

PROMPT: Explain your philosophy of life, your personal set of beliefs. You can do this as an essay or simply in a long journal entry. This is not an easy exercise, but give it a try. We all have beliefs, and yet rarely do we think of them with such cool objectivity. Now's your chance. It may be easier to begin by making a list or a cluster, writing down things you believe, then putting them into cogent sentences and paragraphs.

PROMPT: List as many clichéd truths—truisms, rather than truths—as you can. For example, "time heals everything" (and "all wounds"); "you can't fight city hall"; "what goes around comes around." Then choose one entry from your list and write about it, defending it or exploding it or, perhaps, a bit of both. If you sometimes use one of these clichés in your day-to-day life, take it to task. Argue passionately against its validity. Then rise to its defense. (As the old saying goes, clichés are clichés because there's an element of truth in them. Of course, that sentiment is, in itself, a cliché.)

PROMPT: Create a character who speaks—and therefore thinks—about life in clichés and truisms. Develop the voice, perhaps in a monologue. If the voice interests you, place the character in a situation that challenges and eventually shatters those clichés.

PROMPT: Write about how you came to hold a particular belief, beginning with the event or the person who led you to your conclusion. Move from the specific to the general. After you finish the explanation, review it, asking questions of yourself to lead you to deeper explorations. Does the logic of your conclusion hold up? Does it require a leap of faith? Do you believe this truth more strongly than ever? Have you been too hasty in your conclusion?

PROMPT: Is the glass half-empty or half-full? Without thinking, write your response. Fast. Now take some time and explore in writing why you hold this belief. Then write a brief essay in which you try to convince someone who sees it the other way that you are right. If you want, write a rebuttal to your own argument. Or you can write a short poem, using images to make the same point.

PROMPT: As a sentient adult, you've been well aware for some time that life, indeed, is not just a bowl of cherries. Nor is it only a paper moon. So what is it? Pick a metaphor for life and explore it in a piece of writing. Begin with "Life is just a _____." And you must use a noun, a specific, concrete thing. From that opening metaphor you can move in a number of directions: Write new lyrics to the melody of "Life Is Just a Bowl of Cherries"; write a poem, perhaps using the same meter as the song lyrics; write an essay supporting and exploring your metaphor; begin a scene with a character's statement that "Life is just a . . ."

PROMPT: Find a religious or philosophical quotation that makes a statement about the human condition. Consider looking in the Bible, a book of quotations, the Koran or a book of philosophy. Use that statement as the first sentence in a piece of writing (or as an epigraph to a piece). In the piece, refute or demonstrate the efficacy of the statement.

PROMPT: What favorite line from a movie speaks to your view of the world? Write it down. Begin a piece of writing by explaining the context of the line in the movie: Who says it? To whom? Why? Where? What is its significance? Then explain your affinity for the line, detailing why you believe it is true.

PROMPT: Write a letter to someone whose worldview you strongly oppose. Explain why the person is wrong, making a strong case for your own view of things. Choose a well-known person if you want—a political or religious leader, someone from the media, the local shock jock. Or you can write to someone you know well, preferably someone around whom you've been forced to endure in silence—your sweet but wrong-headed father-in-law, perhaps.

PROMPT: You're very old. You're on your deathbed. (Sorry.) Family and friends gather around you. What do you tell them about life? What advice about living do you offer them? Spill a few pearls of wisdom from your experience.

Philosophical Characters

The themes that run through your writing reflect your beliefs, even if unintentionally. In fact, a good way to gain a clearer understanding of what you believe is to read your fiction with an eye toward theme. What are you saying to your reader? What contradictions and struggles for understanding lie at the foundation of your art? What themes surface in story after story? Some writers and critics feel we tell the same story over and over, in different ways, using different sets of characters. I don't know that this is true or false, but it's fun to think about. What is your story?

You also can use beliefs and philosophies in your fiction to develop characters. Ask yourself, What does this character believe about life and the way the world works? Put the answer on the page and find out what happens. One of the best-known examples of a character stating his philosophy occurs in *The Great Gatsby*, when Jay Gatsby, the stupendously romantic gangster, tells an incredulous Nick Carraway, "Can't repeat the past? Why of course you can, old sport." In that statement of belief, we see Gatsby in all his deluded splendor. Wham. He's right there before our eyes. The line speaks to the heart of the novel's themes, foreshadows Gatsby's ultimate failure and eventually wakes Nick from his moral torpor.

Though I'm loath to place a humble creation of my own right next to

Fitzgerald's shimmering masterpiece, let me offer another example, one in which a character's statement of belief not only placed him more clearly on the page but led me to understand him better. While working on a novel, I was troubled by the protagonist, whom I couldn't fully understand and whom readers didn't find sympathetic enough. I could sense within him a certain strength that I couldn't quite express on the page because I didn't understand it fully myself. After completing a draft of the novel, I abandoned it, but the protagonist, Mitch, popped up later in a short story titled "Touchdown Jesus." In a scene near the end of the story, Mitch, who is in his thirties and down on his luck, speaks to a freckle-faced college freshman named Tom and tries to impart a bit of hard-earned wisdom about the shootings on the campus of Kent State University in 1970. Mitch had been a student there at the time. While writing the story, I read James Michener's *Kent State* and learned that many of the students were shocked when the guards opened fire. The students hadn't realized the guns were loaded. A lot of sixties idealism died that day. And the sentiment seemed perfect for Mitch:

"The gun is always loaded, Tom," Mitch told the boy. "Make no mistake."

With that line I suddenly understood Mitch as I never had during the writing of the novel. The story was published and even nominated for a Pushcart, but I never went back to the novel, which, sadly, is a product of another time and place, another me. My point here, however, is that discovering what a character believes can lead to your understanding him better and can help the reader understand him, too.

PROMPT: Choose a character from a project you're working on or planning to begin. Ask him to explain his beliefs, even if only in a scattered elliptical way. Try to dig into the character's mind and let him talk to you, without forcing it. Put the page away for a few days, then return to it. Any surprises? Does it make sense? Does it fit the character as you knew him?

PROMPT: Create a character who states a belief with which a second character disagrees. Have them work through their differences or simply accept them. A classic example of this situation occurs in Robert Frost's poem "Mending Wall," in which one character states the belief "good fences make good neighbors," meaning that people can get along with each other if they don't try to connect. The narrator does not share this belief. He feels, as Frost clearly feels, that it's much more natural, even inevitable, for people to share their lives with others. Ironically, the neighbor's sentiment has gained wider usage than the narrator's, is even quoted by people: "As Robert Frost said, 'good fences make good neighbors'."

PROMPT: Have a character espouse a viewpoint on life with which you very much disagree, but have the character argue it well, citing examples from her life to buttress her stance. Resist the temptation to make her sound foolish or harsh. If you can, relate the character's view in third person, as if it's coming from the narrative rather than directly from her mouth. The narrative should be sympathetic in its approach.

PROMPT: OK, now you can make it sound foolish. In fact, exaggerate the view. Show it in all its stupidity. For models, look to the great satirists, such as Sinclair Lewis, James Thurber and Dorothy Parker.

A nother great model to use for the previous prompt appears in John Kennedy Toole's novel *A Confederacy of Dunces*, in which the protagonist, Ignatius J. Reilly, is quick to explain his view of life, usually in wildly pompous, hypocritical language. Here is a bit of Ignatius, who is writing (in Big Boy tablets) a preposterously inflated document on the decline of Western civilization:

> After a period in which the western world had enjoyed order, tranquility, Unity, and oneness with its True God and Trinity, there appeared winds of change which spelled evil days ahead. An ill

wind blows no one good. The luminous years of Abelard, Thomas à Becket, and Everyman dimmed into dross; Fortuna's wheel had turned on humanity, crushing its collarbone, smashing its skull, twisting its torso, puncturing its pelvis, sorrowing its soul. Having once been so high, humanity fell so low. What had once been dedicated to the soul was now dedicated to the sale.

Not that Ignatius doesn't have a couple of points worth considering. But his grand style and linguistic ineptitude undercut any point he might make. Toole is having fun with the voice here, as he does throughout the novel. If you want, try the previous prompt again, and strive for the wild absurdity Toole manages to create.

Control

Now that you've had some fun, let's get a bit more serious. There is danger in allowing a character to step up on a soapbox: You can lose control of the narrative. If the character's viewpoint agrees with yours and lies near the story's themes, the character could become simply a mouthpiece and the story could descend into didacticism. Resist this temptation. Especially in early drafts, we sometimes feel overly eager to pump a few bright red thematic flares into the sky above our narrative landscapes. In early drafts, this compulsion is not a problem. It can help us understand the story's themes more clearly and understand the character better. But then we must remove it, relying on drama and indirection to carry forward the themes.

But if you can manage to control the voice—especially difficult in a first-person story—you can create some powerful moments in your fiction. One such moment that I like occurs in Alan Sillitoe's "The Loneliness of the Long-Distance Runner." The speaker is a lower-class boy of seventeen, doing time in a juvenile detention center (called a Borstal, in England) for robbing a bakery. The boy's view of the world is tough and unsentimental, and yet Sillitoe manages to make him sympathetic, even when he's violent. In one scene, the nameless narrator and some friends break up a picnic, scaring away a group of upper-class teens and taking their food. In explaining his actions, the narrator offers a glimpse into his view of how life works:

> Well, I'll always feel during every day of my life like those daft kids should have felt before we broke them up. But they never dreamed that what happened was going to happen, just like the governor of this Borstal who spouts to us about honesty and all that wappy stuff don't know a bloody thing while I know every minute of my life that a big boot is always likely to smash any nice picnic I might be barmy and dishonest enough to make for myself.

A very dark sentiment from a seventeen-year-old narrator, but it is one that speaks to the sense of hopelessness that surrounds his life. By understanding this view, the reader can more clearly understand why the boy acts as he does and can sympathize more fully with his plight. Note, too, that the narrator is far different from the writer. He is not a mouthpiece. His revelation does not smack of didacticism.

PROMPT: Begin a story in the voice of a character who espouses some viewpoint or belief about life. Have the character explain why she feels this way. The character should be different from you in some significant way, and her belief should be clearly not your own. If you want, introduce a second character who does not share this belief, as you did in the earlier prompt.

PROMPT: Place two characters in a room. They have vastly different views of life. Create a dialogue in which these differences become clear to the reader, but don't allow the characters to confront these differences directly. Instead, they might argue or talk about an innocuous subject. For example, a father and son watch a football game and speak mostly about what they're watching. Two sisters meet for dinner in a trendy restaurant. A boss and employee work together in a sales booth at a convention. The different world views, again, should not be stated directly.

Chapter Eleven

The Love You Make

Writing about people helps us to understand them, and
understanding them helps us to accept them as part of ourselves.
—ALICE WALKER

The comedian Lenny Bruce once got into trouble for what the media perceived as an insult to Jackie Kennedy. This incident occurred not long after the president's assassination, after the famous Zapruder tape was released. In his comedy routine, Bruce noted that after the president was shot, while the car was still moving, the First Lady climbed across the trunk in an effort, Bruce thought, to get away. A Secret Service man was running along behind the car and helped Mrs. Kennedy back into the car, which then sped away. Pictures of the First Lady on the trunk of the car were presented in the newspapers and on television as her attempt to help the Secret Service man into the car. Bruce's assessment: "The First Lady was hauling ass."

His point in bringing up this perceived lie was that the media makes heroes from people who are not heroic, who suffer from the weaknesses of human nature from which everyone suffers. This sort of lie, he felt, makes people feel terrible when they cannot reach what is, in fact, an unachievable standard. "Nobody stays," Bruce told his audience. And though he was speaking of Jackie Kennedy, I believe he was also speaking about love. Bruce never fully recovered from his wife's leaving him after their tempestuous marriage. He had grown cynical—or realistic, depending upon your view of love. Love, said Bruce, does not conquer all, and when times get tough, people leave. Even the First Lady ditches the president when the bullets start flying.

Romantic Love

What do you think? Is love really a capricious emotion, subject to the winds of fortune? Or are people capable of staying—not out of fear or comfort or inertia but out of a selfless concern for someone to whom they feel deeply devoted? We're speaking now of the love between mates, between couples, rather than the love we feel for our families and friends.

PROMPT: Write about your beliefs about love, following some of the questions raised above. Is it a powerful emotion? What is the nature of love? How long can it last? Does it inevitably fade? Begin an essay titled "On Love," or write a poem about love. Or, if you prefer, write a scene that dramatizes your beliefs about the nature of love.

I won't tell you what I think, but consider that Bruce's story has stuck with me for a long time. But another line has stuck with me, too. It appears in Woody Allen's *Manhattan*. In fact, it's the last line of the film and thus has a strong thematic resonance. After realizing he has made a stupid mistake in leaving the young woman he'd been seeing, Allen's character rushes to her apartment to beg her forgiveness and win her back. He finds her leaving for a three-month stay in London. Though he begs her not to go, she insists on leaving but promises to return. When he pleads that she'll meet someone new while there, she tells him, "Sometimes you've got to have a little faith in people."

A wonderful and sentimental line. Let's use it for the next prompt.

PROMPT: Make a case for our capacity for love, for our right to deserve "a little faith." Even if you're the most hardened cynic about affairs of the heart, give it a try. If you're a true believer, this one should be easy, but imagine that hardened cynic reading your piece. Anticipate objections and arguments and rebut them.

PROMPT: Write about your first love as an adult or, at least, after the age of sixteen. Give all the details—when, where, why, etc. How long did the relationship last? Why did it end? What did you learn about love from this first experience?

PROMPT: Write about your current love. If you haven't got one at the moment, write about your most recent one. Again, give us the when and why. Describe your mate. What is unique about that person? Which of your partner's qualities do you love most?

PROMPT: Write about your experience with—or desire for—an illicit love. Of course, each of us must define for ourselves what is "illicit," but let's take the view of conventional society: Write about a relationship or encounter you experienced with someone who was off-limits. If you've never had or desired this experience, create a fictional character and recount a fictional illicit love.

PROMPT: Write about "the one who got away," a past love for whom you still yearn, perhaps, or who you feel would have been a good mate. If you don't have such a person in your past, create a fictional character or focus on someone you know who has had this experience.

PROMPT: You're Dr. Frankenstein: Build your ideal lover. List all of the qualities he or she would possess. You may even want to throw in a flaw or two, shortcomings that you'll find endearing. When you've finished your list, create a character sketch of this person, a detailed description.

PROMPT: Write about life with the ideal lover you created in the previous prompt. Where do you live? What do you do? Take time to develop the "happily ever after."

PROMPT: Describe the nature and feeling of love to someone who has never had the experience—a young person, perhaps, or someone who simply has never been smitten. What insights and advice can you offer?

PROMPT: Write about a time when you suffered a broken heart. Explain what happened, how you felt, how you handled it and how you mended yourself. Then write a letter to that person, expressing your feelings—how you felt at the time and how you feel now. Write freely, assuming you won't send the letter.

PROMPT: Write a scene from the point of view of a character being left by another character. If possible, avoid all the clichés of soap operas and televisions and bad books and movies. Unfortunately, that doesn't give you much room to work. It seems that everything on this topic has been said to death. You'll need to reach down into your characters to find something fresh, something particular to them. If you want, keep dialogue to a minimum. Work with action and gesture.

PROMPT: Write about a time when you broke someone else's heart. Again, explain what happened and how you felt. Then write a letter to the person, expressing your feelings. Again, assume you won't send the letter.

PROMPT: Write a scene from the point of view of someone breaking someone else's heart. If you want, recast the scene you wrote above, this time showing it from the other character's point of view. Again, do your best to keep things from veering into melodrama and cliché. Rely on action and gesture. Rely on indirection. The couple could talk about something completely off the subject, making little mention of what's taking place.

PROMPT: Write a scene in which two former lovers meet after many years. What happens? If you've had this experience, base your scene on what happened to you, or change it in whatever way feels right.

PROMPT: What song or songs best capture the nature of love? Defend your choices. Or, if you'd prefer, what song or songs are outrageous lies?

PROMPT: What's the most romantic book you've ever read? What's the most romantic movie you've ever seen? Or, again, what book or movie got it all wrong?

PROMPT: At the end of his short story "The Sensible Thing," F. Scott Fitzgerald writes, "There are many kinds of love in the world, but never the same love twice." Though the statement seems sentimental, it's worth a close look. First, do you feel that it's true? Explain your feelings. Second, write about the kinds of romantic love you've experienced—passionate, blissful, quietly assuring, erratic and unpredictable. Use Fitzgerald's sentence to begin a piece about your own experiences with love.

Sex

We love to write about sex. We love to read about it. It's a universal subject that, even if we live to be a hundred years old, retains its power. If you were flipping through this book in a store, you'd have passed through dozens of pages with barely a glance, but I'll bet if you saw this subhead you'd stop for at least a skim.

Which is why I included it. In truth, sex is tough to write about. We can write about passion and desire and the first stirrings of sex, but the actual sex act, and most of what leads up to it, has been exhaustively well charted and, with some exceptions, doesn't quite work on the page. The act is so primal and focused and is more than the sum total of the physical mechanics. To do it well, you must get into the minds of the characters, make it mean something. If not love, then some sort of connection. As Elizabeth Benedict writes in her book *The Joy of Writing Sex*:

> In the best fiction writing about sex, even if it is a brief paragraph, we come to the end knowing not just "what happened" but something about the characters, their sensibilities, circumstances or inner lives, about the narrator who is relating the events, the concerns of the author—or all of the above. A well-written sex scene engages us on many levels: erotic, aesthetic, psychological, metaphorical, even philosophical.

Her insights apply to nonfiction as well. Beyond the gymnastics—or, as Cathleen Schine put it in *The New York Review of Books*, "tab A being fitted breathlessly into slot B"—we need to provide details on how the sex affects the characters involved. In that way the scene becomes particular and interesting.

PROMPT: Write about what arouses you sexually. Take time to consider what popular media tells you arouses you sexually, and then dismiss it. I don't know about you, but to me, seeing a lover in a setting of candlelight, soft music and flowers through the rosy glow of a glass of wine always feels like a cardboard cutout of romance, someone else's idea of intimacy. To create a scene more your own, spend a little time recalling the specifics of that last really blazing encounter. Who were you with? What triggered your reaction? Where were you? What time of day was it? How did that person make you feel? Randy, yes, but exactly how? Where did you specifically like to be touched? How did that make you feel? Write a few of these scenes, and then give yourself a break. You may need it.

PROMPT: Mine the rich ore of your sexual fantasies. Write about your favorites, the ones you depend upon when you're dead tired and your partner is desperately in the mood.

PROMPT: In her nonfiction book *Aphrodite*, Isabel Allende writes that she grows amorous watching her husband cook. She especially admires his hands and the economy of motion with which he chops and mixes and sautes. She playfully imagines him slowly undressing, as he continues to cook, as a prelude to spontaneous lovemaking. What unlikely settings or circumstances trigger the same response in you? Write a description of what you feel, taking time to linger over the sensual details. Can you speculate on what arouses your desire? How would that desire play itself out?

PROMPT: Write a sex scene in which conflict simmers beneath the surface. What happens next? Do the characters address the issue or continue to bury it beneath the motions of lovemaking? If you want, try both ways. Which one better fits the characters? Which one makes for more compelling drama? Can you recall a similar experience in your own life? If so, write a narrative explaining what happened.

PROMPT: In an interview, Carol Shields said, "The most erotic scene I've ever witnessed was my uncle, bending over at the dining room table to kiss the back of my aunt's neck. It was summertime and she was wearing a sundress and just lifting a spoonful of sherbet to her lips. They were middle-aged then. I was child of nine or ten but I recognized 'it.'" Write about the most erotic scene you've ever witnessed. Like Shields's scene, it can be subtle and understated. Or it could be passionately sexual.

PROMPT: Whom in your past would you most like to make love to again? Set the scene. How would this happen? Detail the seduction.

Or, if you prefer, whom in your present life would you most like to make love to? Again, plot the story of the seduction from start to finish.

Family and Friends

The final type of love we'll look at in this chapter is the love we have for family and friends. We discussed your family in chapter seven, so we won't explore the topic in detail here, but a chapter on love could not be without mention of family. Though I've been a parent for more than ten years, I continue to be amazed at the depth of love I feel for my two sons. They have stirred in me feelings I didn't know were possible before they were born. Dive in front of a bullet for them? No problem. If you're a parent, you know what I mean.

If you're not a parent, these feelings can come from other sources, perhaps your family or a very close friend. For many years I was very close to my brothers and felt a strong bond with them. Perhaps you've enjoyed a similar relationship with siblings. In this section, let's explore your feelings for family and friends.

PROMPT: Write about your relationship with your parents by describing an event from your childhood, an event from your teen years, one from your early adulthood and, depending on your age and the ages of your parents, one from later adulthood. Each event should suggest the nature of your relationship with your parents at the time it occurred.

PROMPT: Make a list of the good friends you've had in your life. Briefly describe each person and the nature of the friendship. Choose one to explore in greater detail. Then write in a more general way about the nature of the friendships you've enjoyed. Do they usually last a long time? What sorts of needs are satisfied by your friendships? Do you consider yourself a good friend? Why or why not?

PROMPT: I once dated a woman whose brother told me, "Friends are just people who borrow things." I remember thinking how incredibly lonely the guy must feel or how friends in his past must have disappointed him. Begin a piece of writing with a sweeping assertion about the nature of friendship, then develop your statement or refute it or just go where it leads you.

PROMPT: Write a scene in which a group of friends get together—to watch a football game, to attend a baby shower. Imagine they share a secret or bad experience of some kind from their past that no one ever discusses. Keep that secret—a robbery in which they all took part, a trip to Florida that went out of control—on the fringe of the discussion, bringing it up slowly until finally it's out in the open.

PROMPT: Some friendships last beyond their natural life spans. By that I mean that many of us have a few friendships that are relics from a different, often much earlier, time in our lives. Though we still like the old friends, we share nothing in common and find we have very little to talk about when we get together. Falling quickly into reminiscence when you do get together is a good indicator that a friendship is well past its prime. Do you have a friendship of this type? If so, write about it. What factors keep it alive? How would you feel if it ended?

PROMPT: A family, perhaps one based loosely on your own family, heads off in the car for vacation or for a day-trip. Describe what happens. The scenario is a classic one in American literature and movies. Two examples that come quickly to mind are John Barth's short story "Lost in the Funhouse" and Flannery O'Connor's short story "A Good Man Is Hard to Find." Read these stories as models for handling this situation. Unfortunately, neither of these trips turns out well for the family. If you have a cheerier trip in mind, you'll want to look elsewhere.

PROMPT: I used "The Love You Make" in the title, so let's end with that, a quote you no doubt recognize from a Beatles song titled "The End." The line goes, "And in the end, the love you take is equal to the love you make." Do you believe that love works in this way—the more we love, the more we are loved? I ask that question, which seems valid, even important, knowing well that the late Chris Farley asked Paul McCartney the same question in a classic moment of *Saturday Night Live.* But I'll ask it anyway. What do you think?

Chapter Twelve

Don't Get Me Started

I write to find out what I'm talking about.
—EDWARD ALBEE

What ticks you off? Poor service in a restaurant? Traffic jams? Incompetence where you work? The injustice of untalented people—far less talented than you, for example—enjoying unwarranted success? We all have our flash points, the buttons that people had better not push. Let's spend some time looking at what makes you good and mad and search there for ideas.

What Makes You Angry?

We like to talk about what makes us angry. We like to write about it. Earlier this year, we conducted focus groups at Writer's Digest Books as part of researching a new line of guided journals. As moderator, I threw out a half-dozen topics for the group's consideration. A few sparked interest; a few sparked yawns. I asked when the members of the group felt most like writing in their journals. "When I'm mad," a woman declared. "I write it down and get it off my chest." Others in the group nearly shouted their agreement. At the next focus group, I offered this topic and the members jumped all over it. We had touched a nerve.

So if you enjoy grumbling in your journal about what ticks you off, as most people do, don't feel ashamed. Enjoy it. Get your feelings out there on paper. If you have a short-fused character, indulge her for a while. Try to find out what is behind the anger.

PROMPT: Let's start with a list. Write down the things that have made you angry in the past week—or the past month, if your week has been mild. Take some time and try to remember all of them, from stubbing your toe on a chair leg to your child's adamant refusal to do what you asked to your senator's cowardly vote on a bill you strongly support. Keep a running tally for a few days, if necessary. Pick one item from your list and freewrite about it, telling in a rush of words (don't sweat punctuation and style at this stage) how you felt and why you felt that way. Can you fashion this into a more considered essay or poem? If you want, pick other items from the list and follow the same process.

PROMPT: Place the items from your list above into categories, such as "home," "the office," "family," "friends," "the news," "social injustice" or whatever categories are appropriate for you. Then add to each list by moving farther back in time—a month, even a year. Write down what you can remember, then pick a category and look for patterns. Is there something at work that angers you on a regular basis?

PROMPT: Make a list of chronic anger sparkers. Pet peeves, if you will. When you finish your list, choose one and freewrite about it. Include examples of when this has occurred and how you reacted. Is there a way to resolve this problem? Write about some possiblities.

PROMPT: Review the list from the previous prompt and look for patterns. What *types* of things tend to make you angry? People who are chronically late? Machines that break down? Kids with attitudes? Parents with attitudes? You will probably spot a few patterns. Choose one and write about it. Explore the reasons behind the pattern. Use examples.

PROMPT: Write about your relationship with anger. Are you an angry person? Do you hold in your anger or let it out? Do you let it out in what could be considered appropriate ways? Do you express anger at the true sources, or do you find other people and things at which to vent? Road rage, for example, is usually the result of anger at something else. The guy who cut us off in traffic is simply an easy target.

PROMPT: Choose someone you know who handles anger well and describe how she does it. If you tend to hold in your anger, you might admire someone who speaks her mind. If you tend to unleash your anger too quickly, you might admire someone who exercises more self-control. Either way, write about why you wish you could handle your anger as this other person does.

PROMPT: If you could embody your anger with an animal, what one would be the most appropriate. Tiger? Vulture? Write about why you chose that animal.

PROMPT: Write a letter to someone at whom you are angry or once felt anger. Really blast him. Then write a letter to that person in a calmer tone, explaining how you feel or felt. This letter can be particularly effective if you didn't show your anger at the time.

PROMPT: Write a letter to someone who is or was angry with you. Apologize, if necessary, or explain your reasons for doing whatever made her angry.

PROMPT: Psychologists tell us that beneath anger lies fear. Think about how this theory applies to you or, if you're writing a story, to one of your characters. In a freewrite, try to dig beneath the anger and find what fears might be causing the anger.

PROMPT: Write an essay titled "On Anger," in which you begin with your own feelings about anger—such as what makes you mad, how you and other people handle anger—and move to some conclusions about the nature of this complicated emotion.

Angry Stories

Now that you've explored your own anger for a while, let's move to using anger in stories. Anger can be a great motivator for writing and can keep you going when the story lags. Some writers nurse anger for years against teachers who told them they couldn't write, using this anger to keep them going when times are tough. Writers also use stories as a place to express anger that they cannot express in their lives. Some of these writers get sued for it, so beware of what you say in print.

Writers use anger at people they know as the basis for stories. Eugene O'Neill's great play *Long Day's Journey Into Night*, published posthumously but written years before his death, seems to explore the anger he felt toward his father. Anger at social injustice has led to great novels, such as John Steinbeck's *The Grapes of Wrath*, Upton Sinclair's *The Jungle* and Richard Wright's *Native Son*. Great characters have been developed who are motivated primarily by anger. Think of Captain Ahab in *Moby Dick* or Allie in Paul Theroux's *The Mosquito Coast*, or Myra in Marilyn French's *The Women's Room*.

If you want an example of an angry character in action, consider the following bit of vitriol from Robert Penn Warren's *All the King's Men*. The novel is based loosely on the political career of Louisiana governor and senator Huey Long, known at the time as The Kingfish, a small-time demagogue who rose to great heights through his powers of intimidation. Throughout much of the novel, Willie "The Boss" Stark rages against anything that stands in the way of his ambitions. In this scene, in a pique of paranoia, he blasts an underling who he feels has betrayed him:

As soon as I opened the door, I ran right into the Boss's eyes like running into the business end of a double-barreled 10-gauge shotgun at three paces, and halted. "Look!" he commanded, heaving his bulk up erect on the big leather couch where he had been propped, "Look."

And he swung the double-barrel around to cover Tiny, who stood at the hearthrug before and seemed to be melting the tallow down faster than even the log fire on the bricks would have warranted.

"Look," he said to me, "this bastard tried to trick me, tried to smuggle that Gummy Larson in here to talk to me, gets him all the way up here from Duboisville and thinks I'll be polite. But the hell I was polite." He swung to Tiny again. "Was I, was I polite?"

Tiny did not manage to utter a sound. . . .

"You thought you'd trick me—trick me into buying him. Well, I'm not buying him. I'm going to bust him. . . . I made a mistake not busting you. But I figured you'd stay bought. You're scared not to."

"Now, Boss," Tiny said, "now Boss, that ain't fair. You know how all us boys feel about you. And all. It ain't being scared, it's—"

"You damned well better be scared," the Boss said, and his voice was suddenly sweet and low. Like a mother whispering to her child in the crib.

Notice that the author modulates the tone of Stark's voice at the end, which paradoxically makes him even more menacing. Characters who are angry do not have to shout. By varying your approach to presenting their anger, you can produce more chilling effects.

PROMPT: Place anger at the center of a scene between two characters, but keep it below the surface. Allow the tension to build slowly. You can end with a blowup, in which the anger finally boils over, or you can resolve the anger, allowing the emotion to dissipate.

PROMPT: Write a monologue in which a character vents his rage. As the monologue develops, add clues that suggest the character is more fearful than angry, or is angry as a result of fear.

PROMPT: Write a monologue in which a character vents her rage, but this time vary the tone of the character's voice. Instead of one long howl, soften the voice, or add a touch of humor. Perhaps the entire monologue can be delivered quietly, the rage burbling just below the surface.

PROMPT: Write a scene, based on a real experience in your life, in which two characters are angry with each other. Do not base the viewpoint character on yourself. Instead, give the viewpoint to the person with whom you argued.

PROMPT: Begin a story with a character in the middle of a rage. The character's anger seems completely inappropriate to its source. For example, a character can be cursing in great anger about a minor inconvenience or disappointment—the local baseball team lost an unimportant game, the cookie jar is empty. As readers watch this character explain—and bellow—his frustration at the characters around him, it becomes clear that the character is angry about something else, which you could name or not.

PROMPT: Write about a social injustice, some issue that makes your blood boil. Begin with an essay, titled "On [issue of social injustice]," and try to get your ideas on the page in an expository way. Then try to move to a less direct approach—fiction or a poem or a script.

PROMPT: Write about something that happened to you that made you very angry at the time but now seems funny. Recall the event in as much detail as possible, writing it down exactly as it happened. Then try to fictionalize the event, adding a few details, sharpening the situation, exploring the dramatic possibilities. Don't feel tied to the story as it happened.

Chapter Thirteen

Your Fifteen Minutes

Let us not be too scornful of fame;
nothing is lovelier, unless it be virtue.
—CHATEAUBRIAND

A ndy Warhol promised all of us fifteen minutes of fame. He promised. I don't know about you, but I'm still waiting for mine. But all of us, in fairness, have had times in our lives when we were in the spotlight, if only in a small way. There have been times, too, when we have met someone famous or been involved in some event that made a stir. In this chapter, we'll look at such times, in hopes of moving our experiences from the private to the public arena.

A friend of my father taught English for many years at a local high school. He was a smart man who in his youth aspired to be a writer, but gave up, for reasons I never knew. He also was a fine baseball player and spent a couple of springs with minor-league clubs. One spring, while playing against the Dodgers' farm team, he faced the great Sandy Koufax, albeit before Koufax found out how to control his fastball. This showdown must have occurred in the late 1950s. With two strikes on him and Koufax blazing the ball into the strike zone that day, my father's friend smashed a single into the outfield. After a drink or two, he would tell that story—his brush with fame.

The husband of a woman who works with my brother was in the armed service in 1963, stationed in Washington, DC. He was one of the guards assigned to Jackie Kennedy on the day the president was assassinated. He remembers that throughout the evening and into the next day, she wore the dress stained with her husband's blood.

Though neither of these men is at all famous, each experienced a brush with fame and has an interesting story to tell as a result. My family and friends are by no means famous, and yet I know at least a half-dozen stories of this kind—a second cousin who starred on a 1950s TV sitcom, a friend's father who landed at Normandy Beach on D-Day, a friend's sister who invented an important synthetic heart valve. In my workshops at writers conferences, I often ask students to write about such moments in their own lives. Some have told fascinating stories. One I remember very well involved a young woman's meetings—two of them, a few years apart—with Indira Gandhi. Both meetings left the woman frustrated. She wanted to express her deeply felt admiration for her hero, and yet couldn't seem to find the right words when she needed them. Though she was disappointed at the meetings, they led to a short piece of writing that moved a roomful of writers. I hope she developed the piece further when she returned home from the conference.

PROMPT: Write about meeting a famous person. Even if it was only a handshake in a crowd, put the event on the page. Freewrite or cluster to stir your memory of the meeting. Tell it as a narrative, step by step, including as many details as you can recall. If you want, take time to do a little research on the famous person. Expand your piece by adding this information to it. When you finish the account of the meeting, speculate on its significance. What did it mean to you, if anything? How did the person measure up to your expectations?

PROMPT: Write about a news event to which you have some connection. Did an important event occur in your hometown? Were you ever involved, even as a bystander, in an event that the general public will remember? Follow the process you used in the previous prompt: Freewrite everything you can remember about the event, form the details and the actions into a narrative, research the event to add relevant background, speculate on its significance to you.

PROMPT: Ask family and friends and colleagues about their own fifteen minutes of fame. Most people have some story to tell. Write down these stories as best you can. Research the people and events mentioned in the stories you find interesting. Is there an article idea here? Do you detect any patterns within the stories? Do you believe all the stories, or have some clearly been embellished in retellings?

PROMPT: Many famous people have appeared in works of fiction. Try this yourself. Write a fictive scene involving a well-known person—historical or contemporary. Try to be true to what you know about the person. If you want, relate the scene from the famous person's point of view. Or, if you want, add a few more famous people to the scene. In the following excerpt from a long scene in Mark Winegardner's *The Veracruz Blues*, the narrator attends a party at Ernest Hemingway's house. Guests at the party include Babe Ruth and former heavyweight boxing champion Gene Tunney. Notice how the author shows the celebrities in actions we recognize from reading about them—Ruth and Hemingway full of bluff and bluster. Notice, too, that he adds specific details to humanize these larger-than-life folks, to make them seem like believable story people rather than like animated monuments:

> Throughout dinner no one spoke to me. Babe Ruth and Ernest Hemingway, both drunk, at a single dinner table, swapping suspiciously exciting tales of manly prowess (here a dead beast, there a pair of friendly twin redheads, everywhere a sweaty triumph), provided little chance for others to talk.
> Above the sideboard were framed photos of Hemingway with famous men and dead animals. I was in none of them. I had taken one of the ones from Paris, a blurry shot of Hemingway and Scott Fitzgerald (in for a brief visit), each in a brand-new beret.

PROMPT: Write a fictive scene in which a character meets someone famous. Perhaps the character could be based on you or someone you know, and the famous person could be someone you admire. Develop the scene as fully as possible. In the following scene from Kim Herzinger's short story "The Day I Met Buddy Holly," the narrator meets a man who he believes is the famous rock-and-roll star. The story does not reveal if the character is *really* Buddy Holly. Instead, it investigates the nature of celebrity and the light they can bring into ordinary lives:

> The sun was shining down onto the top of Buddy's head; like most rock and roll stars Buddy had sort of short hair, with a just a tiny curl coming down in the front. I had to squint to see him.
>
> "Well, usually the trains are here on time," I said.
>
> He lit a cigarette. "Not today."
>
> "No. Not today. There might be something wrong. Maybe a log problem or something. Sometimes we get a log problem in town because of all the lumber companies here. You've probably smelled some of them. Maybe some logs have fallen off and hurt the tracks. That's lumber for you. . . .
>
> "You're Buddy Holly aren't you?" I was surprised at myself, and I thought for a minute that Buddy was going to turn and walk away from me. But he didn't. He took it in stride.
>
> "I wish," he said finally. "My name is Tom Truehaft. I'm from Lake Oswego. I'm a barber."
>
> I looked at his shoes. They were not the shoes of a barber. No barber would have ever known that they have shoes like that.

PROMPT: What famous person do you physically resemble? In other words, who do people say you look like? Write about that resemblance, perhaps in a nonfiction piece in which you could compare yourself to the famous person. For example, many people tell me I look like the actor Chuck Norris—same beard, same build, same coloring. Though Chuck is probably 15 years older than I am, I try not to be insulted by the comparison. In fact, while in Aspen (a place where people expect to spot celebrities), a young family pointed at me and smiled excitedly. I figured out the error but gave them a hale-

and-hearty Chuck Norris wave. Or you could write a fiction in which you *are* the famous person. Or, following the example in Kim Herzinger's story, the story could involve a character who is mistaken for a celebrity. Perhaps the character does little to correct the mistake, perhaps even tries to exploit it.

Two of my favorite books concern meetings with famous people, though in neither case was the meeting the primary focus of the book. The celebrities are used as metaphors, as ways for the writers to explore aspects of their own personalities. In *A Fan's Notes*, Frederick Exley uses football player turned commentator Frank Gifford, whom, before the book was written, Exley met only once, very briefly, when both were students at the University of Southern California. In the novel, which is called a fictional memoir, Exley uses Gifford as a symbol of fame and celebrity, both of which elude the narrator, who is called Fred Exley. Much of the book is a true account of Exley's life. After the novel was published, Exley's first novel, he met Gifford and the two remained friends until the author's death a few years ago.

The other book is Nicholson Baker's *U and I*, a nonfiction account of Baker's adoration of writer John Updike. In the book, and in real life, Baker meets Updike, twice, very briefly. The book investigates a number of literary themes, including the trials of developing one's unique voice and viewpoint while under the influence of another writer's work. Both books take a thin relationship to a celebrity and develop it in powerful ways.

PROMPT: Write about a moment you experienced in which you were celebrated, if only on a small scale. Did you star in a high school play or on a sports team? Have you won a contest? Have you sat on a float in a parade? Have you performed before an audience in any way? Take yourself back to that moment and write it down. After you've finished the narrative part, speculate on what that moment meant to you then and what it means now.

PROMPT: Let's look at your fifteen minutes of infamy. Warhol never said they'd be good minutes, did he? Have you ever had a publicly embarrassing moment? If so, write about it. As with the others, the event need not be of grand import. It simply needs to involve more than family and friends. Did you, for example, fall off that float you were riding on in the previous prompt? The one such moment that comes to my mind is the day in second grade when I forgot to wear a shirt. My family overslept (the only time I remember this happening) and I got dressed in a hurry and rushed off to school with my brother. When we arrived, a few minutes late, my classmates had already trooped off to morning Mass. I found them and breathed a sigh of relief as I settled into the pew with as little commotion as possible. Then I took off my heavy winter coat to find only an undershirt. No shirt. No Catholic-school-issue tie. The kids around me noticed, though I was quick to slink back into my coat and dart to the teacher, telling her I needed to run home right away. But word spread, as it will in grade school, and for weeks I was "the kid who forgot his shirt," even to older kids who didn't know me. Alas. But after years of therapy, I've worked through this traumatic episode, and I can now use it here in this book to put you at your ease to explore your own moment or two of crushing humiliation before a deriding crowd of onlookers.

PROMPT: Write down your dream of a moment in the spotlight. Do you see yourself accepting an Oscar for a screenplay? Catching a Super Bowl–winning touchdown? Saving the lives of millions by developing a cure for a disease? Trying and winning a big legal case? Put yourself in that moment and write about what happens. Indulge the details. Write about what this dream means, what it says about you. We can tell a lot about ourselves and about each other by what we dream of attaining.

PROMPT: Give yourself an award, one, perhaps, that you dream of winning. Write your acceptance speech, thanking those who helped you and offering advice on the nature of the achievement. If you're interested, find copies of Nobel prize acceptance speeches, and read what the winners say about the nature of writing.

PROMPT: Take time to reflect on your characters' moments of glory or dreams of glory. Explore their moments in the sun and the way these moments influenced their lives. A character's dream or memory of glory can be a good place to begin a story. An example that comes quickly to mind is Irwin Shaw's classic short story "The Eighty-Yard Run," in which a man sees his life ambitions fading, his one great moment being a long run for a touchdown while playing for his college team. That moment, which Shaw renders in extensive detail to open the story, haunts him, casting every other event in his life in its fearsome shadow. Another well-known example is Arthur Miller's play *Death of a Salesman*. After Biff Loman's big day in the city championship game, neither he nor his father, Willy, ever achieves such a moment of glory again. The cheers of the crowd, their chants for "Lo-man, Lo-man," echo in Willy's mind years later as his own dreams of success slowly evaporate.

PROMPT: Begin a story with a scene in which a character enjoys—or suffers—a public moment. Take time to fully develop the scene, and, if possible, avoid narrative explanation. Don't tell the reader of the moment's significance; show it. If you want, in the next scene, you can provide a bit of background to establish the moment's particular significance to the character. *Revolutionary Road* by Richard Yates begins with a community theater group performance starring one of the main characters, April Wheeler. The play is a complete disaster. Yates loads his description with specific details, lingering over the painfully bad performance. April believes she is more talented and sophisticated than her neighbors, who watch the play, and she is devastated by her public failure:

She was working alone, and visibly weakening with every line. Before the end of the first act the audience could tell as well as the Players that she'd lost her grip, and soon they were all embarrassed for her. She had begun to alternate between false theatrical gestures and a white-knuckled immobility; she was carrying her shoulders high and square, and despite her heavy make-up you could see the warmth of humiliation rising in her face and neck.

PROMPT: End a story with a character's public moment. The story should build to this moment, in which the character's dream of glory is either achieved or denied. A model for this approach is Beth Henley's play *The Miss Firecracker Contest*, which was filmed as *Miss Firecracker*. Throughout the play, the protagonist, Carnelle, has worked toward appearing in the Miss Firecracker beauty contest. Though she doesn't achieve her goal of winning the contest, she performs well and enjoys her moment in the spotlight.

Chapter Fourteen

All Our Secrets Are the Same

Look, then, into thine heart and write.
—HENRY WADSWORTH LONGFELLOW

I took this title from a collection of *Esquire* fiction, edited by Gordon Lish and published twenty-five years ago. Aside from the smooth and beguiling alliteration of *secrets* and *same*, I've always liked the statement's declarative quality, its confidence in the face of unknowable truth. How can we know if our secrets are the same? Fact is, some of our secrets aren't the same. In this chapter, you'll explore your secrets, and your hopes and fears, your goals and regrets and dreams. We'll focus on the you that doesn't meet the eye.

Writing about this side of yourself can be fun and can be a great source of creativity. If creativity ignites from the spark of conflict and tension, then the tension of concealment serves a writer well. Use it. Write as if you must burn the pages as soon as you finish them. Expose yourself to the white of the page. Some of what you write, of course, may be too personal to show others. We all try to appear calm and capable, in control, masters of our lives. Talk of secrets and lies, guilt and regret, longing, hopes and dreams shoves into the light a more vulnerable part of ourselves. But, with luck, it will be a source of insight, even revelation, for you.

Secrets and Lies

PROMPT: Write about a secret you've held for a long time, which you have told no one. What would happen if you did reveal it?

PROMPT: Write about a time that you revealed a secret, and detail the consequences. Why did you reveal it?

PROMPT: Write about your ability to keep a secret. If you had a secret, for example, would you tell someone like you about it? Why or why not? If you did have a secret, what person in your life would you tell? Why?

PROMPT: Write about a time when you told a secret and found out the person you told revealed it to someone else. How did you feel? Did you confront the person? Describe the circumstances and consequences of this experience.

PROMPT: Write a monologue in which a fictional character reveals a secret. Make it a significant one. Give urgency to the telling of the secret. This situation can add urgency to whatever you write. If you're feeling stale on a piece, imagine it as a secret being revealed.

PROMPT: Write a scene that leads up to the revelation of a secret. If you want, write the revelation first, then go back to the start of the scene and move toward the revelation.

PROMPT: Write a scene in which a character reveals a secret that is actually a lie. What happens next? In a wonderfully human anecdote, Tobias Wolff told of a time in which he was close friends with fellow writer Raymond Carver. The two met often late at night and told the stories of their lives to pass the time—both were insomniacs. Carver's revelations were frequently more powerful than Wolff's, so Wolff one night told the story of his heroin addiction—an outrageous lie. He soon noticed colleagues asking him about heroin or seeming especially sympathetic in a general way. Carver, obviously, had found this secret too juicy to keep to himself. Wolff was faced with admitting he had fabricated the story to make his past seem darker and more interesting, or accepting his new reputation as an ex-heroin addict. One night Carver admitted he'd told the secret and Wolff admitted that the secret was a lie. The pair had a long laugh at their writerly penchant for making up stories and for revealing the secrets of others.

PROMPT: Write about a lie you've told—a whopper, as they say in old movies. Did you fess up later? Were you caught in the lie? What were the consequences? Depending upon how honest a life you've led, you can do this prompt more than once.

PROMPT: Write about a time when someone significant in your life lied to you and you found out the truth. How did you feel? What did you do?

PROMPT: Write an essay titled "On Lying," exploring the nature of lies and lying. Mix personal experience with a philosophical stance.

PROMPT: Write about the worst liar you've ever known, worst in the sense of most ready to lie and then worst in the sense of least convincing. If you want, fictionalize these people and begin a story about one of them, or both of them. Perhaps put them in the same story.

PROMPT: I have a friend who is an excellent liar. His secret: Believe the lie yourself when you're telling it. Begin a story in first-person point of view in which a character reveals his secret of being a good liar. In the story, make clear that at times he is not telling the truth.

PROMPT: Write a scene in which a character lies to another character. Then write a second scene in which a second lie must be told to cover up for the first one. Continue in this way, weaving a tangled web for your character.

Guilt and Regret

Feelings of guilt and regret can be devastating, and they can be tenacious. As much as we are aware of them, try as we might to exorcise them, they can persist. And because we feel them so deeply, they can be a good source of ideas for writing. Sometimes writing about them can be a way to dispel their hold on us. However you approach them, don't ignore them as a source for ideas. In the opening pages of his novel *The Sportswriter*, Richard Ford establishes regret as a major theme by addressing it directly in the voice of his narrator, Frank Bascombe. Bascombe leads a lonely life of failed ambition and a failed marriage, and he copes, too, with the loss of a child. Through most of the novel, he battles regret:

> For now let me say only this: if sportswriting teaches you anything, and there is much truth to it as well as plenty of lies, it is that for your life to be worth anything you must sooner or later face the possibility of terrible, searing regret. Though you must also manage to avoid it as your life will be ruined.

PROMPT: Write about a regret you feel or that you struggled for some time to put to rest. What did you do or not do that led to the regret? How did you manage to put it to rest? How does it affect your life now?

PROMPT: What would your life be like now if you had done or not done something that you regret? Indulge the feeling for a while and write about this different life.

PROMPT: Write a letter to someone explaining a regret you feel that involves this other person in some way. Explain your feelings.

PROMPT: Write about a character who feels deep regret about some part of his life. Put the character in a scene so readers can see his regret in action. If possible, don't address the regret directly. Allow it to inform his behavior, but don't try to explain it.

PROMPT: Create a metaphor for regret, a physical object that embodies the feeling or allows you to explore the feeling in a fresh way. Begin with a metaphorical statement: "Regret is . . ." and move from there. If you prefer to write fiction, use the line in a scene, perhaps to begin a scene.

PROMPT: Write about something that makes you feel guilty—a memory that still has the power to create this emotion inside you. Describe the source of the guilt and how you cope with the feeling.

PROMPT: Like regret, guilt can be a destructive force in anyone's life. Create a character who, unlike Ford's narrator in *The Sportswriter*, has not managed to avoid regret or guilt. Develop a story in which a character's life is nearly ruined by one of these emotions. Though Frank Bascombe is not quite the master of his emotion that he pretends to be, he does manage to persevere (though Ford fans know that in his more recent novel *Independence Day*, Bascombe is still struggling). In Graham Greene's novel *The Heart of the Matter*, the protagonist is ruined by guilt. He has an affair with a young widow, and after early feelings of elation and renewal, his conscience begins to hector him. When his wife returns from her extended vacation, the protagonist, Scobie, becomes ravaged by guilt, which Greene dramatizes in a number of powerful scenes, some of which are set in church. In the following scene,

Scobie, a Catholic, feels he is in a state of mortal sin and therefore cannot take the sacrament of Communion. And yet, if he refuses the sacrament, his wife will grow suspicious and find out his guilty secret. He can see no way out:

> Father Rank came down the steps from the altar bearing the Host. The saliva had dried in Scobie's mouth: it was as though his veins had dried. He couldn't look up; he saw only the priest's skirt, like the skirt of the medieval war-horse bearing down on him: the flapping of feet: the charge of God. If only the archers would let fly from ambush, and for a moment he dreamed that the priest's steps had indeed faltered; perhaps, after all something may yet happen before he reaches me: some incredible interposition . . . But with open mouth (the time had come) he made one last attempt at prayer, "O God, I offer up my damnation to you. Take it. Use it for them," and he was aware of the pale papery taste of an external sentence on his tongue.

PROMPT: Write about a time when you did something hurtful but did not feel guilty. Explore the emotional complexities of the situation and your reaction to it.

PROMPT: Write a scene in which a character professes feelings of guilt but clearly does not feel that way. Use action, gesture and voice to signal her true feelings.

PROMPT: Try the opposite approach to the previous prompt. Write a scene or a monologue in which a character professes to be free of guilt or regret and yet clearly is still struggling with these feelings, perhaps without even being aware of the struggle. Ford uses this approach throughout *The Sportswriter*, as Bascombe continually professes to be free of the past and to enjoy the simplicity of his life, and yet we detect that the issue is more complex, that the narrator has not worked through his regrets.

PROMPT: What are the clichés of guilt and regret, the gestures, actions, statements that typically are used to suggest these emotions? Show these emotions in a character, but find fresh ways to do it. Avoid the bowed head, the angry outbursts, the expressions of self-hatred. In the film *The Apostle*, the protagonist, a hypocritical minister, literally baptizes himself in a river and begins to lead a more honest life, understanding and accepting the sins of others far better than he did before admitting his guilt and regret to himself. Perhaps your character can find a new sense of purpose and direction through these feelings.

Longing, Hopes and Dreams

In her book *Creating Character Emotions*, Ann Hood writes that "even the word 'longing' gives me an ache in my chest." If you've ever experienced longing, you know what she means. By longing, we don't mean the occasional glaze of wistfulness—for the past, for a simpler time—but heartfelt yearning for someone or something. Like all powerful emotions, longing can be a great source of ideas.

PROMPT: Write about someone you long for or have longed for in your past. Perhaps a lost love or a family member who has passed away. Try to describe the feeling and how you respond to this feeling. How long does it last? What usually triggers it? For example, I lost a brother with whom I'd been very close all of my life. He died suddenly at the age of thirty-two. He used to call on Sunday nights, just to talk about the week or whatever. Even though he's been gone for five years now, I still feel a strong sense of longing for him, especially on Sunday nights. When the phone rings, part of me still expects to hear his voice on the other end.

PROMPT: Write about longing by comparing it to a place. What place seems to embody longing or to evoke it? What does longing look like?

I think of some of Edward Hopper's paintings, those empty streets with the long shadows. For me, they manifest longing.

PROMPT: Write about the physical sensations of longing. What does it literally feel like? Give these sensations to a character, adding movement to suggest this emotional state without using the word directly.

PROMPT (this one I borrowed from Ann Hood): "What is the time or person or thing you most long for right now? Write about it as clearly as you can. Describe it with concrete details. Try to evoke the essence of that time or person through sensory triggers. (How did it taste? Look? Smell?)"

Hope is a complex emotion. It's tied to longing, in some ways, but it's more focused and directed, even energetic. While longing suggests a certain enervation, even malaise, hope can suggest positive thoughts, as if we can *do* something to achieve the subject of our hopes. I opened this book by saying that writing is an act of hope, meaning that hope embodies determination in the face of adversity, a belief, despite evidence to the contrary, of a positive outcome. The Buddhists, however, feel that hope leads to illusion, to a grasping after solutions that don't exist. To find our true selves, we must abandon hope, accept that hope leads only to confusion. Psychologists believe that hope slows the grieving process. When we suffer a loss, we tend to deny, to hold onto the hope that the loss we've suffered is not permanent. Until we give up hope and accept the loss, healing cannot begin. So hope has many facets, and for that reason can lead us to interesting ideas for writing.

PROMPT: Write about a time in which you remained hopeful in the midst of anguish or adversity. What was the source of your hope? How did you manage to sustain it?

PROMPT: Write about a character who remains hopeful, partly through denial, and uses that hope as a source of strength. For example, in *Death of a Salesman*, Linda Loman remains hopeful of the family's success despite the turmoil in which they stew. She expresses her hope by exclaiming, at two moments in the play, how "the whole house smells of shaving lotion." She associates that smell with good times and with her sons preparing to conquer the world. Try to find a gesture or line that expresses your character's hope.

PROMPT: Write about a character whose hope is clearly an aspect of denial. Use first-person point of view, allowing the character to express her hope directly while showing through action and detail that the hope is illusory. To sustain our hopes, we sometimes hear and see selectively, focusing on evidence to support our hopes and ignoring evidence to the contrary. Show your character choosing to hear and see only what supports her unrealistic hopes.

PROMPT: Write about a character struggling with hope, trying to be realistic while keeping a positive outlook. In Beth Henley's play *The Miss Firecracker Contest*, the protagonist hopes to win the eponymous contest, though she's not especially pretty or talented, nor is she well respected in the town. When she loses the contest, she feels that she's suffered a broken heart, an overwhelming disappointment, but then doesn't allow herself to dwell in self-pity. She does give credence, however, to the validity of her desire to win the contest, saying, "How much is it reasonable to hope for?"

PROMPT: Let's end on an upbeat note. Write about a time in your life in which you achieved the subject of your hopes, when, in a sense, your dream came true. Or, if you prefer, write a fictional scene or story in which a character's hopes, which at first seem unrealistic, are achieved.

Chapter Fifteen

Minding Other People's Business

I don't see how a writer can operate without going out as a reporter. Think of the feast that's out there.
—TOM WOLFE

G etting ideas is sometimes simply a matter of paying attention. A writer must keep in mind Henry James's famous advice about being "someone on whom nothing is lost." Notice what is going on around you—the people and situations, the places and objects. These can be fodder for your writing and can spark ideas for stories and characters, articles and essays, poems and scripts. Sometimes, as writers, we live a bit too much in our heads, blind to what's going on around us.

We must practice mindfulness, and by practicing we grow better at it. We are more aware of what we're doing and what other people are doing. That awareness becomes our normal state of mind. True, when we're deeply involved in projects, we live in the worlds of the projects. (Let's be honest; part of our interest in the projects is to escape the world around us.) This absorption can make us forgetful, absentminded and unseeing. A couple of favorite examples of this state of mind:

- According to A. Scott Berg's biography of editor Maxwell Perkins, Thomas Wolfe once took Perkins home to Wolfe's apartment, breaking into the place after the key didn't work, then was surprised to find other people living there. Absorbed in his novel, Wolfe forgot he had moved.

- Thomas Edison went to a government office to apply for something (sorry I have to be vague, but I can't find this anecdote anywhere!) but was forced to leave without the document because he couldn't remember his name.

These are great stories, and if you're the writer in your family, you probably have a reputation for being dreamy and impractical. That's OK. But let's try some prompts that will help open your eyes to what's going on in your world.

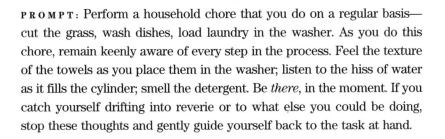

PROMPT: Perform a household chore that you do on a regular basis—cut the grass, wash dishes, load laundry in the washer. As you do this chore, remain keenly aware of every step in the process. Feel the texture of the towels as you place them in the washer; listen to the hiss of water as it fills the cylinder; smell the detergent. Be *there*, in the moment. If you catch yourself drifting into reverie or to what else you could be doing, stop these thoughts and gently guide yourself back to the task at hand.

PROMPT: Read everything in today's newspaper, from the front-page news to the comics to the ads. Don't use the Web site; buy a copy of the paper. Make a list of the stories you find interesting or amusing. Also list any ideas for your writing that you find. Do this for a week. Begin a folder in which to place articles that interest you. Keep this folder active and current. When you're feeling stale or uninspired, a quick shuffle through your folder can help spark some ideas.

PROMPT: Choose three of the articles that offered ideas and try to put them together into a single piece.

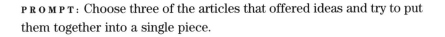

PROMPT: Go to a public place you frequent—the grocery store, church, fitness center. Try to see the place as if for the first time, noticing people and how they behave, the way they speak and relate to each other. Go to a second place and compare the modes of behavior. Do people act differently in church than at the grocery store? Are they less or more guarded? Notice details. Are postures similar or different? Body language?

PROMPT: Go to a public place and eavesdrop. That's right: Invade people's privacy. Of course, don't get caught. But if you feel comfortable with this, try to overhear some conversations. Write down what you hear. Try to record it exactly as it's said. Restaurants are great places to do this. You can be anonymously scribbling in your notebook, not even looking at the people, and writing down what they say. Another great eavesdropping place, according to writer and friend Tom Chiarella, is the airport. You can get pretty close to conversations and yet seem a disinterested bystander. Also, at airports people often are parting. They're trying to sum up, to put everything in order before leaving.

PROMPT: This one I stole from comedian George Carlin. He called it "spy at the airport." He would try to pick from the bustling crowd the person who was an international spy. As a writer, it would be better if *you* played the spy. Give yourself a spy persona and watch people. Something about pretending to be a spy or some type of security person will make you much more aware (not that I've, ahem, done this myself). Write brief observations in a notebook, and keep your eyes and ears open.

PROMPT: Break out of your routine. Wake up at least an hour earlier than usual, and go for a walk or a drive. If you're up very early in the morning, go to an all-night grocery or gas station. Take notes on what you observe, and develop these details into a sketch when you get home. Or, if you prefer, do it the opposite way, staying up an extra couple of hours and venturing out into the world.

Listening for Ideas

Eavesdropping requires sharp listening skills. All of us can become better listeners, and writers need to be especially good. Listen to how people say things, and listen to what they say. The quick aside, the tossed-off anecdote, the boring trudge of a life story can hold ideas for writing.

For example, I spoke at a writers conference a couple of years ago and heard a story that turned into a published article. At breakfast, a woman told a funny story about driving across the country with her mother and daughter. Three generations of women in one car for thousands of miles, from California to Pennsylvania. In the middle of the story, she mentioned stopping in a small Louisiana town at the Bonnie and Clyde museum, noting that the place was tiny and uninteresting and was run by a ninety-year-old man who claimed to have witnessed the famous ambush of the gangsters. The story continued as the three women headed northeast, but that museum and that guide stuck in my mind. The writer did not see an article idea there; it simply wasn't of interest to her. But it was to me. I scribbled the idea in a notebook later in the day and began poking around on the Web, finding out more about the museum. The passing remark became an article that was a lot of fun to write.

PROMPT: Every day for a week, write down something you've learned in a conversation. Impossible for you because your friends and colleagues are boring and uninformed? Fine. Go to an expert. Chat with the manager of a store about the product she sells. Go to the library armed with a dumb question or two. (Librarians love dumb questions. They really do.) Write down what you learn. You can choose to learn about subjects that especially interest you, or you can make your quest for knowledge random.

PROMPT: Begin a scene with a line you've overheard someone say recently. It needn't be a catchy or powerful line. Something mundane will work: "How much are these pants?" "If you're good I'll let you pick out some candy at the counter." "Is he ever on time for a meeting?" Begin there, and move forward, providing a completely different setting and context for the line.

PROMPT: Fill up dead time with observations. Notice the people around you at the grocery checkout. Make mental notes about them, and write down these observations when you leave. Look around you while waiting in traffic. What are people doing in their cars? Car observations are great because, for some reason, we all feel invisible in our cars, as if we're in protective bubbles. People sing to themselves, check out their faces in their rearview mirrors, make out with each other, angrily bang their steering wheels in frustration. Try to pull away a few details each time you sit in traffic.

PROMPT: Spend some time on an elevator, especially if you don't normally ride one. Here you'll find people who have nothing to do or to distract them. Watch body language. If you're feeling bold, strike up a conversation. One way to do this is to ask a question. Watch the person's reaction. Of course, you don't want to seem intimidating in any way. Respect the person's space. But try to get the person talking.

Sometimes we simply find an idea already formed and neatly packaged, there for the taking. A poem in a letter to a friend. A story in an anecdote told to us at a party. A perfect line of dialogue on a soup can. The opening for an essay on a sign in a store window. When such good fortune befalls you, grab it and go. A well-known example of this type of "found" idea is the John Lennon song "Being for the Benefit of Mr. Kite." He found the lyrics to the song on an old poster announcing the attractions at an upcoming fair. He wrote them down and used them verbatim. By pushing them into a more artistic context, the words took on resonance. They gained a new meaning.

These accidents, of course, require that you discover them, that your eyes and ears and writer mind are open to chance. Surely hundreds of people saw that poster, but only Lennon was able to turn it into something bigger, a piece of art. Debra Sparks speaks to this awareness, this keeping one's eyes open for ideas, in her essay "The Trigger: What Gives Rise to a Story?" She recounts going to the Cave of the Mounds, "a rather tacky tourist spot in Wisconsin," with several women, including fellow writer Lorrie Moore. All the women in the group endured a dull tour of the place, except Moore, who, Sparks realized, was taking notes. Then,

> Two years later, I opened up *The New Yorker* and read Lorrie Moore's funny, sorrowful story "The Jewish Hunter," which takes place partially at the fictitious Cave of the Many Mounds in Minneapolis. I felt excited, the way one does when one's a party to another's romance or sees a setup working at a dinner. Why, I had been there! Had seen the initial sparks! And I felt something else, too: jealousy. Sure, we'd all met the guy, but only one of us had the skill to fall in love.

Seeing Beyond the Surface

Before leaving this subject, let's pause a minute to discuss the writer's need to see. In this chapter, we've focused on seeing the world around you, taking time to notice details, striving to become someone "upon whom nothing is lost." With that phrase, James means more than simply noticing the surface of things and reaching for a conclusion. As writers, we must see beneath the surface and beyond it. Tempting as it is, we can't settle for the certainty that some people possess—people who, in fact, are incapable or unwilling to push beyond appearance. Limiting yourself to the appearance of things leads to cynicism or intellectual and emotional blindness. Again, we must see deeper.

This approach involves risk. We must accept ambiguity, knowing that we can't know all there is to know. In his theory of negative capability, John Keats explores this need of the writer to remain open and fluid in his thoughts and feelings. As a creative person, you must accept this challenge, must find a way to balance the practical reality before you with the awareness of the mystery beneath the surface. In his memoir *Nola*, Robin Hemley explores this point with beauty and insight. He objects to the facile wisdom of people who tell you to "see things as they are":

> Beware of people, I think, who tell you this, because they are invariably hiding something. They mean you harm, or harm you, by putting a mask on their uncertainty and calling it certainty. (Like those searchers for Noah's Ark, who are missing the point completely; even if they found the ark miraculously intact, sitting on top of Mt. Ararat, that would show us nothing. It's the story, not the artifact that's important.)

If you want to be creative, you must seek the reality behind the appearance, the story, to use Hemley's example, not the ark. Anyone can see the ark. Anyone can say that if an ark is found, the story is true; if an ark isn't found, the story is false. As a writer and creative person, you must seek the truth in the story even if there never was an ark.

Chapter Sixteen

A Day in the Life of a Writer

The boundaries of our world shift under our feet and we tremble while waiting to see whether any new form will take the place of the lost boundary or whether we can create out of this chaos some new order.

—ROLLO MAY

S hort chapter here. You're going to do most of the work yourself. I'll contain my penchant for verbosity and try to get out of your way and let you get to it. This chapter, which is essentially one long prompt, guides you through the process of writing down everything that happens to you in a single day. The thinking behind the prompt is easy enough to understand: In a single day you can find enough ideas to write about for a good long while. Details, images, dialogue, events—in your life, in the news, in the lives of those around you. We have hundreds, maybe thousands of thoughts, ideas, impressions and reactions that often are forgotten minutes later.

We notice that the roof on the garage takes on a golden hue in the morning sun; our mate always puts milk and sugar in the coffee cup before pouring the coffee; the woman in accounting who usually looks so enervated is suddenly dressing up a bit and has a new spring in her step; drive-time disc jockeys are the most annoying creatures on the face of the earth; the water in the shower is never quite hot enough; the guy in front of us at the grocery checkout is buying enough hamburger to feed Ecuador; we feel a touch of melancholy around seven o'clock every evening. Many, many more.

This exercise is also an exercise in what the Buddhists call "mindfulness." As we discussed in the previous chapter, writers must pay attention; they must cultivate this mindfulness. Again, as Henry James told us, we must "be someone upon whom nothing is lost." An entire day of journalizing everything surely will push us in that direction. Doing this prompt more than once will help, too. The first time you do it, you may be very self-conscious and, perhaps, too aware of your writer's apparatus: the notebook and pen or the tape recorder that you use to record what's going on. Doing it a few times will diminish your concern about the equipment and will allow you to focus more on what you're doing and observing. Also, it helps to try this experiment on various days—a workday and an off day, for example, or a weekday and weekend day.

Your goal here is not to develop material for a single piece but to plump your notebooks with ideas and details. It could lead, of course, to a day-in-the-life piece, perhaps a story or an essay. If you want a model for this form, read F. Scott Fitzgerald's essay "Afternoon of an Author." You'll notice that nothing much happens in it. The events and observations are not pulled tightly together. Observation mingles with reverie. But Fitzgerald does create unifying elements and themes, and the accretion of detail creates a quiet, somber essay about a man moving on the fringe of his own life, dispirited and yet obviously quite aware of the subtle nuances of his life and the world around him:

He went into the kitchen and said good-bye to the maid as if he were going to Little America. Once in the war he had commandeered an engine on sheer bluff and had it driven from New York to Washington to keep from being A.W.O.L. Now he stood carefully on the street corner waiting for the light to change, while young people hurried past him with a fine disregard for traffic. On the bus corner under the trees it was green and cool and he thought of Stonewall Jackson's last words. . . .

The bus was all he expected—only one other man on the roof and the green branches ticking against each window through whole blocks. . . . Somewhere church bells were playing *"Venite Adoremus"* and he wondered why, because Christmas was eight months off. He didn't like bells but it had been very moving when they played "Maryland, My Maryland" at the governor's funeral.

A Day in Your Life

Let's get started. Tonight before you go to bed, spend a few minutes setting up your tools. It doesn't matter if you use a notebook or a tape recorder. You could use, I guess, a video recorder if you want, though that will be a big distraction—to you and to those you meet throughout the day. The point is, use what makes you feel comfortable. Place your notebook—we'll call it a notebook for the sake of convenience and con-sistency—on the nightstand next to your bed. Set your alarm, perhaps a little earlier than normal, to give you time to get this exercise under-way. You'll be writing a lot, so you'll need to adjust your schedule to allow for the added activity.

Decide, too, how you're going to do the writing. You can't scribble a conversation while you're having it, obviously. You could do hourly re-ports, checking in every hour to note what's happened, or, if it works better for you, jump in whenever you get a minute. But don't let more than an hour pass without writing. Too much will be lost. Remember, you're trying to get *everything* on paper. So even if you're thinking that absolutely posi-tively nothing is going to happen, structure your day for writing it down.

When you wake up, grab your notebook and record what you can remember from your dreams. Quickly. They can slip away even as you're writing them down. Scribble everything you can recall.

Get out of bed and start your day, taking your notebook with you. As you go through your morning routine, jot down what you're doing and what you're thinking. It may look like this:

eating a bagel and a banana, coffee. Coffee is too weak again. need to set up time for oil change in Jeep. In newspaper—county commissioners still fighting about where to put the new stadium. Morning sunlight looks warm and yellow on the countertop, pours in through the east window. Packing lunches for kids. Remember when I was in grade school, racing through my lunch to get to the playground where we played big games of catchers, sometimes using the whole parking lot, coming in after lunch our hair damp from running. . . .

And on and on, moving through the day: Shower and dress, drive to work, talk to people, do your job, eat your lunch. And as you experience your day, keep your notes short and simple. They shouldn't be long asides, unless you have a lot of time for writing today and won't miss out on the day by writing about it. Try to make your jottings just little notes to yourself, capturing details, thoughts, memories. Write only what you need to remember the thought or event or detail later.

Whatever you do, don't stop. Trust me on this. Keep pushing ahead. Halfway through the day, you may begin to feel that this day is simply too boring and you'll try again tomorrow. Try again tomorrow if you want, but finish this day. If the day grows too hectic to write about as you go along, shorten your notes to a few words. You will take tomorrow—and the next day and the next day—to flesh out the notes.

Continue taking notes throughout the evening, making the final note as you get into bed and turn off the light. The next day, examine what you've done. Highlight details or events that interest you. If you find nothing of interest, put away your notes for a few days, even a week. When you return to them, you will see them more clearly. Highlight those of particular interest. You will be amazed at how much is there and how much, even after only a few days, that you've forgotten.

Write a piece narrating your day, selectively using what seems to be most interesting. From the distance of a few days or a week, offer insights and observations about the day as you write, enlarging the scope of the piece. If you want, create a fictional character and allow him to experience your day.

Chapter Seventeen

A Life of the Spirit

Everything that I have written has the closest possible connection with what I have lived through inwardly.
—HENRIK IBSEN

Let's close this section by investigating your spiritual life and religious background. Ignore the cliché about avoiding talk of "religion and politics." Use your writing to focus on subjects people tell you *not* to talk about. Question the prevailing Truths. Dig beneath the surface of things to find out what's really happening. This approach confers a deliciously secret, sneaky, cut-through-the-bull quality on your writing, which makes it more fun and more meaningful. It also is what makes writers dangerous folks to be around.

I'm not suggesting that you betray those you love and who love you. I don't share Faulkner's much-quoted belief about a good story being "worth any number of old ladies." But I do believe a writer's job is to seek to find and to represent in writing the truth as she sees it. To question. To risk seeming too negative or too positive or just too nosy. To attempt to say what has not been said, perhaps because no one had the power or the insight to say it right. In her essay "Your Mother's Passions, Your Sister's Woes," Bonnie Friedman articulates the writer's role very well:

> The force of the forbidden draws us. We want its power. We want to use it for our work. We also long to understand the unarticu-

lated, our own most potent reality not yet structured by words. For in fact the secrets we most want to understand are not secrets at all; they are nothing hidden so much as not yet discovered. They are what has been there all along, not furtively denied so much as never consciously noticed.

Sometimes there have been furtive denials, and each writer must decide what can be revealed and what must remain hidden to protect the lives of others. And always we must leaven our honesty with kindness. Pema Chödrön addresses this point in her book *When Things Fall Apart*, and though she focuses in the following quote on looking inward, the same consideration applies when we view the world around us:

> The challenge is how to develop compassion right along with clear seeing. Otherwise, all that happens is that we cut everybody else down, and we also cut ourselves down. Nothing ever measures up. Nothing is ever good enough. Honesty without kindness, humor, and goodheartedness can be just mean. From the very beginning to the very end, pointing to our own hearts to discover what is true isn't just a matter of honesty but also of compassion and respect for what we see.

Hairy Thunderer or Cosmic Muffin

OK, back on task. Let's talk about your vision of a supreme power, an order in the universe, a spiritual center. We explored some of your beliefs in an earlier chapter, but let's take a more spiritual slant in this chapter. Your spiritual beliefs can shed insight into who you are and can lead to powerful writing. Though our spiritual beliefs are important, even, at times, life sustaining, we needn't approach them timidly. As with the prompts in other chapters, take risks here, and have fun.

PROMPT: Write your own spiritual creed, following the form of creeds, beginning each sentence with "I believe . . ."

PROMPT: Take some time to explore your beliefs—or lack of them—regarding a supreme power. How do you perceive this power? What evidence do you find of it in your life, in the world?

PROMPT: Write about your spiritual upbringing. In which faith were you raised? How did this faith shape your early life? What values and sense of morality did it give you?

PROMPT: Write about your spiritual history, picking up where you left off in the previous prompt. Did you fall away from your early faith? When? Have you returned to it? What beliefs have you retained? What spiritual beliefs do you now hold?

PROMPT: Explain your beliefs to someone who does not share them. Be as clear and specific as possible, and try to intuit her objections or disagreements. Respond to them, not as a way to convince the person of the correctness of your faith so much as to help her understand your beliefs better.

PROMPT: Write about a representative of an organized religion—a minister or priest or member of a clergy. Choose someone you admire, explaining why you feel this way. Try it again with someone you never especially liked. If you want, try it with someone who is a spiritual leader but does not speak for an organized faith.

PROMPT: Write about your spiritual practices. Do you attend church or belong to a spiritual organization? Meditate? Take long walks in nature? How do you feel during these times? How have these practices changed and evolved in your life?

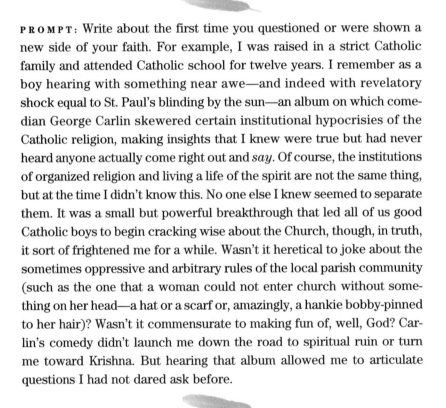

PROMPT: Write about a spiritual breakthrough or revelation you've experienced, a moment of epiphany or understanding that renewed, restored or changed your spiritual beliefs in some way. This need not be a moment in which the clouds parted and celestial trumpets blared. Your experience might have been subtle, its full significance not even apparent until some time later.

PROMPT: Write about the first time you questioned or were shown a new side of your faith. For example, I was raised in a strict Catholic family and attended Catholic school for twelve years. I remember as a boy hearing with something near awe—and indeed with revelatory shock equal to St. Paul's blinding by the sun—an album on which comedian George Carlin skewered certain institutional hypocrisies of the Catholic religion, making insights that I knew were true but had never heard anyone actually come right out and *say*. Of course, the institutions of organized religion and living a life of the spirit are not the same thing, but at the time I didn't know this. No one else I knew seemed to separate them. It was a small but powerful breakthrough that led all of us good Catholic boys to begin cracking wise about the Church, though, in truth, it sort of frightened me for a while. Wasn't it heretical to joke about the sometimes oppressive and arbitrary rules of the local parish community (such as the one that a woman could not enter church without something on her head—a hat or a scarf or, amazingly, a hankie bobby-pinned to her hair)? Wasn't it commensurate to making fun of, well, God? Carlin's comedy didn't launch me down the road to spiritual ruin or turn me toward Krishna. But hearing that album allowed me to articulate questions I had not dared ask before.

PROMPT: Write about a difficult time in your life during which your spiritual beliefs sustained you—or didn't sustain you. Did that experience increase your devotion? Or, if you did not feel sustained, cause you to question your beliefs? Write about the long-term effects of this experience on your spiritual life.

PROMPT: Write about your vision of the afterlife, if you believe in one. If you don't believe in one, write about what happens after we die or, if you prefer, write about your vision of what the afterlife *should* be.

PROMPT: Consider a conventional view of heaven—pearly gates, clouds, angels, harps, etc. Put yourself there. What happens? Have fun with it. While you're in heaven you meet a fictional character who seems in no way heavenly. You wonder why he ended up here. What happens between the two of you as you discover heaven together? If you want, give yourself the opposite fate. You end up in hell—devils, fire, pitchforks, the works. What happens? While you're there, you meet someone who surely should have made St. Peter's cut. Try to find out why he didn't. For a model of fictional heaven, check out Daniel Wallace's hilarious short story "In Heaven These Days."

The Spirit of Your Stories

God, belief, the spiritual life appear in many works of fiction and in film. In the work of William Kennedy and Toni Morrison, for example, the corporeal world and the spirit world are interwoven so that the narratives easily move between them.

Other novels explore the religious facet of our lives, trying to reconcile personal morality and spiritual belief within the structures and codifications of religious institutions, from classic works, such as Nathaniel Hawthorne's *The Scarlet Letter*, to lesser-known ones, such as Harold Frederic's *The Damnation of Theron Ware*. Of course, in most serious novels and stories, characters face moral dilemmas of some sort that call upon their spiritual beliefs or challenge their lack of them.

PROMPT: Write about a time when you were "on the horns" of a moral dilemma, one that challenged or called up your spiritual beliefs to help you make a decision. How did you handle the situation? Would you handle it the same way again? Was your moral compass helpful in providing direction?

PROMPT: Place a character in a situation similar to the one you detailed in the previous prompt, but have the character choose a different course of action. What happens next? Perhaps the character doesn't share your spiritual beliefs. If not, how does this change her actions?

PROMPT: Take a risk and mix the spirit world with the corporeal world. Create a scene in which a character speaks to spirits or spirits speak to each other. This is not an easy task, I know. How to avoid making the spirits sound silly? I can't say for sure. But give it a try.

PROMPT: How large a role do religion and spiritual faith play in your writing? Review some old short stories, essays, poems or whatever you've written in the past, looking for how spiritual faith or the lack of it figures into your work. Look for patterns and write about them.

PROMPT: Write a scene in which a character experiences a vocational calling to be some type of spiritual leader. How does she determine what to do next? Does she follow the call?

Part III

Finding Form

Chapter Eighteen

Of Sonnets and Toasters

Get a girl in trouble, then get her out again.
—KATHLEEN NORRIS

A uthor Michael Martone once proposed a book to Story Press, where I work as an editor, about what he called "appliance fiction." Martone is a brilliant guy with a lot of great ideas. But this one gave us pause: appliance fiction? He explained that technology supplies our lives with many wonderful devices, new ones all the time. When we think we've put ourselves on the very cutting edge of gadgetry, new ones arrive. He felt that these appliances, for lack of a better word, could be a great source of stories, ones that could never have been written in the past. We didn't feel confident we could publish the book, but the idea stayed in my mind. A few months later, I decided to write a story about some type of everyday technology. I would start there and push forward, setting up the story as an exercise, allowing the "appliance" to work as a formal device, something to render form and unity. A few months later I completed a story titled "Redial," about a woman who, by punching the redial button on the telephone every night when she comes home from her late-shift job, discovers her husband is having an affair.

Sometimes finding an idea is as simple as that. Martone later gave the AWP (Associated Writing Programs) fiction-instruction anthology, titled *Creating Fiction* (and published by Story Press, I'm proud to say), a variation on his appliance idea, and I'll begin this chapter on finding form by offering that prompt here.

PROMPT: (by Michael Martone) "Research the history of a common device or gadget, paying particular attention to the compelling social and historical elements that motivated its invention. Have a character use this trivial knowledge, perhaps as an anecdote that informs an activity the character is performing while speaking of or thinking about the device. A character, say, narrates the history of the zipper while making love."

PROMPT: This prompt is from me, but it's based on Martone's ideas from that long-ago meeting. Write a piece using an appliance or technological process or product as the central element in the plot. Use my own story as an example. Another story that comes to mind is John Cheever's "The Enormous Radio." In that story, the radio has magical powers, allowing the young couple to eavesdrop on the lives of their neighbors. If you want to go in a more fantastic direction, following Cheever's example, don't stop yourself.

O ur focus in this chapter is on choosing a form to shape your ideas, and it also explores using form to generate ideas. In the example above, the appliance gives your story a focus, if not necessarily a shape. And it works, in part, because it sets up a task: Find a way to use an appliance. This type of task can free our imaginations by, paradoxically, providing a distraction. You won't worry so much about granting your character an epiphany if you're trying to work a toaster into the story.

Ideas From Form

I'm not a poet. I enjoy reading poetry, but I've never felt the impulse to write it. So I wasn't crazy about having to take poetry workshops in graduate school. I was taking the fiction track in an M.F.A. program, but in order to graduate, fiction students had to take two poetry workshops. But it really wasn't so bad. I had a great teacher, Chase Twichell, who was smart and dedicated and kept things interesting. Her assignments always involved form. Rather than assigning a topic like Write a Descriptive Poem About Your Family, for example, she told us to find a poem we like and write a poem using exactly the same meter. By concentrating on getting the damn meter right, and it was never easy, I lost my self-consciousness and came up with a few nearly mediocre poems, far better than I thought I'd do. The prompts in this section of the chapter are designed to help you get ideas by focusing on form rather than on subject.

PROMPT: Choose a topic you wrote about in an earlier prompt. Now write a sonnet about the same topic. Not sure about the rules of a sonnet? Look them up.

PROMPT: Write a piece of flash fiction—a short story less than five hundred words long—in less than a half hour. Set a timer. Need a topic? Use a prompt from an earlier chapter. Don't spend too much time looking for one. In fact, you may do better by simply flipping to a page and choosing the first one that catches your eye.

PROMPT: Find an essay or story or poem that you like. Outline it, noting turns in plot or shift in topic or approach. Write a piece of your own using the outline, simply changing the topic.

PROMPT: In some of the prompts in the previous section, you created lists. Find two. Don't worry if they're related in any way. It's better if they're unrelated—for example, use the list of five things you'd bring to a deserted island and the list of truisms. Pick an item from each list and begin writing about them, looking for connections. Try to bring them together in a single piece of writing.

PROMPT: Write a story based on a myth or a fairy tale, setting it in contemporary times. For example, you might retell the Hansel and Gretel story using two children you know. If this works for you, pick another myth or fairy tale and try again.

PROMPT: Retell a myth or fairy tale, changing what happens or exploring character more deeply than in the original. For a model, read John Gardner's *Grendel.*

PROMPT: Write a piece of historical nonfiction, recounting an historical event, such as Lincoln's assassination or the stock market crash on Wall Street. But relate the event through the eyes of a fictional character, someone you invent who was an eyewitness.

PROMPT: Write a piece based on a classic story. Jane Smiley used Shakespeare's *King Lear* as a source, known as a metatext, for her novel *A Thousand Acres.* The film *Clueless* was based on Jane Austen's novel *Emma.* The metatext need not be one you deeply admire. In fact, your reason for retelling the story may be because aspects of it bother you. In an interview, Smiley explained her choice of *King Lear:*

> What came first was a long-standing dissatisfaction with an interpretation of *King Lear* that privileged the father's needs over the daughters'. I felt a growing sense of a link between a habit of mind that perceives daughters and children as owned things.

PROMPT: In several interviews Smiley mentions her bringing together several ideas in order to write short stories, comparing the process to placing three or four objects on a desk and moving them around "until you can see some relationship among them." Try this process yourself, but let's, for the moment, take her literally. Gather three or four items from your house and place them on your writing desk. Don't think much about your choices. Just grab three things—a potato, a candle, a jacket. Freewrite about them, looking for connections. Your piece begins with the first object, a scene involving a potato. The plot turns or is complicated by the second object, the candle. The third and, if you want, final scene, involves the jacket.

PROMPT: Write a short story, essay or poem using the form of an instructional article, employing a step-by-step method, such as "How to Know If You're Enlightened" or "Ten Steps to Losing Your Mind." Or try to weave two topics into an instructional piece. In her book *Sugartime*, for example, Susan Carol Hauser explains the steps involved in gathering maple syrup while weaving in meditations on life and nature.

PROMPT: Open a piece with a line of graffiti that you've seen somewhere. Jeff Mock wrote a poem based on a line he read in a men's room in a bar, which, apparently, drew a somewhat philosophical crowd. The line, which he used as the title, was "I Feel More Like I Did When I Came in Here Than I Do Now."

PROMPT: Relate a dream you remember clearly. Write it down exactly as you recall it, presenting the narrative as though the weird dream logic were completely normal. In other words, don't call attention to crazy jumps in time and space or when one character morphs into another. This is a good exercise for breaking down expectations, of allowing your mind to move in unusual directions.

PROMPT: In his book *Exercises in Style*, Raymond Queneau tells the same anecdote ninety-nine times. A man gets on a crowded bus and sees a man accusing another man of deliberately bumping into him. Queneau uses his exercise to explore writing style, but you can use it to explore form. Pick an event, a small one, that you witnessed recently: a car stalled on the highway and another car stopping to help; a man holding a door for a woman and the woman refusing to accept the gesture, insisting that the man go first. Write it as it happened, as you would if recounting the event in a journal or letter. Then write it as it happened but focus only on sounds and smells. Then fictionalize it, adding a few details or a bit of drama. Then write it as a structured poem, a haiku, perhaps, or a villanelle. Then write it in fiction again, this time changing the characters in some significant way, such as their ages, dress or appearances. Then write it in reverse order, beginning with the final action and moving to the first. Then write it in first-person point of view using one character, then first-person point of view using another character. Then write it by setting it in another place—maybe the front door to Bloomingdale's in New York rather than the front door of your office building. If any of these approaches sparks your interest, keep writing. Freewrite or cluster the possibilities of where to go from here.

PROMPT: Think of a situation, perhaps one you created in an earlier prompt. Outline or sketch the story, deciding how you would tell it. Now create at least two other outlines or sketches, telling the story in a different way—different order, different scenes.

PROMPT: Recount a somewhat serious anecdote—a real or a fictional one—in the form of a joke. Use the rhythms and the voice you use when telling a joke, such as premise, setup and punch line.

Choosing Form

You've no doubt had the experience of beginning a piece of writing without knowing what form the idea should take. The idea might spring from real life, but should it be developed as a memoir? Should it be fictionalized? Should you focus on a key moment and turn it into a poem? Maybe you've got a novel on your hands. Of course, your choice of form will influence how you develop the idea. It also will lead to more ideas on the subject.

The answers to these questions are sometimes tough to find, and there are no formulas to apply. The key is working with the idea until you know it well enough to decide which form to use, to allow it, in a way, to choose the form by itself. Sometimes, for example, a personal essay simply grows into a book-length memoir, a short story into a novel. Other times, we decide by experimenting with forms and finding which one works best. Some of the prompts in the previous section can help you play around with form to find the most appropriate one for an idea, but consider a few more to help you explore your options.

P R O M P T : Write about an idea in a few forms, experimenting with ones you wouldn't normally choose. For example, if you usually write short stories, try to render the idea in a poem. If you write essays, see what you gain by developing the idea in a short story.

P R O M P T : Write about an idea by imposing upon it the conventions of a genre you don't normally try. For example, if you're a mystery writer, place your story in the context of a romance. If you're a literary writer, take a stab, so to speak, at a horror story. An example that comes to mind is Thomas Berger's novel *Who Is Teddy Villanova?*, which explores the conventions of the hard-boiled mystery while examining sophisticated philosophical themes.

P R O M P T : Write your story as a play or film script, focusing only on dialogue. Do you find that you need the benefits of description and summary? If so, you may need to render your story as a narrative.

PROMPT: If your story is based on a real experience, write it down exactly as it occurred. How closely can you stick to the truth? Will feelings be hurt or secrets revealed if you use a nonfiction approach? Do you feel limited, even frustrated, by sticking to the actual events? Does the story suggest greater dramatic possibilities than what really happened? If so, move to fiction.

PROMPT: Fictionalize an idea based on a real event but stick to the facts as they took place, simply changing minor details, such as names and the characters' appearances. Is the event believable? Does it seem logical? Do characters act in ways that seem motivated and understandable given what we know of them? Truth *is* often stranger than fiction, but beware that this fact benefits only the writer of nonfiction. The fiction writer must create a sense of believability and logic within the context of the story. Sometimes a true story just doesn't hold water as a fictional piece. The reader won't believe it, even though "it really happened" and even though you're presenting it as fiction, which would seem to eliminate the need for believability. If, for example, your real-life experience involves striking coincidences and unaccounted-for behavior, better make it an essay. This may not seem fair or logical, but as writers we strive to satisfy our readers. In his book *Writing Life Stories*, Bill Roorbach, who writes fiction and memoir, notes with humor that some readers have questioned the truthfulness of his nonfiction, accusing him of exaggeration, while other readers have believed that the fiction is true.

PROMPT: Think of a wild coincidence that has occurred in your life. If a few have occurred, write down all of them in a paragraph or two. Now develop the incident, giving us the necessary background information and specific details. Use this incident in a piece, striving to make it believable, credible. Use the coincidence in an opening scene of a piece, fictionalizing it if you want, and moving forward from there.

Chapter Nineteen

Folks Like You

I let my characters do the talking, simple as that.
—TERRY McMILLAN

There's an old rule about writing that says readers won't care what happens in a story if they don't care who it happens to. If we agree with this statement, then we put character before all other considerations in a piece of writing. In this chapter, we'll focus on getting ideas for characters and on shaping the characters you've developed in earlier prompts. If you're feeling blocked on a character in an ongoing project, perhaps some of the prompts in this chapter can help you break through.

Observing

Developing characters demands a variety of skills—observational as well as writing skills. The first step is choosing a character or group of characters who interest you. Finding such a character may mean hearing a voice in your head, one that compels you to write. Or it may mean seeing a person in your life who intrigues you. The key to creating a great character is something of a paradox: The character should begin as a mystery, and you must work to know as much as possible about the character. Terry McMillan addresses the need for mystery:

> I don't write about characters unless I don't fully understand why they do what they do. And it's sort of like the only way, even if that person is confused and flawed, like most of us are, you get a chance to connect with them.

If you know too much about a character before writing about him, you might grow bored very quickly. The character will offer no surprises, and the piece will lack tension. Compare this situation to having a guest in your home who is unpredictable, volatile. At any moment, the most innocuous topic or comment could set off an emotional outburst. Even an offer of cheese dip becomes fraught with tension. Your character, of course, needn't be so volatile, but he should offer your piece a level of tension. The reader isn't sure what to expect.

But we're getting ahead of ourselves. The first step in evoking people on the page is being observant. Noticing how people act, talk and look—catchphrases, gestures, dress, patterns of behavior. A good writer is always a good observer. You may be way behind on what's in the news and on keeping up with home repairs. And your checkbook balance—forget about it. The roof could cave in and you'd barely notice. But in observing the idiosyncracies of human behavior, you must be sharp, noticing subtle shifts in mood, intuiting thoughts that people attempt to conceal. In an interview, Marge Piercy attributes her sources of characters to talking to people, listening to what they say and being interested in their lives. To sum up, she admits, "I'm a nosy person."

PROMPT: Choose a character who intrigues you, perhaps one from an earlier prompt. Put that character in a brief scene, where you can observe her. Let her interact with other characters while you watch. There needn't be tension in the scene. The character needn't talk about herself. You are trying to see the character in action and to note some observations about her.

PROMPT: Think of a person you know whom, in fact, you've felt that you really don't know at all. Something about the person's behavior simply mystifies you. Write about this person, in descriptions and in recollected scenes. Try to find out more about this person in your writing.

PROMPT: List at least a half-dozen people you know who interest you enough to write about them. Describe why you find them interesting. If you want, re-create them as fictional characters, making up new names and changing some aspects of their personalities, but leaving the real people pretty much as they are.

PROMPT: Combine aspects of two of the people or characters on the list you made in the previous prompt, turning them into a single character, one who embodies elements of both characters. For example, you could combine your brother's appearance and conservative politics with your landlord's *joie de vivre* and love of vintage sitcoms. If you want, place that character in a scene or a situation.

PROMPT: Combine aspects of four of the people or characters on your list, turning them into a single character. Try to pick aspects that are in some way related, making the character complex but not too fractured.

PROMPT: Practice your powers of observation. Go to a party or some group gathering and be consciously aware of what's happening around you. Who taps his foot? Who flounces her hair? Who brags and who mumbles? Who is the liar? Who is trying out a new look? Who fidgets? Who laughs loudly? And listen to what people are telling you and how they speak. Try to pick up on unusual rhythms of speech. When you get home from the gathering, write down your observations. Keep the notebook handy. When you're stuck for a detail or description for a character, your notebook can supply what you need.

PROMPT: Flip through some magazines and find a picture of a person who looks interesting. Don't choose a celebrity or someone about whom you know anything. Don't read the caption. Cut out the picture and put it on your desk. Now freewrite about the person, creating a character sketch. Write about the person's life, her problems and her goals, her background, whatever comes to mind. Move toward some conflict in which the character can be involved. Then write a scene to explore that conflict. If it interests you, keep going. Try this prompt every day for a week, choosing a new picture for each writing day. Keep these characters and pictures in a file and begin building a stable of characters.

PROMPT: Use at least two of the characters from your stable, putting them together in a scene. Force them to talk to each other. If you want, make the scene a first meeting. Put these strangers in a waiting room or on a bus or in an elevator—some place where they will have to talk. Force the proximity.

Getting to Know Your Characters

In the next few prompts, we'll focus on ways to get to know your characters better as you begin working with them on the page. The old saw about knowing what's in your characters' drawers is valid (unlike many old saws). You should know much more about the characters than meets the page. If you're writing narrative nonfiction, the same rule applies, though you may not know what's in their drawers. The prompts that follow can be used on any character. I've kept them generic so you can use them whenever you need them. Also, you can use many of the prompts in section two for characterization. Rather than responding about your own family or favorite things, respond for your character. To avoid repetition, I haven't covered some of these topics again here. In getting to know your character, you will need to know these things, too.

PROMPT: Describe your character's physical appearance—in minute detail. Height and weight, hairstyle, body type, gait, posture, hair color, eye color, nose type and all the extras. Mention, too, the plantar wart on the ball of his foot, and the tiny scar on the left knee where he got stitches when he was seven. What aspects of his personal appearance does he especially like? What aspects are sources of self-doubt?

PROMPT: Describe your character's facial expressions and body language. Describe any tics or physical habits, such as clearing his throat when he's irritated or stroking his chin when he watches TV.

PROMPT: Describe your character's wardrobe. Know everything he wears, but pay particular attention to favorite clothes. What image does this character try to project through clothes, and what does that desired image say about the character?

PROMPT: Describe your character's large possessions: car, home, furnishings, boat. Note what he especially likes among these things.

PROMPT: Describe your character's small possessions, including souvenirs and keepsakes. As in the previous prompt, identify what objects the character likes best. What memories do the favorite objects hold?

PROMPT: Describe your character's interests and hobbies. How active is he in each of the areas? Which hobbies has he abandoned through the years? What is the hot interest of the moment?

PROMPT: Describe your character's personality. Outgoing? Shy? Both? The life of the party but given to melancholy when alone? Give this description some depth. Here's where you are really getting at the heart of the character.

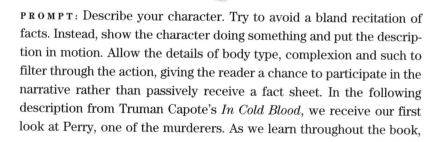

PROMPT: Write your character's life story in a few pages, focusing on the key moments in his life, the turning points.

Rendering Character

Now that you've gotten to know your character better, inside and out, you have to put him on the page. In his book *The Art of Compelling Fiction*, Christopher Leland creates the 7-Ds approach to evoking character: description, declaration, dressing, dialogue, demeanor, dramatics and deeds. Through this method, you show the readers your character, rather than simply telling about him, and it can work for narrative nonfiction as well as fiction. Let's try the 7-Ds through prompts.

PROMPT: Describe your character. Try to avoid a bland recitation of facts. Instead, show the character doing something and put the description in motion. Allow the details of body type, complexion and such to filter through the action, giving the reader a chance to participate in the narrative rather than passively receive a fact sheet. In the following description from Truman Capote's *In Cold Blood*, we receive our first look at Perry, one of the murderers. As we learn throughout the book,

Perry is a paradoxical person, a sentimental songwriter and vicious killer. Capote suggests this paradox in this early description, by focusing on Perry's strangely proportioned body:

> Perry folded the map. He paid for the root beer and stood up. Sitting, he had seemed a more than normal-sized man, a powerful man, with the shoulders, the arms, the thick, crouching torso of a weight lifter. But some sections of him were not in proportion to others. His tiny feet, encased in short black boots with steel buckles, would have neatly fitted into a delicate lady's dancing slippers; when he stood up, he was no taller than a twelve-year-old child, and suddenly looked, strutting on stunted legs that seemed grotesquely inadequate to the grown-up bulk they supported, not like a well-built truck driver but like a retired jockey, overblown and muscle-bound.

PROMPT: Make a few statements about your character. This approach, of course, is more telling than showing, but it can be effective if used judiciously. But be aware that you must support these statements with the actions in your story. As a writing teacher told me many years ago, if you tell us that "Joe was the funniest guy in my graduating class," Joe better damn well be funny. Here is a statement about a character from *The Stone Diaries* by Carol Shields:

> Barker Flett at thirty-three is stooped of shoulder and sad of expression, but women who set their eyes on him think: now here is a man who might easily be made happy.

PROMPT: Show us your character through clothing styles and dress, through his possessions, the things he buys. As with the first prompt in this section, put your description in motion. Allow the reader to make discoveries and reach conclusions about the character. You control the reader's conclusions by selecting the right details, not by directly telling her what to think. In the following description from Nicholson Baker's *The Mezzanine*, we see a character in action, and possessions that help to characterize her quickly:

> "Have you signed the poster for Ray?" said Tina, rolling out in her chair. Tina has lots of hair, moussed out impressively around a small smart face; she was probably at her most alert just then, because she was watching the phones for Deanne and Julie, the other secretaries in my department, until they returned from lunch after one. In the more private area of her cube, in the shadow of the shelf under the unused fluorescent light, she had pinned up shots of a stripe-shirted husband, some nephews and nieces, Barbra Streisand, and a multiply xeroxed sentiment in Gothic type that read, "If you can't get out of it, get into it."

PROMPT: Think of a character you want to write about. Write down her name and her job, such as "Fiona Ferguson, Web designer." In the next three sentences, describe her so that she fits commonly held beliefs or stereotypes about people who do this type of work. In the next three sentences, tell us something about your character that goes against the stereotypes.

PROMPT: Try this variation on the previous prompt. In the game of Taboo, a player tries to describe something without using certain related words. He tries to describe it well enough so that his partner can guess the thing. For example, if the key word is "lipstick," the player can't use words such as "lips" or "mouth" or "make-up" or "kiss." Let's use that approach in describing characters. Choose a character and a job—such as "Fiona Ferguson, Web designer." List all the clichés and stereotypes of someone who does that job. Now write a few paragraphs about the character, but don't use any of the words or phrases on your list.

PROMPT: Place your character in a scene and present him through action and dialogue. Create a situation in which your character is involved, or simply place him in a room with another character or two and focus on bringing him to life for the reader. Try not to move into the character's head, which may be a tempting way to present his feelings. For this experiment, allow us to interpret what he's thinking and feeling through his actions and through what he says and how he says it. In the following scene from Don DeLillo's *White Noise*, the protagonist, Jack Gladney, undergoes a diagnostic interview following exposure to hazardous material. He is nervous, eager for the technician to give him a clean bill of health. But DeLillo gives us no direct statement of Jack's emotional state and gives us few telling descriptions. He relies on the pace of the dialogue and the tone of Jack's statements:

> "Here's where we ask about smoking."
> "That's easy. The answer is no. And it's not a matter of having stopped five or ten years ago. I've never smoked. Even when I was a teenager. Never tried it. Never saw the need."
> "That's always a plus."
> I felt tremendously reassured and grateful.
> "We're moving right along, aren't we?"
> "Some people like to drag it out," he said. "They get interested in their own condition. It becomes almost like a hobby."
> "Who needs nicotine? Not only that, I rarely drink coffee and certainly never with caffeine. Can't understand what people see in all this artificial stimulation. I get high just walking in the woods."

PROMPT: Stay in the scene you wrote in the previous prompt. This time, add details that are more subtle, presenting the way your character does what he does. Try to suggest his level of comfort with the other characters. Is he distracted? Bored? Nervous? Relaxed? Does he have a hearty laugh or a tight one? How does he sit and stand? In the following scene from Anton Chekhov's "The Lady With the Toy Dog," we see the first meeting between two characters who soon will fall in love. Through gesture and dialogue, Chekhov shows us their feelings of nervousness and attraction:

> He snapped his fingers at the Pomeranian and, when it trotted up to him, shook his forefinger at it. The Pomeranian growled. Gurov shook his finger again.
>
> The lady glanced at him and instantly lowered her eyes.
>
> "He doesn't bite," she said, and blushed.
>
> "May I give him a bone?" he asked, and on her nod of consent added in friendly tones: "Have you been long in Yalta?"
>
> "About five days."
>
> "And I am dragging out my second week here."
>
> Neither spoke for a few minutes.
>
> "The days pass quickly, and yet one is so bored here," she said.
>
> "It's the thing to say it's boring here. People never complain of boredom in godforsaken holes like Belyev or Zhizdra, but when they get here it's: 'Oh, the dullness! Oh, the dust!' You'd think they'd come from Granada to say the least."
>
> She laughed.

PROMPT: Use the same scene again, this time focusing on what Leland calls dramatics, how the character carries himself. This mode of presentation is similar to the previous one, but here we're concerned a bit more with tone of voice, the way a character acts and speaks in general terms, rather than in reaction to the other characters around her. In short, we're more concerned with typical behavior rather than the mood of the moment. In the following scene from Flannery O'Connor's "A Good Man Is Hard to Find," the protagonist, known only as "the grandmother," is shown as manipulative and hypocritical. Blind to her own faults, she believes she is a good person who is misunderstood and unappreciated in a changing world that has lost a sense of traditional values. In the following excerpt, we see her sentimentality and racism in action as the family drives down a highway. Her one gesture—"folding her thin veined fingers"—suggests her age and her self-satisfaction:

> "In my time," said the grandmother, folding her thin veined fingers, "children were more respectful of their native states and their parents and everything else. People did right then. Oh look at the cute pickaninny!" she said and pointed to a Negro child standing in the door of a shack. "Wouldn't that make a picture now?" she asked, and they all turned and looked at the little Negro out of the back window. He waved.
>
> "He didn't have any britches on," June Star said.
>
> "He probably didn't have any," the grandmother explained. "Little niggers in the country don't have things like we do. If I could paint, I'd paint that picture," she said.

PROMPT: As F. Scott Fitzgerald once wrote, "action is character." As we've seen, character is more than just action, but action is the primary mode writers use. Put your character in a scene involving some sort of conflict. If the scene you've been developing in the previous prompts does not contain much conflict, try a new one. Give your character an obstacle and test his mettle. In the following excerpt from Lorrie Moore's "People Like That Are the Only People Here," a mother is made aware that her son has cancer. Notice that Moore manages to show the mother's fear without stating it directly. The mother uses sarcasm to mask her feelings, a trait we will see in action throughout the story:

> "The surgeon will speak to you," says the Radiologist.
>
> "Are you finding something?"
>
> "The surgeon will speak to you," the Radiologist says again. "There seems to be something there, but the surgeon will talk to you about it."
>
> "My uncle had something on his kidney," says the Mother. "So

they removed the kidney and it turned out the something was benign."

The Radiologist smiles a broad, ominous smile. "That's always the the way it is," he says. "You don't know exactly what it is until it's in the bucket."

" 'In the bucket,' " the Mother repeats.

The Radiologist's grin grows scarily wider—is that even possible? "That's doctor talk," he says.

"It's very appealing," says the Mother. "It's a very appealing way to talk." Swirls of bile and blood, mustard and maroon in a pail, the colors of an African flag or some exuberant salad bar: *in the bucket*—she imagines it all.

PROMPT: Write about a character whose appearance and actions are far different from her interior self. Place the character in a scene, showing her actions, but occasionally move into her head to show what she's thinking and feeling. A cynical, sophisticated woman, for example, can hold the floor at a party with her wit, but in her mind readers learn of her boredom and loneliness. In her novel *Remember Me*, Laura Hendrie's protagonist, Rose, is known as a fiery, stubborn, independent person, and her behavior around the people of the town where she lives gives credence to this reputation. But Hendrie lets us know that sometimes Rose is on the verge of tears while confronting other characters, that her gruff behavior is a defense against the isolation and powerlessness she feels in a community that has never accepted her.

PROMPT: Write a scene in which your character does not appear. Instead, other characters talk about him, giving the reader a sense of the character through how these characters portray him to each other. If you want to add an extra element of tension, have the characters discuss your absent character unfairly, making him seem better or worse a person than he actually is. Beauty may be in the eye of the beholder, but some characters can be just plain wrong about another character. For example, the title of this chapter, "Folks Like You," is taken from a poem inscribed on Bonnie Parker's gravestone. As you probably know, Bonnie and Clyde were responsible for the murder of more than a dozen people. Here is how her family remembers her: "As the flowers are all made sweeter by / the sunshine and the dew / so this old world is made brighter by / the lives of folks like you."

More Thoughts on Character

As should be clear to you by now, I'm a believer in learning to write by reading. Study the masters. This belief holds true for characterization, maybe even more so than for the other elements of narrative. It's difficult to teach someone how to create compelling characters. This skill requires observing people, knowing your character and mastering the modes of dramatic presentation. We've covered these aspects of the subject. But having the ingredients of a character is not the same as creating a great character. Two cooks can use the same ingredients and have vastly different results.

By studying the masters, you can learn the subtle strategies. Begin by making a list of the characters you like most, the ones you find most memorable. If you read a lot, your list probably will be very long. If you want, include film favorites on your list, but be sure it's the character rather than the actor that you like. My own favorites that come quickly to mind: R.P. McMurphy from Ken Kesey's *One Flew Over the Cuckoo's Nest*, Tom Sawyer from Mark Twain's novels, George Babbitt from Sinclair Lewis's *Babbitt*, Jack Gladney from Don DeLillo's *White Noise*.

After you finish your list, read the story or essay or novel or memoir closely. If you can, read it a few times. Rereading can teach you much about writing. Each time you notice something new. I learned a lot about writing short stories while I was an editor at *Story* magazine. In editing, copyediting and proofreading stories, I'd read them close to a dozen times. Hidden structures would emerge, and I could determine how characters were coming to life or remaining flat on the page.

If a character is not yet working for you, perhaps you need to know him better. If he's not interesting enough, find a strong quality and amplify it. If readers don't find your character sympathetic, find out why. Amplify a few likable traits. In a novel I wrote years ago, my protagonist was too mild to hold the novel together. The secondary characters, who were much more plucky and interesting, stole every scene. In revising some of the early chapters, I realized that the character was always playing the straight man. He was losing the spotlight because I was unconsciously setting him up to do that. I changed his name and made him bigger. With those two simple changes, he became clearer in my mind and more active, more assertive.

P R O M P T : If a character is not working on the page, change some aspect of her personality or behavior. If the character is based closely on you, change more than one aspect. We are always a little ambivalent about characters who are based closely on ourselves. It's tough to get the necessary distance.

P R O M P T : If a character is not doing what you'd like him to do, assess your decision to have the character perform the action. Perhaps the action doesn't feel right for the character because it isn't right. If he must do the action for the sake of the plot, rethink the plot. Try to find another way to accomplish the plot goal. The problem lies there, not in the character.

P R O M P T : Write a scene in which you let loose of your characters. Allow them to do whatever they want. Write down whatever actions occur to you first, without worrying if the action fits the scene or the character as readers know her. This experiment will help you practice letting go of your characters. Some writers have an easy time letting go, especially if they've spent some time with the characters and know them well. Other writers never let go. Vladimir Nabokov once referred to his characters as "galley slaves."

PROMPT: Write a scene in which a character takes a surprising action. Then, on a separate piece of paper, explain the character's motivation. Why is she doing what she's doing? Be as specific as you can be. Go back to the womb if you must. When you feel you have a pretty good understanding (as much as you can ever understand human motivation), move forward with your story. Resist the urge to explain the motivation in the story.

PROMPT: Grab a few characters from your list of favorites. Place them all in a scene. Maybe they're all up in character heaven. Sorry. To evoke these characters, use the strategies you picked up from reading the stories in which the characters appear. Feel free to steal entire paragraphs of description from the originals, if you want. Add to them, echoing the original authors' voices. Have fun with this one.

Chapter Twenty

The Shape of Things to Come

When the plot flags, bring in a man with a gun.
—RAYMOND CHANDLER

S ure, easy for Chandler to say. He wrote hard-boiled mysteries. What if you're trying to structure a memoir? What then, huh? Do you even know anybody who owns a gun? Or how's a gun going to fit into that meditative poem you're trying to shape? Or maybe you're working on a whimsical children's tale. Which of the bunnies in the downy meadow pulls a pistol? Oh, well. Ray was doing his best.

Advice: All advice on structure and plot (and on writing) must be taken at face value. Learn the craft, use what applies to you, and be aware that every piece is a new challenge, a starting from scratch. What worked last time may not work this time. In fact, regard with suspicion any plot that comes too easily. True, sometimes a story will just write itself, all the twists and turns, the scenes and summaries just falling into place. But most times finding the best shape for your story requires some shuffling around. That's our focus in this chapter.

Though structure is a key element in any kind of storytelling, and would seem as fundamental to writing stories as, say, the alphabet, it's a controversial topic. Does one outline or not? How much should one know when beginning? Writers can't even agree on what to call structure. Some writers revile the word *plot* and would never dare to include anything as barbaric as a sequence of connected events in their work. These writers prefer the word *shape*. Other writers feel that *shape* is a pretentious bit of foppery. They feel that any story in which the events can't be followed like shampoo directions isn't really a story. Most writers fall somewhere in between. Some of us tell stories in impressionistic, associative moves, shifting between past and present, between action and reflection. Others think in chronological terms, seeing a story as a grand inevitable sweep. Director John Huston once was asked how he managed to create such unique structures for his films. He replied that he couldn't imagine telling his stories in any other way. He did what came naturally for him. John Irving, in a disarming bit of open-mindedness, feels the writer needs to know the plot before beginning:

> If you don't know the story before you begin the story, what kind of storyteller are you? Just an ordinary kind, just a mediocre kind—making it up as you go along, like a common liar.

John Updike, on the other hand, prefers the common liar approach:

> I really begin with some kind of solid, coherent image, some notion of the shape of the book and even of its texture. *The Poorhouse Fair* was meant to have a sort of wide shape. *Rabbit, Run* was kind of zigzag, *The Centaur* was sort of a sandwich.

So there's no right answer on how to structure your stories. If you want to outline, outline. You won't be a conventional, uncreative lout nor will you be a clear-eyed, commonsense professional for doing it. If you prefer to write until the story finds its own shape, write until the story finds its own shape. You won't be a true artist nor will you be a hopeless fool for doing it. Because this book focuses on getting ideas, we'll concentrate on structuring before beginning, but many of the prompts can be used if you've already begun and are still looking for a shape or if you're stuck in the middle and need to rethink how you've told your story.

P R O M P T : Write or outline your story in chronological order, noting each event on a separate index (3″ × 5″) card. Then shuffle the cards and read the story in a new order. Do this a few times, looking for interesting juxtapositions and for possibilities for creating conflict and dramatic tension. If you prefer, try the cut-and-paste approach. Cut your story into pieces and rearrange it. This latter approach might work better if you've completed a draft of your story.

P R O M P T : Begin a story with a moment of decision or insight, an epiphany that more commonly appears at the end of a story. Then jump backward, allowing the reader to find out what led to the decision. Avoid simply summarizing the events in a narrative flashback. Take readers dramatically up to the moment of decision. Frederick Exley's *A Fan's Notes* begins with the narrator having "what appeared to be a heart attack." When told he's simply been drinking too much, he realizes he has reached a turning point in his life and must begin finding out why he drinks and why he is so troubled. Much of the novel concerns his investigation of how he got to the point where he collapsed.

P R O M P T : Build on the previous prompt. After you've led the reader to the decision, push beyond it. What happens next, as a result of the decision?

P R O M P T : Combine the two previous prompts. Begin with the decision or insight, then allow the character to push forward while filtering past events into the narrative. Lisa Dale Norton uses this structure in her memoir, *Hawk Flies Above*. In the memoir, she confronts the emptiness of her peripatetic life by returning to her childhood home and confronting the demons of her past.

PROMPT: Rather than a decision or epiphany, open with an action scene: Something happens. You can move forward for another scene or two if you want, then jump backward and show what happened that led to that moment. The film *Mildred Pierce* uses this structure. A character is murdered in the opening, Mildred is arrested as a suspect, then she tells the story of her life to explain what happened. Most of the film focuses on her story, returning to the police station only at the end.

PROMPT: Build a story by bringing together two distant—geographically or socially—characters. Begin by focusing on one character, using her in a scene or two, then switch to a second character. Your story will gain structure and tension as you move these characters closer and closer toward their inevitable meeting. For a tour de force example of this approach, read *Continental Drift* by Russell Banks. He brings together two very different story lines: a blue-collar man living in New Hampshire; the geological formation of the Earth's crust.

PROMPT: Read a story or essay or poem or watch a film at least five times. You can use a book-length work if you're feeling particularly ambitious. After the fifth time, write what you've been able to discover about the structure of the piece. Through numerous viewings and readings, you'll be able to pick up on how the piece was put together.

PROMPT: Write an opening scene for a story. You could use a scene you've written in response to a prompt or simply explore a story idea you've had for a while. Next, write a scene in which the key character from the earlier scene is in a different place or different circumstances from the first scene. Then outline—or write about—how he moved from one situation to the next. If the second scene does not close the story, push on. If you want, repeat the process, jumping forward to another place or circumstance and moving the character slowly to that point.

PROMPT: Use a framing device. Write a story in which a character tells a different story, one with a different setting and characters. Of course, the stories need to have some connection. An example: *The Wizard of Oz*. The scenes in Kansas act as a frame for the long section set in Oz.

Shape in Space and Time

Many writers use movement in space and time to provide their stories with structure and unity. They focus on specific periods in time or on journeys from one place to another. This method may seem obvious, but writers often overlook the benefits of this approach. The benefits of a ticking clock—find the villain in forty-eight hours or the world blows up!—are easy to understand and are used often in suspense films and novels. Dramatic tension is immediately evoked. But even if your characters aren't racing against time, you can use time to give your stories a frame.

If you use this approach, find some models and study how the writers suggest time's passage. In a novel I've begun writing, I'm using the Christmas season as a structural device, beginning on the first day of Advent and moving to the Feast of the Three Kings on January 6. If you use a spatial structure, using movement from one place to another, find models to study how the writers suggest this movement. In the prompts that follow, explore the possibilities of shaping your stories by focusing them in this way.

PROMPT: Structure your story by using a specific period of time. Set it in a single day, opening in the morning, ending at night. For a model, read *Ulysses* by James Joyce. Fat chance? OK, find an easier model.

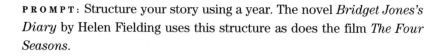

PROMPT: Structure your story by setting it in a weekend. For this one, you can use *Saturday Night and Sunday Morning* by Alan Sillitoe.

PROMPT: Structure your story by using a season. In a famous example, *The Great Gatsby* begins at the onset of summer and ends as the leaves begin to fall.

PROMPT: Structure your story using a year. The novel *Bridget Jones's Diary* by Helen Fielding uses this structure as does the film *The Four Seasons*.

Let's shift the focus to spatial structures. A number of films use coast-to-coast journeys—*Midnight Run* comes quickly to mind. *Dumb and Dumber* provides another example (I know, dumb example. Give me a break. My, um, kids like to watch it.) *Rain Man* covers much of the country. The reader is subconsciously anchored in the story as he locates where he is in relation to the journey's end. For example, if we're headed to Los Angeles, we can plot our course from New York, knowing where we are in the story's arc by knowing where we are geographically. Older films amplified this arc by visually showing the lines on the map—where the characters began, where they are and how far they have to go. *The Adventures of Huckleberry Finn* uses a journey structure, the rafting trip down the Mississippi River providing structure for the picaresque story. The river itself also provides unity, a constant amid the various adventures. Bill Bryson's *The Lost Continent* involves an extended trip through most of the states. *Blue Highways* by William Least Heat-Moon uses a series of trips.

PROMPT: Structure your story by using a trip or journey. Let your reader know the destination early in the story. Note the examples above.

PROMPT: Use a framing device, placing your journey within a larger story. *The Wizard of Oz*, as mentioned earlier, uses this structure. We know that when the group arrives in Emerald City that Dorothy still must find a way back to Kansas and the story's original setting.

PROMPT: The physical journey provides structure and movement to your story and is often used to show changes in a character. The character is in a different place emotionally at the end of the journey. Something has been lost or gained. A friendship has been forged through the events of the trip, as in the film *Thelma and Louise*, or has broken apart, as in Jack Kerouac's *On the Road*. Write a story, or plan one, using the journey to show narrative progression as well as progression within your characters.

An event also can structure your story. Try some of the following prompts to experiment with this approach.

PROMPT: Structure a story around a holiday or birthday. Readers will know how these holidays work and the various stages of preparation and the celebration and will have that structure in their minds as they move through the story. The holiday needn't be the story's primary concern. It can provide a background for the main story, simply working as a unifying device.

PROMPT: Write a story involving a wedding or a funeral or a birth. As in the previous prompt, this activity need not be the story's primary focus. The event can be used as a subplot or background device, providing a silent structure.

PROMPT: Write a story involving a blizzard or a drought or some other type of weather event. The same conditions apply here as in the previous prompts. You could tell the story of a family's unraveling, concentrating on the interrelationships of the characters while using the heavy snow as a counterpoint to the main story, allowing it to provide unity and structure.

PROMPT: Write a story that builds to any of the above times, events or activities. For example, begin a story that ends with a big Fourth of July celebration (and showdown). Or begin with a chilly day or two and build slowly to a blizzard.

Chapter Twenty-one

It All Depends on Your Point of View

I'm about to write a novel. The only problem is I don't know if I am an I or a she.
—ELIZABETH HARDWICK

The title of this chapter is not an overstatement, especially when turning your ideas into fiction, poetry, a script, even nonfiction. Your choice of who tells the story and from what perspective may be the most important decision you make. A good idea can become a great one if presented from the right point of view. Conversely, I've seen many a good idea botched by the point of view.

In attending writers conferences for many years, I've learned that many writers aren't especially interested in discussing point of view. They want characterization. They want plot. Point of view? Yawn, well, OK, if we must. But I've been pleasantly surprised at conferences in the past year to hear so many questions about point of view. A few months ago, a workshop on novel writing was dominated by talk of point of view: How do I know which one to choose? How can I dramatize scenes that the narrator can't possibly have witnessed? Many others.

In the next two chapters, we'll explore this subject in detail, trying to find ideas, shape material you've begun writing already and solve problems that have arisen in your work by helping you see it in a new way. In this chapter, we'll focus on first-person point of view, perhaps the most troublesome of them all, because it's the most tempting to use and it's the most misunderstood.

First Person

A quick review: In first-person point of view, a character in the story tells the story, using the first-person pronoun *I*. A few examples:

I read about it in the paper, in the subway, on my way to work.
"SONNY'S BLUES," JAMES BALDWIN

I will wait for her in the yard that Maggie and I made so clean and wavy yesterday afternoon.
"EVERYDAY USE," ALICE WALKER

I am Gimpel the fool.
"GIMPEL THE FOOL," ISAAC SINGER

I steal.
"LAWNS," MONA SIMPSON

The events of this type of story are related to the readers through the narrative *I*. The readers see, hear, think and feel right along with this character. They are told only what he thinks, knows and does.

PROMPT: Find four pieces of writing that open with the word *I*. (First-person pieces that don't begin with *I* are off-limits for this prompt.) Copy the first few sentences. Then write four of your own openings, all beginning with the word *I*. At least one must follow the Singer example, a statement of identity: "I am _____." Another must follow the Mona Simpson example: "I [action verb]." If you worked the prompts in chapters five and six, you have done this already. Use the ones you've written, and push on for at least three paragraphs. If you haven't done them, do them now.

Here's one I wrote. We'll use this sample throughout the point-of-view chapters to discuss the qualities of each viewpoint:

> I saw Alice walk into the club, radiant in an orchid dress, her hair drawn back in a French braid, just the way I like it. It'd been two weeks since I'd seen her, three weeks since our getaway trip to the shore. But she looked different. Thinner maybe, her skin paler, her dark eyes tense, like she had something on her mind.
>
> But her chin was tilted back in this way she had, like she was some kind of queen. You had to look close to see it was all an act. Like always, she looked around the smoky room, pretending that she was trying to decide where to sit or that maybe she was meeting some people there. Then, like always, she headed for the one empty bar stool at the far end, by the waitress station. I'd put a glass of water there an hour ago to save the seat.
>
> "This seat taken?" she asked, like it was the first time I ever saw her in my life.
>
> Sweeping away the glass and bar nap, I said, "They left," solemn as a judge.

First Person—the Good Stuff

In this example, we can see some of the positive aspects of point of view. First, it supplies an immediate *focus*, a central consciousness: the bartender. He supplies the story with boundaries, a frame to use for shaping this narrative world. This point of view also allows us to establish *conflict and tension* very quickly. Alice looks different, is apparently troubled by something. What gives? This question is then complicated by the game the two play, pretending not to know each other.

First person also gives the narrative *immediacy*, since readers receive the events directly from the bartender, let's call him Jim. With first person, there's no narrative middleman diluting the impact of the drama. Readers feel and think right along with the narrator, and the narrator is taking part in the drama. If they're rooting for him, the narrative stakes are raised for them: To put it simply, if he wins, they win; if he loses, they lose.

First person gives your story a strong *voice*. The voice characterizes Jim and creates a tone for the story. Note that Jim uses slang and that his grammar is not perfect: He uses *like* to render the subjunctive case rather than the correct *as if* or *as though*. Through a unique and vivid first-person voice, you can captivate, charm and seduce your reader.

PROMPT: Push forward with the openings you wrote above, writing at least one page for each one. By the end of the first page, your "I" should establish conflict and tension, and the reader should gain a sense of the character through voice. Tip: Don't go overboard on the voice, especially in using slang and dialect. A little goes a long way.

PROMPT: Begin a story in which the first-person narrator is at work. She'll use jargon and slang to describe what she's doing. To make it easier, give the narrator a job you've done, that you can speak of in the shorthand style we use in our jobs.

First Person—the Bad Stuff

The good news is that some of the bad stuff isn't really bad. You can use it to your advantage if you're clever. But do be aware of the limitations of this point of view. You can avoid roadblocks in your stories by knowing in advance that trouble awaits, and you can be more successful with your ideas if you've found the right perspective from which to tell the story.

The first problem is *limitation*. You're limited to what your narrator can reasonably see and know and feel. If key action occurs elsewhere, you can't render that action dramatically. Perhaps Alice has just been fired from her job in an explosive confrontation with her boss. More than twenty thousand dollars has been discovered missing and all the evidence points to Alice. She declared, but could not prove, her innocence. Since the readers know Jim was working behind the bar, they know he couldn't have witnessed this scene. Alice can tell him about it, but that loses the immediacy, even if Jim imaginatively recreates the scene and relates it directly. He wasn't there.

And then there's the problem of *distance*—your own and the narrator's. If the story is autobiographical and the narrator is a slightly altered version of you, first person is a risky choice. (Of course, if you're writing an essay or memoir, there's no way around this dilemma, but still you should be aware of the pitfalls.) A big, deep, hairy-looking pitfall is the temptation to explain everything rather than showing it. Let's face it, we like the sound of our own voices. And who better than we to tell the readers what they should think about the stories we're telling. Even if you create a voice completely different from your own, you'll grow to like that voice and might be less stingy than you should be with how much that voice gets to talk.

If the story is autobiographical, you also might tend to stick too closely to *what really happened.* In nonfiction, you'd better stick to what happened; in fiction, that's a danger. You're limiting your material and assuming that because the events took place that they possess logic and believability.

For these reasons, I'd advise not using first person if you are too close to the voice or character of your story. Successful first-person point of view *exists* in the distance between the writer and the voice. From that gap blooms the story's conflict and tension, along with a great deal of useful irony. The voice is not only your guiding light through the jungle of plot, it is a device you consciously manipulate. You need to hear it clearly, objectively, from a distance.

P R O M P T : Create a narrative voice that is distinctly different from your own by changing a key element of the character. If you're a woman, write in a man's voice. If you're under thirty, create the voice of a character over sixty. Make a change in appearance or education or background. Put that character at an event or in a scene from your own recent experience—at a friend's wedding, at a restaurant with your mate—and retell the story through this new voice.

P R O M P T : Put yourself in the previous scene, but narrate it again through the voice of the new character. For example, if you placed someone else in the restaurant where you argued with your mate about his family's continuing interference with your lives, allow this new person to observe, perhaps as a waiter or as a nosy patron at a nearby table.

PROMPT: Write about an event from your childhood through your adult eyes, adding perceptions that you could not have known at the time.

This prompt speaks to the next concern in using first person: the problem of *perception*. In our story, the readers will see and know what Jim knows—and what he feels obliged to tell them. This can create difficulties in telling the story. For example, if Jim has worked at the nightclub for a long time, why would he describe it? He's known Alice for a while, so why would he describe her? We avoided this problem by having him describe her because she looks different when she enters the bar. He notices changes and through them we can slip in a few details about her general appearance.

Another aspect of the perception problem concerns the narrator's observational powers. Can the writer, on the one hand, characterize Jim as a self-absorbed dolt and on the other hand have him supply all the specific and particular details necessary to bring his world to life? Possibly, but not easily.

Our narrator Jim seems to be observant, but can readers trust his perceptions? First person always brings up the question of *reliability*. Whenever we tell stories, we have our own best interests at heart, especially when telling stories of some significance to us. As readers and listeners, we automatically reserve judgment. For example, when someone tells you about his divorce, citing all the reasons his wife is to blame, do you believe him, or do you believe you're only getting half of the truth? Conversely, if the speaker, obviously pained by guilt and regret, puts all the blame on himself, do you believe you're getting the full story?

A bit of advice: If your story requires a speaker of absolute truth, first person is not the right choice. The reader can take Jim's word that Alice walks into the bar and peers around the room. The reader can accept that her dress is orchid and that her hair is styled in a French braid. If we establish him as somewhat perceptive, we can even believe that the objective observer would perceive her as self-confident, but this is a mask.

But because Jim is romantically involved with Alice, readers must question his perception of her as "radiant." Is she merely attractive, no more radiant than the last five women who walked in the place? And does she really look like she has "something on her mind," or is this the result of Jim's feeling insecure? Perhaps he's a bit concerned that they haven't been together in two weeks and is seeing everything as significant and negative.

You can take great pains to establish the speaker's validity—choosing the Pope or Mother Teresa to tell your story. But the intelligent reader will still question. This is not a bad thing in itself. Again, choose first person when you want to use the reader's doubt, when the story truly lives within the disparity between what the voice says and what the reader can determine is true. Use that doubt, that disparity, to create and sustain tension in your narrative. In *The Great Gatsby*, when Nick Carraway proclaims, "I am the most honest person I have ever known," Fitzgerald wants us to think, *Yeah, right*. Nick is, in many ways, honest. And he's very observant. He is perceptive and he's selfless enough to empathize with other characters. Good qualities for a narrator. But he's also a bit blind to his own priggishness and to his inability to commit himself to any one side. He tries too hard, in short, to be fair. In some ways, he doesn't quite get the point of what happened in that strange summer of 1922 among the rich and decadent of East and West Egg.

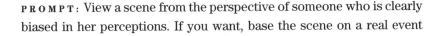

PROMPT: Write a monologue from the point of view of a character who insists he's "telling the truth" about something that happened. Try to show that he doesn't grasp the full story or is fudging that truth a bit.

PROMPT: View a scene from the perspective of someone who is clearly biased in her perceptions. If you want, base the scene on a real event in your own life. Perhaps, this character is jealous of the bride at the friend's wedding. She finds fault with everything she sees. Or perhaps she's trying so hard to "take the high road" that she characterizes the event in a better light than it deserves. Allow the biases to be revealed slowly.

PROMPT: Use the same character and event as in the previous prompt, but don't mention the biases. Try to be more subtle this time, allowing the narrator to appear coolly objective and observant while tainting ever so slightly the details and events.

Whose Story Is It?

You've decided the story needs to be handled in first person. Now you must choose which narrator to use. In short, whose story is it? Our story, for example, doesn't have to be rendered through Jim. Let's switch to Alice:

> I walked into Jim's club—loud and smoky, as always—and looked around for a minute before heading for the last open stool. Though I was happy to see Jim, this was about the last place I wanted to be. The trouble at work was all I could think about, and taking the time to explain it to Jim would require more effort and energy than I could manage.

Same bar. Same action. Different story. It's no longer about a man worried about keeping a budding relationship alive with a woman who might lift him from the tawdry world in which he lives. It's now a story of a woman's struggle after being fired for a crime she didn't commit. In fact, Jim's role might be small, a peripheral relationship for Alice as she attempts to prove her innocence.

We have other options, too. Our scene could be seen through the eyes of a different character, describing Jim and Alice briefly before launching into his own tale of love. He might idealize the young couple, setting them up as a comparison to his own meager love life. Or that character could tell the story of Jim and Alice, working as a peripheral narrator, perhaps a regular customer at the bar or someone who socializes with one of the characters. A peripheral narrator is an excellent choice when dealing with unperceptive characters or ones who are potentially unsympathetic. The narrator's interest in these characters can be used to foster the reader's interest.

Consider, again, *The Great Gatsby*, perhaps the most famous use of this approach. Nick tells the tragic story of Jay Gatsby and Daisy Buchanan, neither of whom is perceptive enough or likable enough to tell the story him- or herself. Nick's fascination with them leads us to care about them. However, the story, in its larger sense, is not about Jay and Daisy. It's about Nick. When choosing a peripheral narrator, know that you're changing the story and its larger implications. The story is always about the person who is telling it. Nick is peripheral to the events he relates, but he is, in fact, the center of the story, which is less about the love affair than about Nick's disillusionment and, ultimately, his moment of awakening.

PROMPT: Pick one of the pieces you wrote in one of the prompts in this chapter. Change the narrator, keeping the piece in first person. The events of the drama can remain the same, but their implications should change now that the narrator has changed. Push forward with this new story.

PROMPT: Write a scene as observed by a peripheral character, someone on the fringe of the action. If you want, choose an event from an earlier prompt and retell it from this new perspective.

A Final Word on First Person

In my experience as an editor, I feel that first person is used too often and for the wrong reasons. Too many writers use it without fully understanding it. Nevertheless, as we've discussed, this viewpoint offers many advantages to your story. There is more to learn about first person than we can explore here. We didn't cover first-person plural, the use of past and present tense, the use of various distances, the use of first person in nonfiction, but there are many good books that offer advice on these subjects. Find them and read them. And when reading a first-person piece, don't believe everything you hear.

Chapter Twenty-two

Other Rooms, Other Voices

Everyone is in the best seat.
—JOHN CAGE

N ow let's look at a few other point-of-view options. As I said in the previous chapter, we don't have the space here to cover them all in the necessary detail. Our goal, instead, is to know enough about point of view to find the full potential in our ideas and, with luck, to generate new ideas.

Second Person

A risky venture, this second-person viewpoint. In it, instead of *I*, the writer uses *you*, as if talking to someone:

> You walk down the street and turn left into Sam's deli, where the smell of cured meats and Sam's delicious salads causes you nearly to swoon with hunger. Sam waves a bustling hello at you and turns to wait on the man in front of you.

The "you" seems to be the reader. Instead, it's an aspect of the narrator, as if the narrator is speaking to herself. The problem with this approach is that it's too apparent, too vehicular. The reader is aware that she's not in Sam's deli, and the reader questions if anyone would talk to herself in this way. In short, readers see the wires holding Superman aloft, making his heroic deeds seem like so much backlot farce.

Can this point of view work? Absolutely. The most commonly cited example—so common I hate to repeat it here—is Jay McInerney's novel *Bright Lights, Big City*. His great feat is that he sustains this point of view for an entire novel, making it, after a while, almost invisible. In the novel, a bright and sensitive young man with lofty aspirations surrenders to his self-destructive impulses while recovering from a divorce and the death of his mother. He abuses drugs and alcohol in all-night forays through the trendy world of New York nightlife, a drastic departure from his normal life. He is living, in a way, outside himself. Through second person, the better angels of his nature attempt to drag him back to safer ground. So the novel becomes a monologue in which one level of the character's consciousness addresses another.

For other examples, see the short story "Lord Short Shoe Wants the Monkey" in Bob Shacochis's collection titled *Easy in the Islands*, or Tess Slesinger's "On Being Told That Her Second Husband Has Taken His First Lover," or Lorrie Moore's brilliant collection of stories titled *Self-Help*. These stories use the conventions of instructional writing, directly addressing the reader but offering advice on subjects such as "How to Be an Other Woman."

Use second person if it feels the most natural way to tell your story, but be aware of its limitations. Even McInerney doubted if this was the best choice as he was writing his novel, which grew out of a short story told in second person. In an interview he reflected:

> I thought, what the hell, I can pull this off for ten or fifteen pages. It just seemed to work, and in the best sense the story seemed, on the momentum of that voice, to write itself. When I went back to the story with the idea of writing a novel, I thought, "I have to change this to first or third." But when I did, the prose went flat. Something drained out of the narrative—a certain distance and a certain intimacy as well. And somehow it wasn't as funny. [The

editor] said to me, "Don't even think about trying to write a novel in the second person." I was almost fatally discouraged by that comment, but since I was already halfway there I just kept going. The moral would seem to be—trust our instincts.

P R O M P T : Shift one of your first-person writings from the previous chapters to second person, substituting *you* for *I*. Note how the piece changes. Assess what you lose and what you gain. If you're taken with the new point of view, push forward with the piece.

P R O M P T : Use second person to write a few pages of a personal essay recounting a difficult moment in your life. Does it supply a pleasing distance? Do you find yourself being more candid? Again, if it works, push forward.

P R O M P T : Let's steal Moore's idea and write a piece using second-person imperative, as if we were writing an instructional piece. But choose a topic that offers narrative possibilities, one you've thought about writing as a story or an essay, and, if you want, choose a subject that the reader really will not want to learn. For example, "How to Wreck Your Car With Style"; "How to Speak to Your Mother-in-Law at Christmas Dinner"; "How to Spend Your Birthday Alone." Have fun with this one.

P R O M P T : Write a poem or narrative piece addressed to a specific reader, as if you were writing a letter to the person.

Third Person

In third person, the most commonly used point of view, the writer refers to the characters by name or uses the pronoun *he* or *she* to tell the story. A few examples:

Her doctor had told Julian's mother that she must lose twenty pounds on account of her blood pressure, so on Wednesday nights Julian had to take her downtown on the bus for a reducing class at the Y.

"EVERYTHING THAT RISES MUST CONVERGE,"
FLANNERY O'CONNOR

He came from the twenty-third floor down to the lobby on the mezzanine to collect his mail before breakfast, and he believed— he hoped—that he looked passably well: doing all right.

SEIZE THE DAY, SAUL BELLOW

To begin at the beginning, the airplane from Minneapolis in which Francis Weed was traveling East ran into heavy weather.

"THE COUNTRY HUSBAND," JOHN CHEEVER

These characters and situations are presented by a narrative voice that exists outside them, and yet the voice can move inside their minds to show their thoughts. The voice in Cheever, for example, is distant, using phrases such as "To begin at the beginning," which make clear that the story is being told by an outside voice. In Bellow, the perspective, still in third person, is much closer to the character, presenting his thoughts and doubts. Let's look at a few of the types of third-person viewpoints.

Omniscient

In the omniscient approach, the voice of the story knows all. It can be in all places and know every character's thoughts. The main advantage of this choice is *flexibility*. We are not limited to the thoughts of a single character. The disadvantage is that the narrative can lack a sharp focus as the voice moves from character to character, from a godlike distance to a detailed close-up. Contemporary writers tend to avoid the omniscient, for technical and philosophical reasons too complex to enumerate here. Omniscience does appear now and again in all its glory, but not often.

PROMPT: Write a scene using the omniscient point of view, moving into and out of the characters' minds, drawing back to make general observations. If you want, create a party scene that includes at least four or five characters. Dip into the minds of at least three of the characters. Also, make a few general observations about the place where the party is held and even make a pronouncement or two about the nature of parties.

PROMPT: You are a supreme being. From your all-seeing, all-knowing vantage point, render a scene based on an experience you've had recently. Make yourself one of the characters and tell what you thought and did, but move into the other characters' minds, imagining their thoughts during the experience. The experience can be something very small—tossing a Frisbee at the park, a trip to the mall. The key is the all-knowing voice.

PROMPT: Use the omniscient, all-knowing voice to present a scene, but allow the voice to be, in fact, less than godlike. Allow it to show biases and to make mistakes in its descriptions or statements.

Objective

Sometimes known as "fly on the wall," this viewpoint does not venture into the minds of any characters. It stands apart, observing the events, describing the details. It reports. That's all. You can move in space and time, report scenes that occur simultaneously, but you cannot enter anyone's thoughts. For an example, let's return to Alice and Jim from the previous chapter:

The young woman in the orchid dress walked into the bar, scanned the crowded tables with one eyebrow cocked. She strolled past the tables and found a stool at the bar. The bartender, a dark-haired man wearing a too-tight black vest slapped a bar napkin in front of her.

The woman said, "Margarita," in a soft voice.

"Sorry, we're all out," the bartender said.

"Out?"

"All out." He looked at her closely, his elbows propped on the bar. "Something else instead?"

No thoughts or interpretations are included in this exchange. The writer simply observes and reports. This viewpoint is attractive for several reasons. The action of the story dictates and supplies a natural focus and gives immediacy to the narrative. Tension arises quickly as the reader tries to understand what is happening, why it's happening and what it means.

The difficulties of this viewpoint should be obvious. You must *suggest* the meaning of actions and details rather than explain them or have characters supply the meaning. If Jim begins wiping shot glasses when Alice arrives, you cannot explain that he always does this when he's nervous. You must suggest his nervousness by describing how he wipes.

This viewpoint is rarely sustained for an entire story and is not used often anymore. It enjoyed a certain vogue in the late 1970s as part of the minimalist era. Raymond Carver, the godfather of minimalism, uses the objective viewpoint with amazing results in some of his early stories. Read his "Why Don't You Dance?" for a great example of this viewpoint at work. The classic example of the objective approach is Hemingway's story "Hills Like White Elephants," in which a couple debates whether or not the woman should have an abortion. We enter neither character's mind. In fact, they don't even directly state what they're discussing.

PROMPT: Describe a room using the objective viewpoint. Simply state the details. Don't speculate on who lives there or on the person's traits or tastes. But do select details that will show what the person is like by what is in her room.

PROMPT: Place a character in a place where he feels uncomfortable, a hotel lobby, perhaps, where he knows no one. Or, if you prefer, a dinner party at which he knows everyone but still feels out of place. Describe the character from an objective viewpoint, showing his discomfort without mentioning it.

Limited

Much more common in fiction and poetry written today is the third-person limited approach. In this one, we use the pronouns *he* and *she*, but we enter the mind of only one character at a time. As writers, we enjoy the tight focus of first person but can drift back to a more objective perspective, as in this version of our story:

> The bar at the Marriott hotel was exactly like all the business bars in all the airport hotels in America—sterile, graceless, a little sleazy. Not the kind of place a woman especially enjoys entering alone, unless she's powerfully assertive or trained in the martial arts.
>
> Alice Downy was neither. When she entered the bar, she kept her eyes trained on Jim, the bartender, with whom she was having what she sometimes allowed herself to call "a relationship." After the day she'd had, it was a relief to see him. He was, in a way, such a wonderful man.

In this description we shift the narrative distance, moving from a general assertion about the bars in airport hotels, which is not necessarily Alice's perception, to the statement that Jim is "a wonderful man," which definitely is Alice's perception. We cannot, however, now jump to Jim's point of view unless we're using an omniscient viewpoint. In the limited approach, we are limited to Alice.

PROMPT: Retell your story from the previous prompt, this time in limited third person, from a character who is not you. Pick someone else. Then, if you want, try it again from the character who *is* you.

Shifting Perspective

In contemporary novels, it's common for the author to use third-person limited but shift the focus from one character to another, a shift usually signaled by a chapter or section break. We could open our story with Jim as our narrative eye, then, in chapter two, switch to Alice. This approach allows us to enjoy the focus of a single character without creating a claustrophobic narrative, one too tightly absorbed with a single character.

You may want to limit yourself, however, to a few characters or you risk muddling your focus. Readers often want a character or two to root for and identify with. If you switch back and forth between a number of characters, this pleasure is tougher to achieve. Of course, if your story needs more shifts, make them. Some writers use quite a few third-person viewpoint characters. Robert Stone's *Damascus Gate*, for example, employs at least a half dozen. But he relies on plot and setting to keep the reader anchored, and he's not especially concerned with the reader's rooting for someone. He is using a broad canvas to paint a picture of the sociopolitical forces at work in the Middle East. Again, know your goals in your story to make the best choice in point of view.

PROMPT: Write a scene in which a store is robbed. The cast: the robber, the store employee, a shopper. Relate the event three times, each from a third-person limited perspective of a different character. This approach is know as the Rashomon Effect, taken from *Rashomon*, the famous film by Akira Kurosawa, in which the same story is told from various characters' perspectives.

Some writers even shift between third person and first person. In *The Barracks Thief*, Tobias Wolff shifts from third to first person even while focusing on the same character. He also shifts between past and present tense. It's a very short novel and technically brilliant and ambitious. To get some ideas on how you can manipulate point of view, it's worth reading. These shifts between first and third person are growing more common in fiction, but be aware of what you're doing and know why you're doing it.

That advice applies to all point-of-view choices. Like Jay McInerney, you must trust your instincts. You also must know your goals for your piece and know whose story you want to tell. These are not simple decisions but can be great fun to make.

Chapter Twenty-three

Vast Is the Power
of Cities

Caress the detail, the divine detail.
—VLADIMIR NABOKOV

I n two earlier chapters, we explored writing about places—places
you've lived, places you want to go. Now we'll look at ways to use
place and descriptions of places and things in your writing. Let's begin
with a question: How large a role does place play in your writing? Think
for a moment before you answer.

Next, a few more questions. Do you base your fiction in your hometown or, perhaps, a fictionalized version of your hometown? Is your
novel set in your ideal hometown, a place you've never been and that
probably doesn't even exist? Do you usually use natural settings, or are
you drawn, instead, to describing people packed onto dirty sidewalks?
Are your stories set in the present time or in an earlier historical era?
Do you tend to move around in place and time?

No matter what you're writing, remember that readers want to feel
anchored in a place and time. Think about your own favorite stories,
novels, movies, poems. Odds are that you immediately recall images of
the place where the story is set: the hardscrabble farmland in Robert
Frost's poems, the grimy New York docks and streets in the essays of
Joseph Mitchell, the golden fields of Nebraska wheat in Willa Cather's

My Antonia. The details of time and place are the stuff of storytelling. We'll discuss quality vs. quantity later in this chapter, but keep in mind that your job as a writer is to transport the reader. A sharp sense of place makes the process more powerful and pleasing.

P R O M P T : List all the places you've written about, or as many as you can recall. After making the list, review it, looking for patterns, types of places to which you're especially drawn. Think about, or write about, the nature of these places and your connections to them. Note, too, which places played a large role in their stories and which ones were nearly invisible.

P R O M P T : Describe the place where you are sitting now. Freewrite the details you observe—and push yourself to observe a lot of details. Describe the people you can see, the architecture and the furnishings. Use your senses. After you've written down what you see, close your eyes and focus on sounds and smells. Now open your eyes and pull the description into a few paragraphs.

P R O M P T : Choose two characters you have written about or two people you know in real life, and put them in the place you just described. If possible, pick two people who would feel out of place here. Give them a reason for being here, and record what they say to each other. One has coerced the other into coming here. From your freewrite in the previous prompt, select details to use in your drama. Use the place as part of the drama.

P R O M P T : Buy some old postcards at an antique store. (They're usually very cheap.) Choose ones that have writing on the back. Begin a story, set in the time the postcard was sent, about a person or group of people going to that place. Or, if you prefer, begin with a description of the place pictured on the postcard. Your character is looking at this place as your story begins.

Setting as Character

One of my favorite novels is Sinclair Lewis's *Babbitt*, set in the mythical town of Zenith, a midsize Midwestern city based, in part, on my hometown of Cincinnati. (Though the novel is a broad satire that pokes no end of fun at Zenith the Zip City, our city paper mentions this connection with pride every few years in some feature story on "literary Cincinnati.") George Babbitt, the boorish, boosterish protagonist of the novel, loves his city, as does, in his own way, Lewis. Consider this description, which opens the novel:

> The towers of Zenith aspired above the morning mist; austere towers of steel and cement and limestone, sturdy as cliffs and delicate as silver rods. They were neither citadels nor churches, but frankly and beautifully office buildings.

And, later in the chapter:

> Cues of men with lunchboxes clumped toward the immensity of new factories, sheets of glass and hollow tile, glittering shops where five thousand men worked beneath one roof, pouring out the honest wares that would be sold up the Euphrates and across the veldt. The whistles rolled out in greeting a chorus cheerful as the April dawn; the song of labor in a city built—it seemed—for giants.

Notice the many functions of this description. It establishes clearly, if indirectly, the setting of the novel. It establishes that setting will play a large role. It also establishes the novel's tone—arch, satirical, romantic. The ordinariness of Zenith is heightened by the hyperbole in the description. Mundane products are destined for exotic locales; the shops are "glittering." And yet specific details abound: "sheets of glass and hollow tile," "steel and cement and limestone." Lewis takes time to anchor that arch tone, which gives it weight rather than an airy smugness.

PROMPT: Follow Lewis's lead. Describe a mundane setting in an exaggerated tone. Make a backyard birdbath a hallowed sanctuary; turn a suburban street of look-alike houses into a place of exotic intrigue. Tip: Choose a place you know well so your tone will be anchored with specific details.

PROMPT: Reverse the previous prompt. This time, describe an extraordinary place in mundane terms. Reduce the Grand Canyon to a big hole in the ground.

PROMPT: Describe a place from a first-person perspective of someone who has strong opinions about the place. Try to show that the person is coloring the readers' view of the place. For example, a man who was jilted returns to the home he shared with his ex-wife. A woman who owns a restaurant that she loves views it from the kitchen on a busy Saturday night.

PROMPT: Try the previous prompt again, but this time don't let the reader know why the view is colored. The character simply describes the place in a particular tone of voice. For examples, consider the following, borrowed from John Gardner's *The Art of Fiction*:

> Describe a building as seen by a man whose son has just been killed in a war. Do not mention the son, war, death, or the old man doing the seeing; then describe the same building, in the same weather and at the same time of day, as seen by a happy lover. Do not mention love or the loved one.

The Importance of Description

We can see in these prompts how description provides a rich backdrop for drama and how it characterizes the observer and influences the reader. Good description of place can—and should—perform a variety of narrative functions. Beginning writers too often ignore this fact. Many of the short stories I read while at *Story* magazine or continue to read in writing contests lack the richness of place. Today's writers, fearful of losing the reader, don't include the details that, in fact, are crucial to their stories. They hold to their hearts Elmore Leonard's advice to "leave out the parts readers skip."

Or perhaps the problem is that the writer hasn't imagined herself fully into the place. She doesn't truly see it herself and is therefore unable to render it for the reader. This flaw often occurs in stories we are too anxious to complete. We want them out there, making the rounds, getting published. I've spoken to numerous editors who complain about reading skeletal early drafts submitted as completed stories and novels. Fiction lies in the details. Don't make the mistake of sparing them. Throughout this book, you've plumped your store of details and images. Use them. And push yourself deeper into the places you're writing about. If you're writing a memoir, be sure that what you're seeing is on the page.

The key to good descriptions lies in selectivity. Today's reader is, without question, less patient than ever before. Rhapsodic passages glorifying setting for its own sake won't work anymore. Descriptions that are little more than weather reports will be skipped. But ignoring everything but drama isn't the answer either, because the drama has no scenic context, no frame. The voices call out from a void. As the writer, you must construct a stage from which your characters can speak, a stage that adds dimension to what your characters say, that affirms or contradicts their lines, that provides an extra nub or two of meaning.

In his nonfiction book *U and I*, Nicholson Baker takes exception to the argument that descriptions merely clog the narrative:

> The only thing I *like* are the clogs . . . . I wanted my first novel to be a veritable infarct of cloggers; the trick being to feel your way through each clog by blowing it up until its obstructiveness finally revealed not blank mass but unlooked-for seepage-points of passage.

Baker, admittedly, is a special case, an exceptionally talented novelist who can do what few of us could even attempt. The first novel he mentions is *The Mezzanine*, a tour de force of description. In it, readers' normal expectations for drama are frustrated over and over as very little happens. A man who works in an office goes to a drugstore during his lunch break to buy shoelaces. He buys them and returns to his office. That's it. But Baker's powers of observation are so amazing that the novel works on a variety of levels. I am not suggesting that you must pause the action in your current novel or memoir or story for a detailed review of office supplies, but if you feel your descriptive powers need improvement, read Baker's novel.

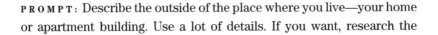

PROMPT: Describe in great detail some object of seemingly minor importance—the rust-eaten basketball hoop on your garage, for example; a curling iron; a stick shift. Get up close and really eyeball the thing, noting every tiny nuance of detail. Try this experiment on a few objects. After you have at least a few paragraphs, allow yourself to move from the object into free associations. What does that plant stand remind you of? How is it emblematic of plant stands everywhere? This prompt will help you practice your powers of observation and will help you move from the specific to the general. It also will allow you to linger, at times, on a description that is important to your story.

PROMPT: Begin with the image you described in the previous prompt. A character is looking at the thing, as if it has some great significance. Decide why it is important to the character and move forward. For example, your character might find the curling iron in her boyfriend's apartment, but it is not *her* curling iron.

PROMPT: Find a short description in a piece you've written. Now, as backyard quarterbacks used to say, go long. Expand it to at least twice the length. Add details or describe more intricately those you've included.

PROMPT: Describe the outside of the place where you live—your home or apartment building. Use a lot of details. If you want, research the building, finding out when it was built and by whom and maybe even the names of some of the people who live there. Find out, if you don't know, its style of architecture. Take time to fully develop this portrait of a place.

Selectivity

Despite Baker's defense of descriptive "clogs," you do need to handle them deftly. The key, again, is selectivity. In workshops, students are sometimes amazed that the rest of the class doesn't "get" their stories. Very often the problem lies in selection of detail. The writer either shows us nothing, having a clear view of the place in his own mind, or shows us so much that we don't know what's important. Selectivity means showing just the right details that bring a place to life and rooting those details deeply into the lives of the people in the story. Richard Russo makes this point brilliantly in his essay "Location, Location, Location: Depicting Character Through Place." At one point he discusses the sense of place in John Cheever's Shady Hill stories. Shady Hill is based in part on Cheever's town of Oneida in the Hudson Valley. He knows it well. Russo remembers wonderful descriptions of the place and recommends the stories to a student who is having problems with description. The student reads the stories but finds little description. Russo rereads them himself and is shocked that the student is right:

> The deep sense of place that emerges from the Shady Hill stories has more to do with life's rhythms, where things are in relation to other things, whether the characters can walk there and how long that will take, whether they'll drive or take the train. We won't be told that the cocktail shaker is pure silver; we'll be told that it's sweating in the lazy Sunday mid-morning sun.

The point here is that Cheever's descriptions evoke a strong sense of place and yet are nearly invisible. The pace of the stories is not slowed, and yet the reader perceives the story world clearly. The world of the story is clear in Cheever's mind, so clear that he can evoke it with a few deft strokes. True, the setting is based on a town he knows well, which, I guess, argues for writing about places you know. But if you spend enough time in an imagined world, you will come to know it well enough to write about it.

P R O M P T : Revise the long descriptions of the building where you live and of the short description taken from a piece of earlier writing, this time selecting only a few details, the most telling ones. Then review both descriptions of each subject. Which one works better?

P R O M P T : Review pieces of your writing, looking for ways to sharpen the sense of place. Are there too many details? Too few? Do the details suggest "life's rhythms" Russo mentions in his essay? Choose at least three details that could be improved, either through better placement or greater specificity. Choose at least three details that could be deleted.

P R O M P T : Describe your neighborhood. Freewrite a list of descriptive details about it, then choose two or three details from your list, searching for those that are most emblematic of the place, the ones that best characterize it. If this is difficult, push deeper and add details to your list. Try again. If this is simple, you're not doing it right.

Authoritative Description of Place

When you know a place, or a type of place, very well, you can not only find the specific details, you can speak in broad terms about it. In an earlier prompt, we moved from the specific to the general. Now let's try it the other way, moving from general to specific. In this passage from *Babbitt*, Lewis speaks not specifically about Zenith but generally about cities:

Vast is the power of cities to reclaim the wanderer. More than mountains or the shore-devouring sea, a city retains its character, imperturbable, cynical, holding behind apparent changes its essential purpose.

PROMPT: Previously, you wrote a specific sensory description of the place where you're sitting now. This time, make a few general observations about the type of place you're sitting in now. Address the nature of coffeeshops or libraries or even living rooms—wherever you're sitting. You don't need to use Lewis's high-blown language, but do speak with a declarative authority. Tell us what we need to know about such places, what we may not have considered before. If you want, adopt Lewis's tone and try again. This may seem silly, but give it a try. Have fun with it. Write at least a paragraph or two in this way. Then, if you want, and if you're sitting in the same place you described in your earlier writing, shift to the more specific details you generated in the other prompt.

PROMPT: Describe two places and compare them to each other. Choose places that are very different. For example, compare the Vatican to a laundromat, the Oregon Coast to a strip mall. You may find this impossible to do, but keep trying. Look for ways to connect these places, if only in the most peripheral ways. The point is to see beyond the surface, to avoid the easy detail, the most obvious modifiers. Anyone can talk about the awesome splendor of the Grand Canyon; only you will find it as eternal as an all-night gas station.

Chapter Twenty-four

It Was the Best of Times

It's appropriate to pause and say that the writer is one who, embarking upon a task, does not know what to do.
—DONALD BARTHELME

Quick—what novel begins with the words in this chapter's title? Anyone who didn't blurt out *A Tale of Two Cities*, go to the back of class and read your Dickens. This is one of the most famous openings in literature, and it continues to hold its power: "It was the best of times; it was the worst of times." With this seemingly paradoxical statement, Dickens announces he will work on a large canvas, that he will range from best to worst, that he will speak from high omniscience about times, historical eras. With this line we pass into a novel of grandeur and high stakes that concerns the lives of a great many people.

A good opening suggests the nature of the story about to be told. It locates the reader, if not in the story's place and time, then in the approach of the story—its tone and narrative stance. Otherwise, there are no rules about what constitutes a good opening. If it works, it works. The reader is engaged and moves forward. If not, the reader stops reading. Writers need to rely on their judgment when assessing their opening sentences and paragraphs.

Great Openings

One way to develop criteria for judging the effectiveness of your openings is to review ones you especially like, ones that resonate in your mind, ones that, when you first read them, carry you into the pieces. As you review openings, look for patterns. Try to determine what ingredients you tend to enjoy and admire. Here are a few of my favorites:

> When I was a windy boy and a bit,
> And the black spit of the chapel fold,
> (Sighed the old ram rod, dying of women),
> I tiptoed shy in the gooseberry wood. . . .
>
>   "LAMENT," DYLAN THOMAS

> You had to get out of them occasionally, those Illinois towns with the funny names: Paris, Oblong, Normal. Once, when the Dow-Jones dipped two hundred points, the Paris paper boasted a banner headline: NORMAL MAN MARRIES OBLONG WOMAN. They knew what was important. They did! But you had to get out once in a while, even if it was just across the border to Terre Haute, for a movie.
>
>   "YOU'RE UGLY, TOO," LORRIE MOORE

> In a little house, in a little village, not far away from Thunderbolt City, lived a whistle fixer named Lunchbox Louie. He had a wife named Bigfoot the Chipmunk, and a little son named King Waffle.
>
>   *THE WUGGIE NORPLE STORY*, DANIEL PINKWATER

> Lolita, light of my life, fire of my loins. My sin, my soul. Lo-lee-ta: the tip of the tongue taking a trip of three steps down the palate to tap, at three, on the teeth. Lo-lee-ta.
>
>   *LOLITA*, VLADIMIR NABOKOV

Once I got started writing, more favorites flooded into my mind, but these few will do to start. Notice that all have a striking use of voice; all have a certain playfulness of tone and language. If you asked me before today what I like in an opening, I don't know that I would have rattled off those qualities, but that seems to be true. What qualities do you notice as you think about your favorite openings?

P R O M P T: List ten openings you like. Look for patterns. What qualities do many of your favorites exude? Then look at the openings in your own work. Do they take a similar approach? Do they exude similar qualities?

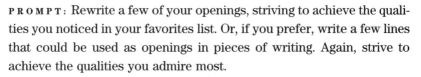

P R O M P T: Rewrite a few of your openings, striving to achieve the qualities you noticed in your favorites list. Or, if you prefer, write a few lines that could be used as openings in pieces of writing. Again, strive to achieve the qualities you admire most.

P R O M P T: Steal an opening line or sentence from one of your favorites. Cut away the next lines and substitute lines of your own. Try to match the tone and voice of the authors whose work you're borrowing.

Types of Openings

Just as there are no rules for what constitutes a great opening, there are no rules regarding what type of opening works best. Your opening must perform a few functions to be effective, one of which is to match the story that follows. An opening can do any of the following:

- Set the scene.
- Create mood.
- Introduce characters.
- Introduce situations.
- Establish place and time.
- Introduce conflict.

It needn't do all of these, but it had better do more than one. Most of all, it must interest the reader, as we discussed in the previous section of this chapter. It can do this in a variety of ways. Let's try some of these approaches.

PROMPT: Find a collection of pieces—stories, essays, poems, whichever form you prefer—and read the opening of each piece. Choose five to seven that you especially like. Using the same approach as the author, relying on description or drama, narrative or dialogue, setting scene or jumping into conflict, write five openings of your own.

PROMPT: Open a story with a dialogue. A famous model for this approach is the opening of Ernest Hemingway's "The Snows of Kilimanjaro":

"The marvelous thing is that it's painless," he said. "That's how you know when it starts."

"Is it really?"

"Absolutely. I'm awfully sorry about the odor though. That must bother you."

"Don't. Please don't."

The first speaker is dying while camped in the plains of Africa. The opening brings us immediately into the story, its characters and conflict.

PROMPT: If you have an ongoing project, consider moving a scene that appears later in the piece to the opening. Does it work?

PROMPT: Write an opening dialogue in which one character asks a question of another character or characters. The response will move the scene forward and, with luck, get you rolling on a piece. *A Clockwork Orange* by Anthony Burgess opens with four "droogs" sitting bored in a milkbar, trying to think of a bit of mischief to undertake. The novel begins with one droog asking the others, somewhat ominously, "What's it going to be then, eh?"

PROMPT: Begin in the middle of a scene or event. Keep pushing forward rather than stopping to inform the reader of background details. Known as beginning in medias res, in the middle of things, this opening supplies a quick start to your story. As Richard Hugo writes in *The Triggering Town*, "When the poem starts, things should already have happened." Myriad examples of this type of opening exist. It's especially plentiful in movies and action novels.

PROMPT: Write a few paragraphs in which a character introduces himself as though beginning an autobiography. Don't directly state any conflicts, any hardships or situations, but try to imply what hardships the character has suffered or will suffer in the story ahead. For example, consider this opening from Marilynne Robinson's *Housekeeping*:

> My name is Ruth. I grew up with my younger sister, Lucille, under the care of my grandmother, Mrs. Sylvia Foster, and when she died, of her sisters-in-law, Misses Lily and Nona Foster, and when they fled, of her daughter, Mrs. Sylvia Fischer.

Though this character does not directly state her young life has been filled with tragedy and abandonment, the point comes through clearly. Her not saying it makes the opening powerful. Can you use your paragraph as an opening for something longer?

PROMPT: Use the same approach as in the previous prompt, but try it in third person, as if you're writing a biography.

PROMPT: Begin with a statement, a general observation that you or a character makes. Remember Tolstoy's statement about families, mentioned in a previous chapter. Or consider this statement that opens the memoir *Blue Highways*, by William Least Heat-Moon:

> Beware thoughts that come in the night. They aren't turned properly; they come in askew, free of sense and restriction, deriving from the most remote of sources.

Try to move quickly from the general statement to specifics of your story. In *Blue Highways*, for example, by the end of the first paragraph, the narrator has lost his job and found out his estranged wife is seeing another man. Tip: Find a general statement somewhere in your writing. Move it to an opening and begin the piece there.

PROMPT: Begin with a statement of fact. Scan earlier prompt writings for a simple statement, nothing monumental, perhaps a line that appears in the middle of a longer piece. Freewrite or cluster using this focus. Mark Richard began his story "Strays" with a line that kept nagging at him, though he had no idea what it meant: "At night stray dogs come up underneath our house to lick our leaking pipes." To write the story, he put the statement in a character's voice and pushed forward.

PROMPT: Richard began his story "Her Favorite Story" by picking a single word and deciding, arbitrarily, to start there. He chose the word *in* and created his first sentence: "In Indian this place is called Where Lightning Takes Tall Walks." Begin a sentence with a preposition: *about, above, after, at, below, by, for, from, in, of, on, over, to, up.* Then follow that sentence with at least one paragraph. If you feel a spark, keep going. If not pick a different preposition and try again.

PROMPT: Begin with a paragraph of description. Set the scene for the drama to follow. Be sure your description introduces an element of tension or conflict, or achieves something beyond mere scene painting. Focus on details that will bring the setting quickly to life.

PROMPT: The Bible opens with "In the beginning . . . " Let's use that, but rather than following with "God created the heavens and the earth," use something different, something that creates a situation you want to explore. The sentence should suggest that whatever occurred "in the beginning" is about to change. For example, "In the beginning, Dave really didn't care for Andrea" or "In the beginning, Charlie was sure no one would find out who was siphoning money from the employee 401(K) fund."

A Few Tips About Openings

Openings can be tough. Sometimes you can block yourself by trying too hard to get them right. This can prevent you from moving forward and from finding other ideas for your pieces. A commonsense tip: Begin later in the story, starting with a scene or idea you planned to introduce later. Then, when you have a draft or when you're really cooking on the piece, come back to the opening.

Sometimes we put too much pressure on the opening, sweating out every word until we've forged an absolute zinger. By trying too hard, working and reworking it, we end up with a stiff, overwrought paragraph or we lose the momentum of our idea. If your opening is labored and forced, read your piece and look on page two for a better place to start. When you wrote the interior paragraph, you were less self-conscious, weren't forging a masterpiece to hook the reader. The reader probably will glide easily into the narrative.

PROMPT: Write a paragraph or two to open a story. Really work those paragraphs, establishing character, plot, setting, tone, voice and atmosphere. Then put those paragraphs aside and begin again, simply telling the story.

PROMPT: For fear of losing the reader, we sometimes hype the opening, shooting off all sorts of narrative fireworks—arguments, fistfights, lovemaking, guns blazing, life decisions made and announced in rhetorical flourish. The questions then become: How do I top this? Where do I go from here? So much noise also can put off the reader. The writer appears too eager for attention, like a slick salesperson or a child showing off. Rather than intrigued, the reader is repelled. Find an opening of this kind in your files and rewrite it, taking a more natural, more subtle approach. If you don't have this type of opening, write one, as an exercise in what not to do.

PROMPT: Begin a story with the blare of an alarm clock. Your protagonist awakens for the day, showers, dresses, eats breakfast and heads out to begin his day. Sometime early in the day, a conflict arises. Drama begins. Now, cut all the paragraphs leading up to the moment of conflict. In her book *Building Fiction*, Jesse Lee Kercheval warns writers about the "alarm clock" opening, noting that too often this approach delays the start of the story. If your story opens with the character in any way getting ready for the drama to begin, cut to the drama. This is not a hard-and-fast rule; some of the openings I cited earlier don't begin with action. But dramatic openings are the easiest for many writers to achieve, and are the least risky. However, if you can begin with a powerhouse voice or compelling language, and you feel confident that with that approach you can carry the day, go for it.

PROMPT: Find an unfinished piece or one that has never satisfied you. Write a new opening, beginning in a different place. Write the piece from that point forward, filtering in scenes and description from the earlier work.

PROMPT: Try the cut-and-paste method. Find an unfinished piece or one that has never satisfied you. Cut your piece into sections or paragraphs and rearrange them. Look for interesting juxtapositions.

Chapter Twenty-five

A Sort of Miracle

Most writers enjoy two periods of happiness—when a glorious idea comes to mind and, secondly, when a last page has been written and you haven't had time to know how much better it ought to be.
—JOSEPH PRIESTLY

A few years ago I interviewed Rick DeMarinis for an article on the writing craft. At one point I asked him for tips on endings. "I can't really say much about how to write endings," he said. "For me, they're always a sort of miracle." This statement from a man who had published many short stories and a handful of novels? But if you've ever struggled to find the right ending for a piece, you probably did feel like you'd need nothing less than a miracle.

Endings are hard.

People can't live happily ever after. All the characters can't die. Your protagonist can't wake to find it all a dream. Even the sacred epiphanic moment, when the character comes to some type of realization, is feeling a bit shopworn these days. The mystery can be solved, the lovers united, the foe vanquished, everyone sadder but wiser; but still, striking that last note in a way that will give it depth and resonance, that will make it sound like just the right note, as satisfying and surprising as it is inevitable, ain't easy.

How many times do we read stories that engage us only to feel disappointed at the end? How many complaints about endings have you heard in workshops and writing groups? Years ago there was a popular joke about the unpleasing open-endedness of stories in *The New Yorker*: "Why do they put the author's name at the end of the story? So you'll know it's over." Then there are the "endings are hard" legends, such as the one about Hemingway rewriting the final paragraphs of his novel *A Farewell to Arms* forty-seven times. But we are writers, and even if it takes "a sort of miracle," we must write our endings.

P R O M P T : Write about an ending you struggled to write. What problems did you face? Are you satisfied with the ending as it stands? If not, consider ways to revise it. Does the problem exist in the ending, or does it lie elsewhere in the piece?

P R O M P T : If you're struggling with an ending at the moment, put the piece away and force yourself not to look at it. If possible, don't even think about it. Don't work on any other sections of the piece. Nothing. Forget about that piece. After a week (and you should wait longer), read the piece from start to finish. Have you discovered any new possibilities for endings? Does the problem lie in the ending?

Before moving on, I must admit that even discussing endings in a book of this kind is difficult. By ending, do we mean the climax of the narrative or the last paragraph or the last sentence? Though the age of the epilogue appears to have passed, the denouement remains with us. In choosing "favorite endings," I have, for the sake of simplicity reprinted final paragraphs. But even the power of these is lost without an understanding of what has come before, without the steady accertion of event in language of the piece, without the tingle of exhaustion still alive from the resonating climax. The topic, however, remains important, so on we go. Endings are hard.

Great Endings

As we did with beginnings in the previous chapter, let's look at a few endings that work. Begin by finding and writing down your favorite endings, at least five or six. Here are a few of mine:

And with Footers beside him, and Martin trailing with an amused smile, Billy went out into the early freeze that was just settling on Broadway and made a right turn into the warmth of the stairs to Louie's pool room, a place where even serious men sometimes go to seek the meaning of magical webs, mystical coin, golden birds, and other artifacts of the only cosmos in town.

    BILLY PHELAN'S GREATEST GAME, WILLIAM KENNEDY

"Well, darling—" he began. His right hand came up and touched the middle button of his shirt, as if to unfasten it, and then with a great deflating sigh he collapsed backward into the chair, one foot sliding out on the carpet and the other curled beneath him. It was the most graceful thing he had done all day. "They got me," he said.

    "A GLUTTON FOR PUNISHMENT," RICHARD YATES

He gave her the answer he had planned. He told her his name. Then he told her who he was and what he had done.

    "FOLEY THE GREAT," TOM CHIARELLA

There are, of course, many others. Classic ones, such as the endings to "Araby" by James Joyce, and Fitzgerald's *The Great Gatsby*. There are more contemporary examples, such as in Lorrie Moore's "People Like That Are the Only People Here," Norman Mailer's *Ancient Evenings* and Don DeLillo's *White Noise*.

PROMPT: In the same piece of writing you chose as a favorite, flip back to the climax or the dramatic moment to which the piece has built. Does it satisfy you? Write about the connection between the climax and the end of the piece. How are they complementary or different?

P R O M P T : Sometimes an ending doesn't satisfy because you simply don't want to leave the piece. You want to remain in that world. Allow yourself this pleasure by continuing the story on your own. What happens next?

P R O M P T : Rewrite a famous ending, or one you know well. Save the character who dies at the climax. Get those loves together. Change a bittersweet ending to a happy one, or change a happy one to tragedy.

P R O M P T : If you're having trouble with an ending, study how the endings on your favorites list work. Imitate a few of them in tone, language or approach. Now, go back to the ending in your own piece. Have any of your favorites sparked an insight or idea that helps your own ending?

P R O M P T : Write an ending for an unwritten piece. In other words, write the ending first. A number of writers do this on a regular basis, using the ending as a destination to guide the writing of the piece. Katherine Anne Porter, for example, used this approach:

> If I didn't know the ending of the story, I wouldn't begin. I always write my last line, my last paragraph, my last page first.

Why Endings Work

In the previous section, you examined why you like the endings on your favorites list. You tried to discover why they work. I tried to do the same with the endings I cited. I like the rhetorical flourish of the first one, from William Kennedy's novel, because the lyricism provides a nice counterpoint to the mundane details being described. There is a fine mix of notes in the paragraph, celebratory yet sad, mystical yet gritty. These tones fit the novel up to that point, and provide a compelling music with which to leave the story behind. In the Yates story, the final note is harder, more closed-ended. The story recounts a man's struggle at work, his attempt to find a place for himself in the world. He doesn't share his struggle with his wife. The "they" have been after him since the start. In the end, they get him. Like a sharp crack, the story ends. There is no denouement, no trailing off. Both endings fit what has come before.

The Ending Fits

A good ending provides closure in which character, plot, theme and tone match what precedes them in the story. If the star-crossed lovers in *Casablanca* had hightailed it across the tarmac, leaving Ilsa's husband behind, we would not be happy. We have watched the characters make sacrifices for a larger good throughout the film. To fight the Nazis, they have put themselves at risk and have grown from the experience. They have cast aside their personal desires for more significant goals. Their final parting is inevitable, and we feel the sadness of that parting even as we admire its nobility. The ending fits the characters.

The movie *Rain Man* also closes with a parting. Charlie must watch as his autistic brother, whom he has fought to keep with him in Los Angeles, returns to Cincinnati. In the film we watch Charlie grow from selfish and defensive to open and caring. That new openness allows him to let his brother go. If he had tried something foolish or sneaky to keep his brother, we wouldn't believe it or enjoy it.

Throughout John Steinbeck's *The Grapes of Wrath*, we are aware of the theme of resilience. Though the Joads lose everything and endure many hardships, their spirits remain alive. When Rose of Sharon feeds the starving man with milk from her breast, we see the theme of the resilient human spirit once again. Her action fits the theme of the novel (which should appear on any list of great endings).

PROMPT: In an on-going piece, determine if your ending fits what has come before it in plot, character and theme. Ask: Would the character

I've presented do this? Does my theme change, presenting a new perspective at the end?

The Reader's Expectations Are Met

Sometimes an ending doesn't work because you haven't been leading the reader to this moment, or line. The reader is confused about the story or has taken a completely different path. When you've written a draft you feel has the right ending, reread the piece to be sure you have led the reader to this point. Inexperienced writers are sometimes surprised to learn that readers have not been following the lines the writers think they've drawn through their narratives. Writing a story can be like dropping popcorn to mark your trail through a forest: You have to know what clues the readers are finding, and that they are following you. This does not mean the ending can't hold a surprise. But the reader's reaction should be, "Aha!" rather than, "Huh?" The surprise should delight, not mystify. The reader should not feel manipulated or tricked.

PROMPT: Outline a story that leads to a surprising conclusion. In your outline, put in clues that could lead the reader to this conclusion. If you choose to write the piece, work to conceal those clues.

You can prepare the reader through foreshadowing—lines, details, scenes that suggest what is to come. Again, you're not "giving away" the ending. People still come to stories of all kinds for the purpose of finding out "what happens." But foreshadowing what happens unifies the story, gives the reader that sense of "I think I know what's going to happen," which you can control and shift and change. A friend and I read a mystery a few months ago, and we were both a little irritated to learn that we could not have predicted the murderer. A few key clues were not mentioned, or were buried so deeply that instead of feeling pleasantly surprised, we were both annoyed.

The Ending Unifies the Piece

One way a writer creates good endings is by bringing back images and details that appeared earlier in the piece. This technique adds a satisfying sense of recognition and pulls the piece together, amplifying its unity. The most common method for nonfiction writers is to refer back to the opening. This approach creates a full-circle effect, though through much use this can seem forced and obvious. But it can work if it is used well. It can even work in fiction. Many of us saw it for the first time in S.E. Hinton's classic young adult novel *The Outsiders*, in which the last line repeats the first. Quentin Tarantino uses a variation of this approach with startling results in his film *Pulp Fiction*: Characters planning a robbery in the opening scene disappear from the film until the final scene, during which they attempt the robbery.

PROMPT: Read a piece in progress with an eye toward image and detail. Find one or two that can be used at the end to unify the piece and amplify the themes.

PROMPT: Read the opening paragraphs of the piece with an eye toward picking up something to use at the end. Is a question raised that now can be answered? Can a line of dialogue be echoed? Can a statement be restated with new meaning?

A s Rick DeMarinis told me, endings require "a sort of miracle." They are rarely easy. Writing about endings isn't easy, either. (Notice the repetition of the opening remarks with which I'm making an obvious and very clumsy attempt to end this chapter.) If you're having problems with your ending and the earlier prompts haven't helped, try a few more.

PROMPT: Change your approach to the ending. If you're fading out, try to be more abrupt. End at the climax. Try ending with a line of dialogue. If you're already ending with a scene, try description, handling the final action in a narrative rather than a dramatic way.

PROMPT: Write at least four possible endings to your piece. End in different places in the piece, or try different methods as you did in the previous prompt.

PROMPT: Look for the ending a few paragraphs prior to where you're trying to end. The piece may be finished already, and you're trying to force it farther than it needs to go. This approach also can end the piece in a nice way because when you wrote the line you weren't envisioning it as part of the ending.

I really will end now, by leaving you with an anecdote about endings. John Cheever was struggling for an ending to his story "The Country Husband." He had wrapped up the action and resolved the themes of the story but could not think of a good last line with which to end. Nothing seemed to work. Then, when he was walking through his home, not even thinking about the story, the last line came to him in a flash. He used the sentence exactly as it came to him. Here is the final paragraph of the story:

"Here pussy, here, poor pussy!" But the cat gives her a skeptical look and stumbles away in its skirts. The last to come is Jupiter. He prances through the tomato vines, holding in his generous mouth the remains of an evening slipper. Then it is dark; it is a night where kings in golden suits ride elephants over the mountains.

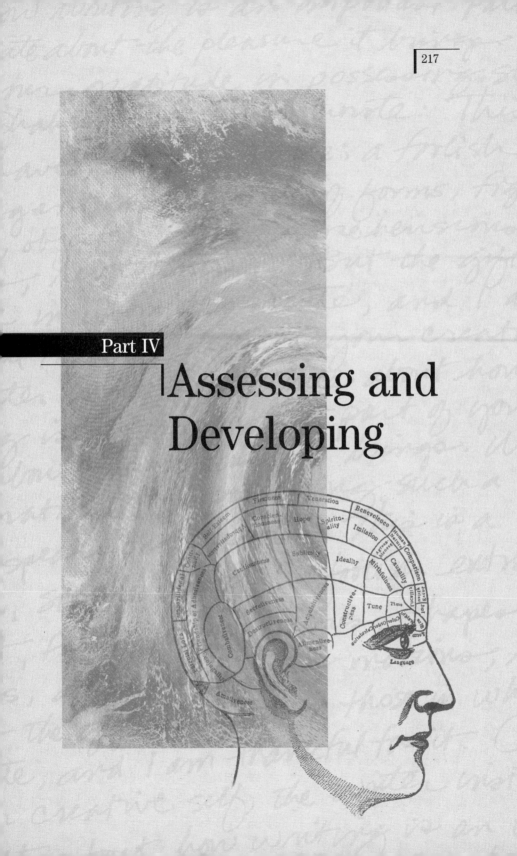

Part IV

Assessing and Developing

Chapter Twenty-six

What's at Stake?

I would never write about someone who was not at the end of his rope.

—STANLEY ELKIN

In this section, we'll look at ways to assess and develop ideas, a crucial phase in the writing process. As we discussed in the first chapter, every writer has a lot of ideas. The key is getting the most from those ideas and from yourself. If you've worked your way through this book, you've generated a lot of ideas and many pages of writing. Now let's take time to add to those ideas, to find new ways of seeing those ideas. When you're feeling stuck on a project, unable to move forward with it, you may want to flip to this section, where we'll discuss how projects can go wrong. You may find out what's holding you back on a piece, why your interest in it has flagged.

In this chapter, we'll begin with a question.

What's at Stake?

This question is raised often in writing workshops, usually after several people seated at the table have made fumbling attempts to articulate why the competent story in question doesn't quite grab them. Following these attempts to get at the source of everyone's discontent, one member of the group will ask the dreaded questions: "What's at stake in this story? Why should I care about what happens?" Editors and agents ask these questions too, usually while writing rejection slips. "What's at stake for these characters? Why would a reader care what happens?"

Because the question speaks to a fundamental flaw in the story, one not easily fixed, we don't like to hear it asked of our work. We can repair a sloppy scene, a slow beginning, an awkward shift in point of view, but "What's at stake?" tells us that even though the story is well written, containing pleasing turns of phrase, engaging characters and vivid descriptions, the reader doesn't care enough to find the story interesting. The story is not bad; it's boring.

PROMPT: Write about one of your pieces that began with an exciting idea but never achieved its potential. Speculate on what went wrong. Did you finish the piece? Does it now languish in a drawer? Or did you finish it but then lose interest in it?

When we hear this question, we might get defensive, proclaiming that what is interesting or boring is a matter of taste. And if only one or two readers tell you they weren't engaged, you may be right in chalking up their disinterest to taste. But if a number of readers tell you that, or, more importantly, you find your own interest waning, then you probably have a problem. You wonder what went wrong. The germinating idea seemed good at the time, the situation ripe with dramatic possibilities. Why, then, did the piece not take flight? A number of issues could be at work here, but "What's at stake?" is worth asking.

How important is the conflict to the characters in the story? What consequences does your character face if the colliding forces don't resolve themselves to his advantage? In short: what if he doesn't get what he wants? What does he lose? To give your story the tension it needs, the stakes must be high. If you're writing a thriller, the stakes could be as high as the fate of the world. If you're writing a mystery or crime novel, the stakes could be a matter of life and death. If you're writing a more literary novel, the stakes may be more internal, but they must be of great significance to the protagonist and the characters around her. If you're writing a memoir or any piece of dramatic nonfiction, the stakes must be high. The outcome must matter to someone—and matter a lot.

PROMPT: Review a few of your story ideas and drafts, asking yourself what's at stake for the characters or people in the piece. Are the consequences high enough to sustain tension in the narrative? Will the reader witness one of the most significant moments in a character's life? Is the decision, event, action or dramatic element crucial to the future of the character, changing her life forever? Is the character desperate? If you're not sure what's at stake, dig deeper, by writing about the character and exploring the situation. At some point in the writing of a piece, you should know why the events matter to these characters.

If you find that the stakes are not high enough, assess your choice of this story. Why is it important that you tell it? Why is this moment important in the lives of the characters? Is this *the* most important moment? Is the character, as Stanley Elkin states in the epigraph to this chapter, "at the end of his rope"? Perhaps you've focused on the wrong moment or not fully understood the significance of the story. Think about it.

Upping the Stakes

Ask yourself how you can make the situation more significant, more ticklish in its ramifications. For example, your character is sick of his job and decides to quit. This decision means he will have to find a new job to support himself and his family. Quitting a job without having another one is always cause for some anxiety. Will the new job be even worse? Will he have to change himself in some way to make the new job work? Important questions. But are these questions significant enough to the character? Maybe.

But what if the job he's leaving had been The Dream Job when he landed it three years ago? His disillusionment with a sought-after career path has left him confused, searching for direction. He now not only needs a new job, he needs a new life plan. The stakes are a little higher. And what if right after he makes the decision to leave the job behind, his wife tells him she's pregnant? Money will be tighter than ever. And what if the person who hired him is a beloved uncle who risked his own position to bring in the favored nephew? Quitting will break the uncle's heart. Or what if he *must* quit because of improprieties that sometime soon may come to light? I could go on, of course, but you get the point. We have raised the stakes, added new and powerful forces to the initial conflict.

PROMPT: Choose a character and a situation to write about, one you created in an earlier prompt or one from an ongoing project, perhaps one you've abandoned for the moment. Write about the conflict in which the character is involved, explaining it to an imagined reader. Write about the character's dilemma. Write about the character's goals. What does she want, and what forces are preventing her from getting it? Now, raise the stakes by changing the obstacle, making it larger in some way.

PROMPT: Use the process as described in the previous prompt, but this time change a relationship with another character (preferably the protagonist) in some way, as we did in the example above by bringing in an uncle. Would a conflict with a friend be intensified if the friend were changed to a sibling? Would a conflict with a friend be intensified if the friend also were a neighbor or colleague? Would the conflict be intensified if you introduced an element of rivalry?

PROMPT: Use the process again, this time changing the character in some way—changing age or gender, level of income. If she is single and childless, give her two children and an ugly divorce. If he is thirty years old, consider how the conflict would change if he were forty-five.

PROMPT: Use the process again, this time adding a new obstacle. If the conflict focuses on love, add a financial element. Now the conflict involves love and money. If the conflict focuses on money, add a love element or one involving the threat of violence.

PROMPT: If you have a project that has gone flat for you, find the place where the character is "at the end of his rope." If many pages precede this moment, consider cutting or condensing them. If you can't find such a moment, consider how you can create one. In both cases, focus on that moment, expanding and deepening it. Your interest in the project may return.

PROMPT: Outline a story with enormously high stakes—a life-or-death situation. If you tend to write more internal narratives, take a chance here and put the lives of everyone in the world in jeopardy (or do something else of dramatic significance). Flesh out your idea, jotting notes about how this situation would develop. If you like the idea, begin a scene. If it's just not right for you, you have the benefit of working with an idea that involves very high stakes.

PROMPT: Create a situation or use the one from above. Write a scene that introduces the conflict. In the next scene, allow this conflict to cause the stakes to be raised. Write at least five scenes, raising the stakes a bit higher in each scene. For example, a woman loves a man who does not return her feelings. But she must have him. They were in love once, and she was happier than she ever thought possible. Now that he's left, she's bereft. She feels she can't go on without him. In the next scene, her desire for him leads her to hatch a scheme to steal money from her employer in order to afford an expensive vacation to the place her ex-lover always dreamed of going. The stakes have been raised. The man refuses the vacation and says he is in love with someone else. The stakes go up. The protagonist decides she must confront her rival but first begins to spy on the couple to assess the level of their relationship. And on and on.

Consider Your Reader

We've focused on raising the stakes for the characters in your piece; now let's consider what's at stake for your reader. Are you writing about a situation that concerns your reader? Will the reader care about your characters and be eager to find out their fates? The reader must feel sympathetic to the situation or you will lose her. Again, this raises the question of interest. Some readers will be more drawn to a story of endangered animals than others. Some won't care what happens to a steelworker in Duluth; they want adventure and intrigue. Some of them will yawn at still another tale of the free world's imminent destruction; they want to find out more about someone who faces the problems they face.

As you asked yourself what your character wants, ask yourself what your reader wants. If she's looking for escape through adventure and romance, make sure you deliver that. Long passages of introspection in a thriller will bore the reader. Lots of race-and-chase in a literary novel will bore the reader. The stakes should be high in any piece, and keeping the stakes high for the reader depends upon knowing what the reader values. The reader comes to our writing far less concerned with us, the writers, than with themselves. They want insight or escape, or both, which is a tough balance to strike.

If you've understood your reader's goal in reading, you still need to face the question of sympathy. Will the reader care what happens? The reader will care more, as we've discussed, if more is at stake for the character. The reader also will care if the character is interesting and engaging, if not necessarily likable. A likable character helps, no question. With an unlikable character, you risk losing your reader, no matter how high the stakes, but characters don't have to be likable to be interesting.

PROMPT: Imagine your readers. Who are they? What interests them? Why will they care about the story you want to tell? Now review your story, reading it through the eyes of those imagined readers. In what ways does the story connect—or fail to connect—with those readers?

PROMPT: If your protagonist is vastly different from you, give her one aspect of personality that will make her in some way similar to you. If your protagonist is very much like you, give him a trait that you don't possess but that you admire.

What's at Stake for You?

Why do you want to tell this story? Why are you writing it? Are you writing to understand a personal experience? Are you exploring an issue that interests you? Are these characters running around in your head, begging to be put on the page? Are you looking for a byline or publication credit? Whatever your reason for writing, you should be aware of its influence on the piece itself. The greater the need to write the piece, the greater the urgency in telling this story, the more energy the piece will possess.

Perhaps the problem with that flat story we discussed earlier in the chapter is simply that you don't care enough about the characters and the situation. It may be an interesting story but doesn't connect with you on a personal level. Perhaps you're trying to resurrect a story that once was important but belongs to a different time in your life.

PROMPT: Explain your reasons for writing a story to an imagined reader. Tell him why the story is important to you, why you feel compelled to write it.

PROMPT: Try to make the story more important to you by assessing how much you care about the protagonist. What might you change that would make you care more? What change would give the story greater urgency for you? Can you add an element that reveals something about you or focuses on a subject that is important to you?

Chapter Twenty-seven

Sitting Still

The discipline of the writer is to learn to be still and listen to what his subject has to say.
—RACHEL CARSON

L ife is complicated. At any one time, we feel a range of emotions, and aspects of our lives can be at any number of stages: Work is going well, the kids are sick, health is fine, money is tight, the marriage could be better, we have many wonderful friends. That's why the question, "How's it going?" is so pointless. Which "it" does the person want to know about?

In stories, we try to streamline the lives of our characters, giving some sense of order to the chaos. We focus on a single "it." Sometimes, however, we focus too narrowly, and a good idea doesn't develop into a good piece. I call these pieces one-note wonders, and such pieces end up disappointing the reader as well as the writer. In this chapter we'll investigate ways of assessing your writing, in search of ways to avoid the one-note wonder.

Many Notes

One-note wonders fail from too heavy a reliance on the generative premise. We ask "what if" and come up with a good idea for a story, but we fail to complicate that idea in interesting ways. We lock into the first idea and fail to push beyond it. In the previous chapter, we focused on upping the stakes to make our ideas more interesting. Now we focus on enlarging the story, to contradict it, to add elements that will create new tensions. In his essay "On Defamiliarization," Charles Baxter discusses this point with his usual insight. In the excerpt that follows, he reflects on why a competently written story, submitted by a student in his workshop, is dull, despite interesting situations. After the story's strong opening, Baxter finds

> [t]he story's initial surprises began to seem less wonderful, even though its details were excellent, and the story was never anything but truthful. But the story had begun to read itself too early, and before long it was always and only about one thing, with the result that all the details fit in perfectly. All the arrows pointed in the same direction. When all the details fit in perfectly, something is probably wrong with the story.

What's wrong with perfectly fitting details? Nothing, of course, unless they fit so well because we're not digging deeply enough. The story skates along the surface. The reader knows where we're headed and may or may not be interested in joining the inexorable march to the end. As writers, we, too, might get bored, putting the idea away for a while, and maybe never coming back to it. We think that, in the end, the idea just wasn't good. The real problem, however, lies in settling in too quickly, in not pulling, as Baxter writes, "something contradictory and concealed from its hiding place."

For example, a few years ago I read a story for a contest. It began well. The writing was crisp, the details nicely chosen. The situation was interesting: A marriage was crumbling under the weight of the wife's new job, a high-paying job that demanded more of her time and energy and was changing her values in significant ways. By page three, the situation was in place. I'd seen a few of scenes in which the couple confronts the change in their lives. In the next scene, the couple argued again about this issue. Next scene: more issue, husband angry and confused, wife changing. Next scene: the same. You get the point. One note, played over and over. A good idea for a story, but no complications. So if you feel ready to chuck a piece of writing (or if you feel a piece is finished), read it again, looking for dramatic possibilities, places to add new elements, ways to push beyond the familiar or what "really happened." Try to surprise your reader, and yourself.

PROMPT: Write three separate scenes from three experiences in your life. In each scene, show yourself in a different light. For example, write about a time when you were very kind and selfless, another in which you were cruel and selfish, still another when you were righteous and indignant about someone else's behavior. Don't simply change your mood. Go deeper than mood, presenting three people—all of them you—who seem fundamentally different from each other. Perhaps these scenes can be pieced together into a longer work, though you'll need to write intervening scenes. But they will show a character in a compelling, dimensional way.

PROMPT: Review a piece of writing that is not going well. Outline it by noting each scene and describing, in a sentence or two, what happens in the scene. Are the scenes enlarging the story, adding new elements, or complicating the initial situation? Or are they all doing much the same work, hitting the same note?

PROMPT: Pick a character you created in an earlier prompt or one from an ongoing project. Give the character an emotion, or an emotional reaction, that contradicts what readers know of him. For example, a character who has been cynical and aloof is moved deeply by another character. Your wisecracking detective, for example, perceives the beauty of another character's selfless gesture; a character who has been passive takes action. It needn't be a significant shift or a permanent one, just a moment in which you present the character in a new light. For example, in "A Father's Story," Andre Dubus shows us a character who is honest and kind, a caring father, a religious man. In the story his daughter tells him she has hit a pedestrian with her car and left the man on the side of the road, assuming he is dead. Rather than calling the police, the father goes to the site of the accident, finds the body and leaves, telling no one. The moral ambiguity of his action surprises us, and he grows as a character.

PROMPT: Pick a character or situation you've created in an earlier prompt or one from an ongoing project. Write down what happens next. If you've already planned the next step, write down your plan. If you haven't planned it yet, take some time and do that. After you've finished, put your written plan aside and write down a new idea. If, for whatever reason, the first plan cannot be implemented, what would you do? Develop the second idea. This exercise helps you escape the obvious choice, the one that is overly familiar. In her book *The Passionate, Accurate Story*, Carol Bly advises to avoid using the first idea that occurs to you while writing. She suggests pushing deeper, where you will find a more original and compelling idea.

PROMPT: Write a short monologue for a character that demonstrates an aspect of her personality readers have not seen before. If the character has been ambivalent, let her take a stand. If a character has been compassionate, let her unleash a bit of cruelty. In his story "In the Garden of the North American Martyrs," Tobias Wolff presents a character who is very nervous about landing a job teaching history at a college. As we do when we're trying to please people, she is agreeable, despite feeling a bit bullied by the hiring committee. In her final interview with the committee, however, she attacks, recounting the atrocities committed by Iriquois Indians, describing in detail their methods of torture. The chairman of the committee tries to stop her speech, but she persists, switching to the tone of a righteous prophet:

"Mend your lives," she said. "You have deceived yourself in the pride of your hearts, and the strength of your arms. Though you soar aloft like the eagle, though your nest is set among the stars, thence I will bring you down, says the Lord. Turn from power to to love. Be kind. Do justice. Walk humbly."

It's a triumphant moment for the character, and we see much more than a victim finally taking a stand—a familiar climactic scene in movies. This stand is fueled by hurts and losses that have nothing to do with the committee, whose actions have not warranted quite so intense a jeremiad. The character, Mary, is presenting a new and surprising side to her personality.

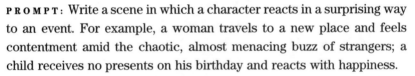

PROMPT: Write a scene in which a character reacts in a surprising way to an event. For example, a woman travels to a new place and feels contentment amid the chaotic, almost menacing buzz of strangers; a child receives no presents on his birthday and reacts with happiness.

PROMPT: Write a true account of an experience in which your own reaction surprised you.

Adding More Elements

Sometimes a piece is just too small. It lacks the necessary elements to sustain the reader's interest, like a song with a simple melody that, by the end, has lost its magic. By adding new elements, you can create resonance and interesting layers of action and meaning. You add a harmony line, which augments the melody. You add an interesting bass line and percussion, perhaps even horns.

I learned this lesson again last year with the article on Bonnie and Clyde that I mentioned in an earlier chapter. If you recall, I got the idea for the article in a conversation with a woman at a writers conference about a trip she took with her mother and daughter. She mentioned visiting the Bonnie and Clyde museum and enjoying the museum's color-ful caretaker. For the article, I would visit the museum, talk to the care-taker, soak up some local flavor, provide a bit of background on the gangsters. I told a friend, who is also a gifted writer, about my plan. He liked the caretaker and wondered about doing a short audio documen-tary. That idea proved too impractical, but in researching the museum, he found out about an annual Bonnie and Clyde festival held in the tiny town where the museum is located. The festival featured a bizarre mix of small-town Americana—funnel cakes, kiddie rides, a parade—and bloody reenactments of the famous ambush in which Bonnie and Clyde were killed. We decided to collaborate on a piece combining the festival, the museum and the caretaker. We pitched the idea to a magazine.

The editors liked the idea but wondered if we could frame it with details from the 1967 film about Bonnie and Clyde to fit an upcoming theme issue. We said fine. But the editors still felt the piece lacked a certain gravity. Could we add a more topical element? Something a little weightier. At that time the news was full of stories about high school students shooting each other. In such a climate, should a festival be dramatizing gunplay to attract visitors? We added this element, which also complicated the tone of the article. How could we mix the wacki-ness of the festival with the tragedy of dead teens? And we later learned that the festival itself was held by desperate people trying to keep their dying little town alive. This element had to be included.

As you can imagine, structuring the piece was not easy. We were given a limit of 3,500 words, so some great stuff had to be cut. Even the colorful caretaker, the one who attracted me to the story at the start, did not make it into the final piece. But the editors were right. The article turned out far better than if I'd have kept to my original premise.

PROMPT: Return to an idea you've abandoned and add a new element to it, an element that does not seem to be related. Try the mix-and-match approach, choosing two dissimilar elements from two lists. Look for connections within the topics as you write about them. Allow your-self to see both topics in new ways. The connections may not be apparent at first, but the topics could resonate on a deeper level. If you find that the topics simply don't gel in your mind, try two others, but don't give up too quickly. In her book *Refuge*, Terry Tempest Williams combines dissimilar topics: breast cancer and the fight to preserve a wildlife refuge. In her book *Hawk Flies Above*, Lisa Dale Norton combines her search for spiritual wholeness with a study of the ecology of the Nebraska sandhills.

PROMPT: Use the same approach as in the previous prompt, but this time add an element that's more closely related to the triggering idea. For example, the elements in the Bonnie and Clyde piece are related. For another example, in his book *Far From Home*, Ron Powers writes about the decay of small-town America as exemplified by Cairo, Illinois. After a section on Cairo, he shifts his focus to the upscale town of Kent, Connecticut, showing how it has grown from an insular community to a commuter village dominated by people who work outside the town. He then moves back and forth between the towns, enlarging his thesis and creating a richer book than a focus on either town would allow.

PROMPT: Add a third element to either of the two pieces you created in the previous two prompts. If using the first piece, which combines two different topics, add a third element that is closely related to one of the topics. If using the second piece, which combines closely related topics, add a third element that's vastly different. Work to enlarge the piece, striking even more notes than you could have struck before. For an example, let's look at "Safe Forever," a short story by Rick DeMarinis, in which several elements are combined into a unified whole. The story concerns an eleven-year-old narrator who is coping with life, with his mother and her live-in boyfriend. The boy vends ice cream for the boyfriend, and this arrangement is a further source of conflict. In one scene, the boy discovers his mother and her boyfriend in bed with another woman. The boy has a strange little scene with the woman as she leaves their house. Certainly these elements give the author plenty of material with which to create a richly textured story. But DeMarinis also includes a friend for the narrator. The boys go swimming, see a ball game, build models and even explore sex together, through reading medical textbooks and spying on a girl in their neighborhood. Late in the story, the friend contracts polio. The narrator visits his friend in the hospital, sees him encased in a hideously clicking iron lung. The story is set in the weeks following V-J Day, when the country was undergoing an awkward yet heady transition to postwar life. Soldiers were returning and life was changing. DeMarinis uses all of these elements to create a powerful story that is thick with detail and incident but doesn't seem dense. He uses the elements to complicate and enlarge each other.

C an a story be too complicated, too heavily nuanced? Absolutely. And simple stories can work very well. But many more stories suffer from being too familiar and too thinly imagined than suffer from too many complications. The point to this discussion is to explore the dramatic potential of an idea. Strive for freshness and surprise. When you find your piece simply has too many elements, subordinate or cut one. Look for ways to balance the elements. This can be difficult, but it's worth the try. In a short story I published years ago, I focused on two brothers trying to forge a new relationship by confronting the memory of their dead father, who remains a ghostly presence in their lives. In revising, I added a third brother, who also never appears in the present action of the story, who left the family and disappeared. Somehow the balance never worked, the third brother adding more distraction than resonance, perhaps because his role is too similar to the father's. Cutting the brother and, perhaps, adding a new element may have helped. But I learned through the story how better to balance various elements, which helped make future stories richer and more complex.

Everything Turns Into Everything Else

I took the title of this section from a friend's poem. It speaks to the topic at hand, which is to experiment with ideas by relating them to something else. To get at the truth of something—an experience, a concept—we sometimes need to focus on a different thing. This approach can shed light on our original topic and free us of the burden of "what really happened" or the "real" nature of the thing. For example, we can try to understand the elation we felt in a particular moment by focusing on a different moment. If you're trying without success to capture something on the page, shift the focus to something else and see if your vision can take hold there.

PROMPT: Write about a real experience, trying to re-create the events and how you felt at the time. Then write about a different experience, a wholly fictional one, that conveys the same feeling—another character in a different situation who experiences the same thoughts and feelings you experienced.

PROMPT: Let's try simile. In conversation we sometimes describe how we felt by comparing it to something else. When describing a wildly self-destructive time in our lives, we might say, "It was like driving a hundred miles an hour on a winding road." Rather than write about the real details of this time in your life, put a character behind a wheel at a hundred miles an hour. Describe how he feels. Try at least three different similes to evoke an experience.

PROMPT: Play word association with yourself. Focus on the experience you want to evoke and write down whatever words or images enter your mind. Don't censor. This process is similar to clustering in that you tap into your unconscious mind, looking for images and associations rather than for memories. This can be a good way to break through blocks, too.

PROMPT: Play "as if." Focus on the experience, then write "It's as if [fill in the blank]." Make a list of "as if" statements until one frees you by offering a fresh insight into the character or situation. Again, write down whatever comes to you, even if it seems to have no relation to what you're seeking.

PROMPT: Make metaphors. Lots of them. Compare one noun to another: a kite to a handkerchief, a lighthouse to a stick of candy. Let yourself go and write all over the page. Copy the ones you like best, for future use. If you're stuck on how to describe an object or an emotion, use this approach. Push through the most obvious metaphors, the ones that come to mind first. Take some chances.

Chapter Twenty-eight

Tell It Slant

Adam was the only man who, when he said a good thing, knew that nobody had said it before him.

—MARK TWAIN

E mily Dickenson gave us some great advice on how to shape an idea: "tell the truth, but tell it slant, success in circuit lies." That's what we'll do in this chapter: look for ways to slant your idea to make is as affecting as possible. We take the time to look for fresh ways to approach an idea for a number of reasons, one of which Mark Twain speaks to in this chapter's epigraph. Other writers have come before us. They have developed their ideas in certain ways that make it tough for us to do the same. The reader has heard the story before and is thus a little tough to reach. Even if we're writing without a reader in mind, other than ourselves, to get at the truth of something, to summon the emotions we want on the page, we can't always take the direct approach. We must experiment, try new angles, new voices. That's what we'll do here.

Indirection

A pair of men wait to die, stranded in the snow, perhaps, their car has broken down, they have no radio or telephone, and no way back. Perhaps a thaw will come or a forest ranger will pass by. But probably not. Probably they will freeze to death. This scenario holds many dramatic possibilities. It offers conflict, tension, suspense. If you have done your work as a writer, you have developed these characters enough that the reader knows them well and cares about them.

Your first impulse may be to have them talk about their impending death, to admit to each other their fear, their regrets, their dreams that will never be realized. Or they could talk about hot dogs. Really. That would probably be a better approach. Maybe they could debate the chances of their college football team having a winning season next year. This approach is called indirection. If you follow your first impulse and allow the characters to voice their concerns, you defuse the tension in your story. You're pointing too directly at the source of the tension. But by using indirection—or, to use Dickenson's words, by telling it slant—you allow the tension to build beneath the surface. The tension informs every word the characters say, and the reader participates. She knows what these guys are feeling and brings that knowledge to the discussion of hot dogs. She is more engaged in the narrative because she is interpreting it. She is playing a part in it.

PROMPT: Create a scene in which two characters face a significant conflict. It need not be life or death, as in the scenario I created above, but it should be important to the characters. Let the reader know the conflict through detail and description. Then create dialogue in which the characters don't directly address their conflict. They speak on a completely unrelated topic.

PROMPT: Revise a scene you've already written by relying on indirection. Choose a scene in which the characters directly address their concern. For example, if you have a scene in which a couple argues about a problem, allow them to argue, but don't mention the problem. Or, you may not even allow them to argue, keeping the tension beneath the surface.

PROMPT: Write a scene in which a character receives very disappointing news. Rather than show the disappointment, she does something else, perhaps focuses on refinishing an old chair. Suggest her emotional state through her actions.

PROMPT: Write about an illuminating moment in your life, a time when you learned an important lesson or gained an important insight. Describe the scene exactly as it happened, but don't mention the lesson or insight.

PROMPT: Write about a relationship in your life—or make up a relationship between two characters—by showing the characters doing something together. They could work together to fix a car, or they could attend a concert, or they could zip a Frisbee back and forth. Suggest the nature of the relationship by how they do the thing. Who leads and who follows? Who knows what he's doing and who doesn't? Do they talk to each other and share the experience in a positive way, or does it lead to disagreement? Take this one wherever it wants to go. The only rule is that the pair can't make direct statements about themselves or the relationship.

PROMPT: If you're blocked on a scene in an ongoing piece, step back and try to decide ways to approach the drama through indirection. Perhaps your feelings of frustration with the scene rise from its seeming flat and predictable. You may be right. Work to find a fresh point of entry and keep the tension beneath the surface.

Writers and Their Symbols

Beginning writers sometimes ask when is the best time to put in the symbols. They have taken literature classes and learned that the color white symbolizes purity, water symbolizes rebirth, babies symbolize innocence, a physical deformity or a scar symbolizes a psychological or emotional problem. We can debate the use of symbols for hours, but our goal here is to find ways of using one thing—a physical thing—to suggest or amplify something else, usually an emotional state. The use of symbols is simply another type of indirection, a way of showing without telling, a way of allowing the reader to participate in the narrative. Seen in this light, the debate about whether or not something *really* symbolizes something else, or whether or not the author *really* intended to put in the symbol becomes moot. A symbol is seen as a technique, a way of expressing an emotion or idea.

Short story writer Andre Dubus once made this point very well in an interview. He was asked if the chips of ice that a son feeds to his dying father are symbolic of the son's love. Dubus said the ice wasn't symbolic of the love, it *was* the love, a silent expression of the son's feelings for his father. In your own writing, view symbols in this way—as a means to make your story more powerful and a way for your reader to become more deeply engaged in the story by participating in it.

PROMPT: Find a couple of key details in a story you're writing. Try to find a way to use them to suggest the emotional state of a character. For example, a man who cherishes his high school swimming trophy might be locked into the past, unable to see a future as bright as the days that are now behind him.

PROMPT: Find an object to describe that you can use to embody an emotion. For example, if those two guys stranded in the snow are slowly losing hope, rather than state their fading hope, you could describe their broken-down car sinking ever more deeply into the snow. Is the car symbolic of their hope? Perhaps. But it also *is* their hope. Without the car, they are stuck in the snow and sure to die.

PROMPT: Give a character an object that she carries everywhere with her or, perhaps, something she always wears. Try to suggest through this object something important about the character. If the character wears a locket containing a picture of her family, what does this say about her? If a character keeps a picture in his wallet of a woman who left him long ago, what does this say about him? If a character always has a fresh condom in his wallet, what does this say about him?

PROMPT: Associate an object or an action with someone in real life. Does someone you know have a cherished possession or a unique ritual? Describe it. Use that object or ritual to begin a character sketch or essay about the person.

PROMPT: Begin a sketch or story by comparing a character or real person to a natural object—a mountain or a flower or a river. Following the comparison, move into your piece, explaining what you mean by the comparison or narrating an event that will illustrate why this comparison is valid.

Exploring Avenues

As we discussed in the previous two chapters, sometimes we lock into a piece too soon, feeling that it *must* be told in a particular way. We limit the possibilities of our ideas before exploring them and experimenting with them. This syndrome can be especially tough to break through when we have finished a first draft. The words take on a certain inevitability, as if the piece can only take that form and no other. Let's try some ways to see a piece in a new light.

PROMPT: Change narrative distance. If you're telling a story from the point of view of a child, for example, try telling it from the point of view of an adult, looking back on the experience. If you're recounting a memory from your point of view as an adult, switch to your view of it as a child. To make this switch more easily, use present tense, relating the experience as if it were happening right now.

PROMPT: Change emotional distance. If you're writing about something that happened long ago, an event that you have processed and now can see from a calm, philosophical viewpoint, shift to a more emotionally charged view, placing yourself in the passion or confusion or elation of the moment.

PROMPT: Change spatial distance. If you're writing about the city or town where you live, move yourself in your mind to a distant place. Try to see the setting and events, as if from far away, from a place you've left behind.

PROMPT: Fictionalize a true story. If you're writing a personal essay or memoir, change a few of the elements in the piece—names, characters, settings, even events, if necessary. Stay true to the emotions and ideas of the story, but change the particular details.

PROMPT: Change the form. If you're writing a personal essay, tell the story in a narrative poem. If you're writing a script, shift to the short story form.

PROMPT: Change the nature of the characters. If you're telling a story of three people, for example, turn them into something else—dogs or apples or angels dancing on the head of a pin. Or, if you're feeling less adventurous, simply change the genders. Stay as close as possible to the events of the story as you imagined them before shifting the characters.

PROMPT: Change the ages of the characters. If you're writing a story of the friendship between three teenage girls, turn them into septuagenarians. As above, don't change what happens in the story. Simply change the ages of the people involved.

PROMPT: Tell your story as a fly on the wall, offering no entry into the minds of the participants.

PROMPT: Focus on one of the five senses in a description of a place or in a scene. For example, in a scene that occurs between two sisters raking leaves in their yard, focus on the smell of the leaves, the smell of the autumn air, the smell of a meal cooking nearby or the smell of burning leaves.

PROMPT: Repeat the previous prompt, describing the same place or scene by focusing on a different sense. Avoid the sense of sight.

PROMPT: Use a frame to tell your story. In other words, tell your story within a larger story, opening with the larger one, then moving into the smaller one, then returning in the end to the larger one.

PROMPT: Rewrite a story by shifting point of view. For example, move from first person to third person or change the point-of-view character. If you're feeling bold, try using a collective point of view, telling your story in the voice of a particular group. William Faulkner tells his short story "A Rose for Emily" from the point of view of a town. In his novel *The Virgin Suicides*, Jeffrey Eugenides uses the voice of a group of men, all of whom knew the sisters who commit suicide.

PROMPT: Describe a tropical ocean resort without mentioning the beach or the ocean. If you can, avoid describing the types of objects that would appear in a promotional brochure for the place.

PROMPT: Use the same approach as you used in the previous prompt to write or revise a description of a place in a new or ongoing piece. For example, if you're writing about a farm where you grew up, try to describe it without focusing on the details the reader would expect when reading about a farm: no barns or chickens or tractors or fields of grain. Push yourself to evoke the farm through fresh, particular details.

PROMPT: Place at least two characters in one of the descriptions in the previous two prompts. Set them in motion by forcing them to react to the setting, making the setting a source of conflict or tension. For example, a couple vacations at the resort you described earlier. He's hoping it will be a second honeymoon; she's worried about the expense. Or perhaps you could use the farm from your personal experience to show two fictional characters unfamiliar with the place. They could be two people from the city who have never spent time on a farm.

Chapter Twenty-nine

Anything Is Beautiful if You Say It Is

Write it as it is, don't try to make it like this or that. You can't do it in anybody else's way—you will have to make a way of your own.

—SARAH ORNE JEWETT

T he title of this chapter is one of my favorite titles, taken from a Wallace Stevens poem. As with many of Stevens's poems, I love the title and can't figure out what the hell the poem is about, so if you're a Stevens scholar, please don't write to me about the inappropriateness of the poem to the topic of this chapter. I'm admitting it. But the statement in the title does speak in certain ways to the roles of tone and theme, two important elements in narrative writing. This chapter continues our focus on assessing and developing ideas. In other chapters in this part of the book, we've looked at ways to make more from an idea by mining its dramatic possibilities, by enlarging its scope, by using indirection and looking for new ways to tell the story. In this chapter, we'll look at making a good idea better by focusing on tone and on theme and the ways you put forth those elements of your story.

Tone

In a glossary of literary terms, tone is usually defined as the attitude of the author toward his material. Tone is created through the words you use and, to a lesser extent, the things you choose to present. We can describe the tone of a work just as we would describe the tone of someone's voice while speaking: sarcastic, bombastic, lyrical, warm, frank, cynical, sentimental or whatever. Notice the tones in the following excerpts, and the ways the authors use tone to amplify their material:

I'm inside the King Fok Club—a Hong Kong mah-jongg parlor and lounge frequented by drug couriers, numbers runners, transsexual prostitutes, and off-duty cops. The band stand is a green blur of jade drumsticks as the topless all-girl trio sweats through an aerobic repertoire of Buddy Rich covers. I'm dancing with Antoinette, who's so gorgeous it's hard to believe she was a man once—not only a man, but a Golden Gloves middleweight champion and then the head of a teamsters local that was considered the roughest on the East Coast, but let me tell you, she is absolutely ooh-la-la.

ET TU, BABE, MARK LEYNER

People came down to the water's edge, carrying lamps. Most of them stood on the shore, where in time they built a fire. But some of the taller boys and younger men walked out on the railroad bridge with ropes and lanterns. Two or three covered themselves with black grease and tied themselves up in rope harnesses, and the others lowered them down into the water at the place where the porter and the waiter thought the train must have disappeared.

HOUSEKEEPING, MARILYNNE ROBINSON

I wish I could swing up into the sky, up into the clouds. I might be able to fly around the whole world and not hear my brothers, Oliver and Eugene, cry in the middle of the night anymore. My mother says they're always hungry. She cries in the middle of the night, too. She says she's worn out nursing and feeding and changing four boys is too much for her. She wishes she had one little girl all for herself. She'd give anything for one little girl.

ANGELA'S ASHES, FRANK McCOURT

Mark Leyner employs a dazzling voice and a hip, ironic tone.

Marilynne Robinson uses a direct, understated tone, which presents the powerful moment in a controlled way. Frank McCourt integrates the voice of a child into his tone, giving his paragraph a wistful and sad lyricism.

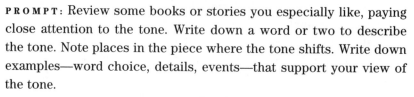

PROMPT: Review some books or stories you especially like, paying close attention to the tone. Write down a word or two to describe the tone. Note places in the piece where the tone shifts. Write down examples—word choice, details, events—that support your view of the tone.

PROMPT: Choose one of the favorites you reviewed in the previous prompt, and copy the tone as closely as possible in a passage of your own. Your subject can be vastly different from the subject in your favorite. If you want, borrow words and phrases from the favorite. When you finish, assess how well the tone fits your passage. Does it help the material? Hurt it?

In assessing an idea, which you'll use either to explore material or to generate material, be mindful of your attitude toward it. As we've discussed in earlier chapters, ask yourself why you want to write about this subject. There is no right or wrong answer. If your answer is to express nearly homicidal rage at a lover who spurned you, that's OK, though you may want to clear a final draft with your ex-lover's attorney before trying to publish the piece. The key lies in knowing your attitude, understanding it, so that you can use it to shape the material rather than allow it to spin out of control.

In beginning to write about a subject, you may not know your attitude. That's OK, too. Often we discover our relationship to our material as we write. At some point, however, perhaps in revision, you need to come to some conclusions about the tone of the piece and your stance with the material. Does emotion cloud the logic of the piece? Does it dominate the material to the extent that the reader is not allowed to make discoveries for herself? Does it charge the piece with energy, carrying the reader along in a powerful way? Ask yourself these questions. You may need a bit of distance on the idea or piece before you can provide yourself with accurate answers.

The next question you need to ask is whether you have chosen the best tone for the piece. Just as a good idea can suffer from being too limited, it can suffer from an inappropriate tone. My advice is to gauge the tone against the material, looking for ways to freshen the material and surprise the reader. This approach demands that you understand the reader's expectations. For example, our first impulse may be to tell a story about the death of a loved one in a solemn, even reverential tone. (Tip: Editors read hundreds of such stories.) That tone can be numbing. By adopting a different tone or by mixing the solemnity with other tones, you can give the idea a fresh spin, making it more affecting for the reader. Amy Hempel takes this approach in her much-anthologized short story "In the Cemetery Where Al Jolson Is Buried." The story concerns a young woman whose best friend is dying in a hospital. Rather than focusing on the tragic aspects of this situation, Hempel uses a light touch and a quick pace, even adding humor, which make the situation vivid and real and, therefore, quite powerful. The tone doesn't undercut the dark elements of the story. Through contrast, it intensifies them, as Hempel modulates from repartee to sudden admissions of the impending death:

> She is flirting with the Good Doctor, who has just appeared. Unlike the Bad Doctor, who checks the I.V. drip before saying good morning, the Good Doctor says things like "God didn't give epileptics a fair shake." He awards himself points for the cripples he could have hit in the parking lot. Because the Good Doctor is a little in love with her he says maybe a year. He pulls a chair up to her bed and suggests I might like to spend an hour on the beach.
>
> "Bring me something back," she says. "Anything from the beach. Or the gift shop. Taste is no object."
>
> The doctor slowly draws the curtain around her bed.
>
> "Wait!" she cries.

I look in at her.

"Anything," she says, "except a magazine subscription."

The doctor turns away.

I watch her mouth laugh.

For another example, consider Joseph Heller's novel *Catch-22*, which concerns life in the army during World War II. Novels have been saying war is hell for a long time, so Heller takes a different approach, telling his story of war's insanity as a broad satire. Characters are drawn as caricatures, and scenes are developed with humor. The hellishness of war is revealed in sharp relief.

PROMPT: Develop an idea you've been considering by adopting a tone different from one you would normally use. If you write in a straightforward tone, try to add a bit of lyricism. If you tend to write in a serious tone, add humor.

PROMPT: Write a piece in which you vary the tone. As we looked at ways to vary action in the chapter on complicating ideas, vary the tone. This will give you new notes to hit and will keep the reader interested.

PROMPT: Write about a serious subject in a humorous way, dipping occasionally into seriousness as a contrast. Then try the reverse: Write about a humorous subject in a funny way. If you're feeling bold, push the tone to the extreme; risk offending the reader with your humorous treatment of a serious subject.

PROMPT: Write the same scene in three different tones. Present the details and the characters in a way that fit the tone. Then, try to combine the tones in a single scene, modulating the tone to surprise the reader. Work to make the transition feel natural, effortless.

Voice

Voice is closely related to tone, as in "tone of voice." Both grow from word choice and from the material you're writing about in the piece. Tone has a bit more to do with what you say; voice has more to do with how you say it. A writer's voice also filters into everything she writes, no matter what the topic. You might write an essay with an angry tone, or a love story with a lyrical tone, but your writer's voice will shine through. As a writer, you may have a penchant for long sentences, or strong verbs, or a particular rhythm and color of language that grows out of who you are as a person.

Some writers struggle to find their voice. Advice: don't. You don't struggle to find your voice when you speak; no need to struggle to find your voice on the page. By writing a lot, you'll begin to develop a clearer voice, but this development won't involve much struggle. Again, it will grow out of who you are as a person: your personality, how you see the world. If you strain to affect a writerly voice or persona, the strain will show. Your writing will ring false, and worse, it won't convey your true thoughts and feelings.

I worked with a writer once who was a shy, taciturn person. Her voice on the phone sounded taciturn as did her writing, though on the page she also possessed a crisp, understated economy. The message on her answering machine was a different story. A well-meaning friend perhaps had told her she sounded dour in her recorded greeting, so she tried to pump up her energy with a "Hi! This is _____!" She sounded like she was on fire. Like flames were licking their way up her leg as she put her message on the tape. In short, the strain showed.

PROMPT: Read a few pieces of writing you've done recently. Describe the voice. How does it sound, and how is that sound created? What types of words are used? How long are the sentences?

PROMPT: Choose a few pieces of published writing that have distinctive voices—authorial voices, that is. We'll get to character voices in a minute. Then choose a subject to write about and imitate those voices as well as you can. If you are in a playful mood, try a parody of the author's voice. People love to parody Hemingway—those terse, laconic sentences, that genuflection before place names that now seems so pompous. People parody Faulkner, too—his long sentences that go on for half a page, his images of a strife-torn South.

PROMPT: Find a writer's voice that you like a lot. Find a writer's voice that doesn't engage you at all. Study them closely. How are they different? How are they similar? Try to find the ingredients that make the one voice appealing and the other unappealing.

Some writers have said they found their natural voice when they found the material they most wanted to explore. If you find that your voice rings false, that the voice on the page is not the one you hear in your head, maybe the problem lies in the material. When I was in college, I enjoyed F. Scott Fitzgerald's wonderfully lyrical voice—its elegance and sharp sense of profundity. I tried desperately to imitate it. Not a bad model to take for a twenty-year-old apprentice. Unfortunately, I also wrote about the same subjects Fitzgerald wrote about in his work, and I didn't know beans about life on the Riviera or in 1930s Hollywood. When I began writing about the world I knew, one that connected with me on a variety of levels, things fell into place.

PROMPT: Review the material you focus on in your writing. Are you writing about a world and about people that you know and love? As an experiment, write a short piece on a subject important to you, one you know well. Then write a short piece on something you don't know well.

Then read both pieces. Are the voices similar? Is one more engaging than the other? Why?

Character Voices

A character's voice can be much different from your own. Character voices can be fun to create. The writer becomes an actor playing a role. If you have a good ear for voices, use this talent in your work. It can be great source of ideas. Many writers speak of getting ideas for their work by hearing a voice in their heads. They follow the voice to the story, almost like taking dictation.

PROMPT: Find a few pieces of fiction with strong narrative voices. Try to imitate these voices, using their rhythms and inflections, but allowing them to tell a story different from the one in the published piece. If you can't find a piece of writing that works, try one of the following models:

> This is a story about the one time I outfoxed Hollywood. Open on me arriving at the Pierre Hotel for a script conference with Sandra Moxie, a short, fiesty, singer slash actress with a brash, almost harassing style and the uncanny ability to turn around on a dime and become quite touching. Or at least *most* people felt she had that ability. In her recent appearances, I myself had felt that you could see the machinery, that she was telegraphing her touching stuff with the result that it wasn't all that touching. But let that pass. For the moment, let's just say that she was touching enough to get the job done.
>
> "AN IRONIC YETTA MONTANA," BRUCE JAY FRIEDMAN

> What strange and unlikely things are washed up on the shore of time. I have in my possession a tattered photograph album full of snapshots of my stepmother as a young woman. Very pretty and sweet she was, with a fur muff and a picture hat and skirts almost to the floor.
>
> *SO LONG, SEE YOU TOMORROW,* WILLIAM MAXWELL

And you, are you married? he asks, stroking my jaw. I half-frown. You know, thinking that shoulda been his first question, whether I'm married or not. I'm wearing a wedding ring, but there's women who wears wedding rings that ain't married, just so's they don't have to deal with every joker. Least if you's a woman from the *Looking for Mr. Goodbar* generation.

    THE HEALING, GAYL JONES

Each voice is unique. Friedman's narrator is full of the bluster, jargon and cynicism of Hollywood. He uses short, choppy sentences, uses words like "machinery," "outfoxed," and "singer slash actress." Maxwell's narrator, on the other hand, has an elegant, almost haughty voice. Jones uses dialect to create her narrator's voice, creating an intimate, informal tone for the character.

PROMPT: Write three paragraphs, each one in a distinctly different voice. Choose the one that interests you most and write a page in that voice. If a story begins to develop, move forward.

PROMPT: Write a scene in which two characters converse in distinctly different voices. They can be from different regions of the country, from different countries, or from different economic or social backgrounds.

PROMPT: Try the same approach as in the previous prompt, but this time but the differences in voice more subtle. For example, one character might have some type of verbal tic, or a habit of repeating himself.

Theme

In some of the earlier chapters we've mentioned theme, but let's take a little time before we part to discuss it further. Theme is related to tone in that it grows out of your attitude toward your material. It also grows out the material. Themes are best expressed when they're not directly expressed. A theme is not a moral. Some beginning writers confuse the two. The culprits: television and literature classes. On television, episodes are wrapped up in tidy packages. We're told what to think, so we don't have to bother figuring it out ourselves, thus keeping our minds free for munching Fritos. Even the grim, award-winning reality shows slam home their themes of the week with much fanfare, though the award-winning actors usually do this in grim tones, which makes us think these really are "reality" shows and that these really are actors.

Television is fine. We all watch it. If you want to write for television, watch it a lot. If you don't, don't. It screws up your writing, I firmly believe. Too much television will inculcate you with the pace and rhythms of television episodes (and will make you docile and stupid, but you'll think you're smart because you will repeat smart-sounding lines from television shows, as if you thought of them yourself, but that's just an authorial aside). You'll also adopt the television habit of delivering the theme like a lukewarm pizza. Here it is! Here's the point of the story!

A writer I know who is also a university teacher told me recently that many of his student's stories sound like "really bad Aesop." He meant that the students were telling morality tales rather than stories that truly interested them. Here the other culprit rears its head. We've all been through the English class find-the-symbols-in-the-haystack ringer, and in five hundred words we must explain who, in this week's classic tale, man is versing: Nature? Society? Himself? As with television, there's much to learn in English class. But when you're writing, your theme should be implicit, and part of the act of writing should be discovering and developing theme.

OK, enough of the grouchy lecture. You understand my point. Your theme is a vital aspect of your piece. But don't allow it to overwhelm your material, and don't shape the material solely to fit a theme. If you want to write about injustice or greed, the nature of love, the nature of family, great. Those are important subjects. Knowing that you're writing about those subjects is enough to give your piece focus. You needn't tell your reader what to think about those subjects. Investigate what you think about them, and tell a good story.

PROMPT: Review some of the pieces you've written in the past, perhaps in response to some of the prompts in this book. Look for common themes. Do you return to the same themes again and again? If so, write about this theme. Why does it interest you? Why do you keep returning to it?

PROMPT: If you're stuck on a piece, write about the themes you're exploring in it. How are those themes manifest in the story? Is the theme serving the story? Is the theme an organic part of the story? Or is the story straining against a thematic harness that no longer works, that is imposing limits?

PROMPT: Explore the Seven Deadly Sins in seven brief sketches. You may want to freewrite or cluster first. For a personal essay, write about times in which you committed each of the sins. For fiction, write scenes or create situations in which each of the sins in involved. One rule: don't mention the sin. Allow it to work behind the scenes, as a theme that informs the writing but is not addressed directly.

PROMPT: Pick a theme to write about by asking yourself a question that you can try to answer in a story. For example: What is the nature of community? What is the nature of love? Loneliness? Confidence? Do a freewrite on the theme or place a key word in a circle and begin clustering. When you have some ideas, begin writing. Don't worry about staying on track. Sometimes we believe we're writing on a theme only to find another theme, perhaps one more important to us, takes over.

A Final Word

Responding to a cheering call for an encore, comedian Dennis Miller returned to the stage, thanked the audience for their applause, and said: "If I had anything else to say, I'd have said it." I feel a little bit that way in these final paragraphs. We've discussed many topics, and though there are many more to cover, we can't cover them here.

But even a book of this kind needs closure, some final note to strike, though it's not as if I'm sending you off to begin writing. You've been writing your way through the book. I do hope you've written some pieces that you've enjoyed and that you now have a fat notebook bursting with ideas. Continue to explore them. Keep adding to the notebook. Keep writing. You will make something beautiful.

Index

The Adventures of Augie March, 65

The Adventures of Huckleberry Finn, 168

"Afternoon of an Author," 130-131

All the King's Men, 101-102

Allen, Woody, 53, 89

Allende, Isabel, 94

Ancient Evenings, 210

Anderson, Sherwood, 73

Angela's Ashes, 245

Anger, 98-101

  using, in stories, 101-104

Aphrodite, 94

The Apostle, 119

Apple, Max, 68

Appliance fiction, 140-141

"Araby," 210

The Art of Compelling Fiction, 153

The Art of Fiction, 193

Austen, Jane, 143

Automatic writing, 37-38

Awakening the Warrior Within, 15, 31

Babbitt, 160, 192, 197-198

Baker, Nicholson, 109, 155, 194-195

Baldwin, James, 172

Banks, Russell, 166

The Barracks Thief, 188

Barth, John, 96

Baxter, Charles, 227

Beliefs

  spiritual, 134-137

  understanding, 80-83

Bellow, Saul, 65, 184

Benedict, Elizabeth, 93

Berger, Thomas, 146

A Bigamist's Daughter, 18

Billy Phelan's Greatest Game, 210

Blue Highways, 168, 204

Bly, Carol, 229

Brainstorming, 37

Bridget Jones's Diary, 168

Bright Lights, Big City, 182

Bruce, Lenny, 88-89

Bryson, Bill, 168

Building Fiction, 206

Burgess, Anthony, 202

Burroughs, William, 40

Callan, Dawn, 15, 31

Capote, Truman, 38, 153

Carver, Raymond, 114-115, 186

Casablanca, 212

Catch-22, 248

Cather, Willa, 190

Cavewriting, 39-40

Chandler, Raymond, 163

Character(s)

  developing, through observation, 148-151

  famous, 105-109

  getting to know, 151-153

  as mouthpiece, avoiding, 86-87

  philosophical, 83-86

  physical appearance, 152

  rendering, 153-160

  setting as, 192-193

  voices, 251-252

Cheever, John, 70, 141, 184, 196, 215

Chekhov, Anton, 157

Chiarella, Tom, 124, 210

Chödrön, Pema, 1, 24, 134

Clichés

  and beliefs, 81

  of guilt and regret, 119

The Clockwork Orange, 202-203

Clueless, 143

Clustering, 38-39

A Confederacy of Dunces, 85-86

Conflict and tension

  enough of, to interest reader, 218-220

  increasing, 220-223

  through first-person point of view, 173

Continental Drift, 166

"The Country Husband," 184, 215

The Craft of Fiction, 24

Creating Character Emotions, 119
Creating Fiction, 141
Creativity
　enemies of, 12
　joy and gratitude from, 9-11
　leading life of, 25-26
　techniques, 36-40
Criticism, of self, 17-19

Damascus Gate, 188
The Damnation of Theron Ware, 137
Darkness Visible, 18
"The Day I Met Buddy Holly," 108
Death of a Salesman, 111, 121
DeLillo, Don, 156, 160, 210
DeMarinis, Rick, 208, 214, 232-233
Description
　importance of, 193-196
　of place, authoritative, 197-198
　See also Details
Details
　about character, 152-153
　noticing, in native place, 70-71
　selecting, 196-197
Dickens, Charles, 199
Dickey, James, 45
Drinking: A Love Story, 55
Dubus, Andre, 229, 239

Easy in the Islands, 182
Eavesdropping, as source of
　ideas, 124-127
Eberhardt, Isabelle, 74
"The Eighty-Yard Run," 111
Emma, as metatext, 143
Endings, 208-209
　great, 210-211
　reasons for success, 211-215
"The Enormous Radio," 141
Et Tu, Babe, 245
Ethnicity, as source material, 64-66
Eugenides, Jeffrey, 243
Events
　recording day's worth, 129-132
　writing about, 78
"Everyday Use," 172

"Everything Else Falls Away," 22
"Everything That Rises Must
　Converge," 184
Exercises in Style, 144-145
Exley, Frederick, 109, 165

Fame, brushes with, 105-106, 110-111
Family
　love of, 95-97
　as source material, 61-64
A Fan's Notes, 109, 165
Fantasies, sexual, writing about, 94
Far From Home, 232
A Farewell to Arms, 209
"A Father's Story," 229
Faulkner, William, 243
Felicia's Journey, 77
Fiction Writer's Workshop, 1-2
Fielding, Helen, 168
First-person point of view, 172-178
Fitzgerald, F. Scott, 83-84, 92, 130, 210
Fitz-Gibbon, Bernice, 25
Focus, through first-person point of
　view, 173
"Foley the Great," 210
Ford, Richard, 116-118
Form
　choosing, 145-146
　ideas from, 141-145
The Four Seasons, 168
Frederic, Harold, 137
Freewriting, 36-37
　See also Automatic writing
French, Marilyn, 101
Friedman, Bonnie, 133
Friedman, Bruce Jay, 251-252
Friends, love of, 95-97
Frost, Robert, 85

Gardner, John, 21, 143, 193
Genre. *See* Form
"Gimpel the Fool," 172
The Glass Menagerie, 58
"A Glutton for Punishment," 210
God, faith in. *See* Spiritual beliefs

"A Good Man Is Hard to Find," 96,
    157-158
The Grapes of Wrath, 101, 212
The Great Gatsby, 83, 168, 177,
    179, 210
Greene, Graham, 117
Grendel, 143
Guilt, and regret, 116-119
Guterson, David, 18-19

Hauser, Susan Carol, 144
Hawk Flies Above, 165, 232
Hawthorne, Nathaniel, 137
The Healing, 252
The Heart of the Matter, 117-118
Heat-Moon, William Least, 168, 204
Heller, Joseph, 248
Hemingway, Ernest, 78, 168, 202, 209
Hemley, Robin, 128
Hempel, Amy, 247
Hendrie, Laura, 73, 159
Henley, Beth, 112, 121
"Her Favorite Story," 204
Heritage, as source material, 61
Herzinger, Kim, 108
"Hills Like White Elephants," 186
Hinton, S.E., 214
History
    personal, as source material, 61-66
    of places, 69
    spiritual, 135
Hood, Ann, 119
Hope, 120-121
Housekeeping, 203, 245
Hugo, Richard, 203
"The Hummer," 54

"I Feel More Like I Did When I Came
    in Here Than I Do Now," 144
Ideas
    from form, 141-145
    getting, 2
    good, going deeper with, 226-230
    listening for, 125-127
    sources of, 6-7

awareness of surroundings as,
    122-124
ethnicity as, 64-66
family as, 61-64
talking about, as enemy to creativ-
    ity, 15-17
See also Creativity
Identity, finding own, 44-48
Immediacy, through first-person point
    of view, 173
In Cold Blood, 153-154
"In Heaven These Days," 137
"In the Cemetery Where Al Jolson Is
    Buried," 247-248
"In the Garden of the North American
    Martyrs," 229-230
Indirection, 236-238
Instincts, trusting, 31-32
Interests, writing about, 52-53
"An Ironic Yetta Montana," 251-252
Irving, John, 164
Iyer, Pico, 76, 79

Jen, Gish, 20
Jones, Gayl, 252
Journaling, 35
The Joy of Writing Sex, 93
Joyce, James, 167, 210
The Jungle, 101

Kennedy, William, 137, 210-211
Kent State, 84
Kercheval, Jesse Lee, 206
Kerouac, Jack, 37, 80, 169
Kesey, Ken, 160
King Lear, as metatext, 143
Knapp, Caroline, 55
Knott, William, 24

"The Lady With the Toy Dog," 157
"Lament," 200
Lane, Barry, 39-40
"Lawns," 172
Leland, Christopher, 153
Lennon, John, 126

Lewis, Sinclair, 160, 192, 197-198
Leyner, Mark, 245
Lies, secrets and, 114-116
Likes
  and dislikes, writing about, 53-57
  literary, 58-59
Limited point of view, 187
Literary likes, 58-59
"Location, Location, Location: Depicting Character Through Place," 70, 196
Lolita, 200
"The Loneliness of the Long-Distance Runner," 86-87
Long Day's Journey Into Night, 101
Longing, 119-120
"Lord Short Shoe Wants the Monkey," 182
The Lost Continent, 168
"Lost in the Funhouse," 96
Love, romantic, 89-92

Mailer, Norman, 210
Manhattan, 53, 89
Martone, Michael, 140-141
Matthews, William, 54
Maxwell, William, 251-252
McCourt, Frank, 245
McDermott, Alice, 18
McGuane, Thomas, 7
McInerney, Jay, 16, 182-183
McMillan, Terry, 149
McTeague, 58-59
"Mending Wall," 85
Metatext, 143
The Mezzanine, 155, 194-195
Michener, James, 84
Midnight Run, 168
Mildred Pierce, 166
Miller, Arthur, 111
Mindfulness, 129-132
The Miss Firecracker Contest, 112, 121
Mock, Jeff, 144
Moore, Lorrie, 127, 158, 182, 200, 210
Morrison, Toni, 137

My Antonia, 190

Nabokov, Vladimir, 200
Narrative, keeping control of, 86-87
Narrator, choosing, 178-179
Native Son, 101
The New York Review of Books, 93
Newspaper, as source of ideas, 123
Nola, 128
Norris, Frank, 58-59
Norton, Lisa Dale, 165, 232
Novakovich, Josip, 1-2

Objective point of view, 185-187
Observations, 126
  beneath surface, 127-128
  to develop character, 148-151
O'Connor, Flannery, 96, 157-158, 184
Omniscient point of view, 184-185
On Becoming a Novelist, 21
"On Being Told That Her Second Husband Has Taken His First Lover," 182
"On Defamiliarization," 227
On the Road, 80, 169
One Flew Over the Cuckoo's Nest, 160
O'Neill, Eugene, 101
Openings
  great, 200-201
  tips for, 205-207
  types of, 201-205
The Outsiders, 214

The Passionate, Accurate Story, 229
The Passionate Nomad, 74
"People Like That Are the Only People Here," 158-159, 210
Piercy, Marge, 149
Pinkwater, Daniel, 200
Place, 190-191
  appealing, 74-75
  authoritative description of, 197-198
  as character, 192-193
  disappointing, 75-77
  evoking, 67-68
  native, 70-73

Plot. *See* Structure
Point of view, 172-189
Pound, Ezra, 68
Powers, Ron, 232
Procrastination, as enemy to creativity, 13-14
Publication, writing for, vs. for pleasure, 22-24
Pulp Fiction, 214

Queneau, Raymond, 144-145
Quindlen, Anna, 56

Rain Man, 168, 212
Reader
    concerns of, 223-224
    meeting expectations of, at ending, 213
Reading
    learning characterization through, 160
    as warm-up, 35-36
"Redial," 140
Refuge, 232
Regret, and guilt, 116-119
Religion. *See* Spiritual beliefs
Remember Me, 159
Revolutionary Road, 111-112
Richard, Mark, 204
Risk-taking, 32-33
Ritual, family, writing about, 62
Robinson, Marilynne, 203, 245
Roorbach, Bill, 68, 147
"A Rose for Emily," 243
Russo, Richard, 70, 196

"Safe Forever," 232-233
Saturday Night and Sunday Morning, 168
The Scarlet Letter, 137
Schine, Cathleen, 93
Second-person point of view, 181-183
Secrets, 113
    and lies, 114-116
    writing about, 62

Seize the Day, 184
Self-criticism, 17-19
Self-discovery, exercises for, 45-48
Self-Help, 182
Senses, exercises focusing on, 55
"The Sensible Thing," 92
Setting. *See* Place
Sex, writing about, 92-95
Shacochis, Bob, 182
Shakespeare, William, 10, 143
Shaw, Irwin, 111
Shields, Carol, 94, 154
Shifting point of view, 188-189
"Shipping Out," 56
Sillitoe, Alan, 86, 168
Simpson, Mona, 172
Sinclair, Upton, 101
Singer, Isaac, 172
Slesinger, Tess, 182
Smiley, Jane, 143-144
Smith, Lee, 22
Snow Falling on Cedars, 19
"The Snows of Kilimanjaro," 202
So Long, See You Tomorrow, 251-252
"Sonny's Blues," 172
Space and time, creating structure with, 167-170
Sparks, Debra, 127
Spiritual beliefs, 134-137
The Sportswriter, 116-118
Stafford, William, 30
Steinbeck, John, 101, 212
The Stone Diaries, 154
Stone, Robert, 188
Story
    adding elements to, 230-233
    angry, 101-104
    defined, 2
    exploring different avenues for, 240-243
    reasons for writing, 224-225
"Strays," 204
Structure, 163-167
    in space and time, 167-170
Stygo, 73

Styron, William, 18
Sugartime, 144
The Sun Also Rises, 78
Symbolism, 238-240

A Tale of Two Cities, 199
Talking, as enemy to creativity, 15-17
Thelma and Louise, 169
Theme, 252-254
  and beliefs, 83
Third-person point of view, 183-187
Thomas, Dylan, 200
A Thousand Acres, 143
Tone, 244-249
Toole, John Kennedy, 85-86
Travel, appeal of, 74-77, 79
Trevor, William, 77
"The Trigger: What Gives Rise to a
    Story?" 127
The Triggering Town, 203
Twain, Mark, 160
Tyler, Ann, 16

U and I, 109, 194
Ulysses, 167
Updike, John, 164

The Veracruz Blues, 107
Victim mentality, as enemy to creativ-
    ity, 14-15
The Virgin Suicides, 243
Voice, 249-252
  character's, 251-252
  control of, 86
  strong, through first-person point of
    view, 174
  See also Tone

Walker, Alice, 172
Wallace, Daniel, 137
Wallace, David Foster, 56
Warm-ups, 34-36
Warren, Robert Penn, 101-102

Webbing. *See* Clustering
When Things Fall Apart, 1, 24, 134
White Noise, 156, 160, 210
Who Is Teddy Villanova? 146
"Why Don't You Dance?" 186
Why I Write, 22
"Why We Travel: A Love Affair With
    the World," 76, 79
Williams, Tennessee, 58
Williams, Terry Tempest, 232
Winegardner, Mark, 107
Winesburg, Ohio, 73
The Wizard of Oz, 167, 169
Wolfe, Thomas, 26, 122-123
Wolff, Tobias, 114-115, 188, 229
The Women's Room, 101
Work space, 26-28
Wright, Richard, 101
Writer's block, combating, 40-41
Writer's guilt, 19-22
Writing
  about likes and dislikes, 53-57
  acknowledging difficulty of, 8-9
  place for, 26-28
  preparation, 34
  for publication, vs. for pleasure,
    22-24
  regularly, 7, 9, 12, 24
  state of mind, 30-33
  time for, 29-30
  vs. other responsibilities, 20-22
  See also Automatic writing, Cave-
    writing, Freewriting, Journaling
Writing Life Stories, 68, 147
Writing prompt, as warm-up, 35
Writing as a Road to Self-Discovery,
    39
The Wuggie Norple Story, 200

Yates, Richard, 111, 210
Yielding, to receive ideas, 30-31
"Your Mother's Passions, Your Sister's
    Woes," 133-134
"You're Ugly, Too," 200